Cool Cats,

and Other Beastly

Expressions

▼

Christine Ammer

HOUGHTON MIFFLIN COMPANY   Boston • New York

Library of Congress Cataloging-in-Publication Data
Ammer, Christine.
    [It's raining cats and dogs—and other beastly expressions]
    Cool cats, top dogs, and other beastly expressions/Christine Ammer.
        p.   cm.
    Originally published: It's raining cats and dogs—and other beastly expressions. 1st ed. New York : Paragon House, 1989.
    Includes index.
    ISBN 0-395-95730-3
    1. English language—Etymology.   2. English language—Terms and phrases.   3. Zoology—Nomenclature (Popular)   4. Animals—Folklore. 5. Figures of speech.   I. Title.
PE1583.A46   1999
422—dc21   99-24727
                                                                  CIP

For information about this and other Houghton Mifflin trade and reference books and multimedia products, visit The Bookstore at Houghton Mifflin on the World Wide Web at
http://www.hmco.com/trade/.

Illustrations by Cathy Bobak
Book design by Margaret Ong Tsao

Manufactured in the United States of America

DOH 10 9 8 7 6 5 4 3 2 1

Contents

For Brian, Lauren, and Paul

Preface

An extraordinary number of words and expressions in our language are related to animals. Some are simply descriptive, transferring a marked animal characteristic to human affairs—the eagle's keen sight, the pig's greed, the whale's size. Others are more elusive, and their origins, ranging from Biblical times (such as *scapegoat*) to the recent (*skunk works*), are fascinating to trace.

The 1,200 or so terms in this revised and expanded edition are arranged in nine animal categories: cats, dogs, domestic fowl, farm animals, wild mammals, birds, reptiles and amphibians, insects, and marine animals. They are roughly alphabetical within these categories, but the reader searching for a term is advised to consult the complete index at the back of the book. The same is true for cross-references, printed in small capital letters (as in see BLIND TIGER).

The author is deeply indebted to a long line of eminent etymologists, linguists, and lexicographers who collectively represent centuries of work in tracing the origins of the English language. This book is but a modest compilation of the results of some of their fine scholarship. Grateful acknowledgment also is made to the many friends and acquaintances who have helped to improve it, pointing out terms and sources and current usages. Their assistance greatly smoothed the way.

Quick
as a
Cat

Since the times of ancient Egypt, where the cat was held sacred and killing one was punishable by death, cats have been an object of fascination and, for the most part, admiration. The speed with which they pounce on their prey, their haughty aloofness, their grace and agility—all are recorded in everyday phrases in our speech.

Unlike their main domestic rival, the dog, cats seldom are the source of disparaging simile. Such terms as the agile *cat burglar,* the suave *cool cat,* and provident *fat cat* by far outnumber the cowardly *scaredy-cat* or spiteful *catty* remark.

The word *cat* can be traced back to Latin *cattus,* via Old English *catt* and Middle English *catte,* but its ultimate origins have been lost.

Cat and Mouse

> She watches him as a cat would
> watch a mouse.
>
> —Jonathan Swift,
> *Polite Conversation* (1738)

Just as arrogant playfulness marks the cat's toying with a hapless captive, so those in authority are said to play *cat-and-mouse games* with a trapped victim. In 1913 the British Parliament passed the Cat and Mouse Bill (more officially, the Prisoners Temporary Discharge for Ill Health Bill) to counter the hunger strikes of imprisoned suffragettes who thus were becoming popular martyrs. The law provided that hunger strikers be released when their health began to be impaired, but that on recovery they must return to jail to complete their sentence.

Playing cat and mouse, in the sense of pursuit and evasion, is also used less formally, in a more playful sense. It is, in fact, the name of a children's game in which a designated "cat" chases a "mouse" in and out of a circle formed by the other children.

At least one authority believes that *catnap,* used since about 1820 to mean a short light sleep, originated from *cat-and-mouse games.* Supposedly a cat playing with a mouse it has caught will sometimes feign sleep, encouraging the mouse to run away so that the cat may pounce again—*quick as a cat.*

A wide-awake cat is an inestimable boon to the household plagued by mice. Hence it is obvious that when the cat is absent the mice will have free rein. *When the cat's away, the mice will play* is a proverb in many languages, first appearing in this form in English in the 17th century. (Earlier variants date back to the Roman writer Plautus.) That the mice might want fair warning of the cat's return was noted by William Langland, who in *Piers Ploughman* (c. 1377) recounted Aesop's fable about the mice that wanted a bell placed around the cat's neck so as to hear it coming in time to escape. However, not one of the mice was brave enough to volunteer to *bell the cat* and thereby sacrifice its life for the common cause. "It is one thing to propose and another to execute," Aesop concluded. Ever since, to bell the cat has meant to take a chance and face danger for the good of the majority.

While cats are valued for hunting pests, they do not always discriminate among their prey, and the cat that goes after its owner's prized pet bird or goldfish may be in for a good scolding. To *look like the cat that swallowed*

the canary has meant to look guilty but smug since at least 1871, and the term turns up in several American mystery stories of the 1930s and 1940s, including Dashiell Hammett's *The Maltese Falcon.*

Our neighbor's cat, harking back to its fiercer ancestors in the wild, has a passion for chipmunks, field mice, robins, and the like. She proudly deposits their corpses at her owner's doorstep, a common practice that gave rise, about 1920, to the expression *to look like something the cat dragged in,* an accurate description of utter bedragglement.

Among the oldest sayings about cats is *A cat may look at a king,* meaning an ordinary person has certain rights even in the presence of a superior power or authority. It comes from the German *Darf doch die Katze den Kaiser ansehen,* which supposedly alludes to a visit of the Emperor Maximilian I in 1517 to the shop of a printmaker whose cat stared at the emperor throughout the visit. However, it may have appeared in print even earlier, and there is a French equivalent, *un chien regarde bien un évêque* ("A dog may look at a bishop"). By 1546 it appeared in English in John Heywood's proverb collection, and many times thereafter, but it is heard less often today.

Cats in Chorus

Let Hercules himself do what he may,
The cat will mew and dog will have
his day.

—William Shakespeare, *Hamlet*

Cats mew in distress, purr in contentment, hiss in anger, and howl or screech in rutting time. The catbird is so named because one of its calls sounds like a cat's mew (see also CAT-BIRD SEAT). A *cats' concert,* usually a nocturnal event, is a discordant din, and *caterwauling,* from Middle English and Middle Dutch words meaning "tomcat" and "wailing," came by the 14th century to refer to the ugliest of feline noises. Similarly, *catcall* denotes whistles, screeches, and other rude sounds of displeasure made at performers by dissatisfied audiences; this term dates from about 1700.

All the more surprising, then, that *the cat's meow,* not necessarily a pleasing sound even to the ardent cat lover, became a slang term for utter excellence (along with the equally unlikely *cat's pajamas* and *cat's whiskers*). It seems to have originated in American girls' schools during the late 19th century and became very popular during the roaring twenties, when Clara Bow, the fabled "It girl," was widely regarded as "the cat's meow."

Cats' Tails

What a monstrous tail our cat has.

—Henry Carey (1687-1743),
The Dragon of Wantley

The *catkin,* from words meaning "little cat," is the inflorescence of birches, oaks, and willows, most notably the *pussy willow,* named for its resemblance to a cat's freely swinging tail. The same is true for the tall, reedlike marsh plants with furry spikes that have been known as *cattails* since Chaucer's day.

The *cat-o'-nine tails,* named for the same resemblance but having nothing soft or fuzzy about it, is a whip with nine lashes fastened to a handle. Once widely used to punish offenders in the British armed services, it was not formally abolished as a punishment until 1948. Sometimes called simply *the cat,* it began as a cat-of-three-tails, but during the 17th century it acquired six more, supposedly because a flogging by a "trinity of trinities" would be more effective.

The whip in turn may have given rise to the expression *no room to swing a cat,* used to describe very cramped quarters by Tobias Smollett, Charles Dickens, and Mark Twain, among others. However, there are several other theories as to the origin of this term, all involving cruel pursuits. Some say that, *cat* being an old Scots word for "scoundrel," the term refers to a criminal swinging from the gallows. Others say it came from the sport of swinging a cat by its tail to serve as target practice for marksmen. And still others say it came from the practice of tying a cat inside a leather sack that was hung from a tree and used as an archery target—a moving one, since the cat naturally would thrash about. To hit such a target the archer must watch carefully to *see which way the cat jumps,* a phrase still used for observing events closely in order to predict their final outcome. "I would like to be there," wrote Sir Walter Scott in his *Journal* in 1826, "were it but to see how the cat jumps."

A Cat's Demise

> This fiber analysis is not going to
> work out. . . . But there's more than
> one way to skin a cat.
>
> —Richard Preston,
> *The Cobra Event* (1997)

Why one should do so at all is problematical, but *There's more than one way to skin a cat* first appeared in print in John Ray's proverb collection of 1678, in slightly amplified form ("There's more than one way to skin a cat without tearing the hide"). It then meant, as it still does, that more than one solution or path of action is available. In the 19th century a similar phrase with the same meaning was *There is more than one way of killing a cat besides choking him on cream,* but it is the older version that has survived.

From far more recent times we have the stock-market term *dead cat bounce,* meaning a slight upturn in a security whose price had dropped sharply, which raises false hopes of a continued rise. The analogy of *bounce,* which here signifies "temporary increase," to the behavior of a deceased pussy makes no more sense than the temporary price change itself. However, one stockbroker has suggested that it alludes to throwing a dead cat from a tall building, where it might bounce when it landed but would not come back to life.

As for how the animal came to die in the first place, one might speculate that *curiosity killed the cat.* This seemingly ancient adage was only first recorded in O. Henry's 1909 story *Schools and Schools* ("Curiosity can do more things than kill a cat"), and its exact present wording not until 1922 (in Eugene O'Neill's *Diff'rent*). It has just about replaced the earlier *care killed the cat,* dating from Shakespeare's time, *care* here meaning "worry."

And then we have the colloquial and controversial Southern expression, *dead cat on a line,* used to indicate that something is suspicious, that things are not as they should be. The origin is disputed. Some say the "cat" here is actually a *catfish* (so called for its feline, bewhiskered visage) and that the saying alludes to finding a dead catfish on a trotline (one with numerous hooks), revealing that the line's owner has not checked it daily, as he should. Others believe it alludes to the practice of drowning an unwanted litter of kittens, one of which might be pulled up on someone's fishing line. The true origin is unknown.

A Cat Has Nine Lives

> *One of the most striking differences between a cat and a lie is that a cat has only nine lives.*
>
> —Mark Twain,
> *Pudd'nhead Wilson* (1893)

Given the cruel treatment it sometimes suffers, it's just as well that *a cat has nine lives,* a reference to the fact that it often lands on its feet uninjured after a seemingly bad fall. The secret to this feat is the cat's ability to right itself while falling and to spread out its limbs horizontally, like a flying squirrel. An ancient Hindu scribe named Pilpay (or Bidpai) is credited as the first to record this remarkable but clearly fictional characteristic about 300 B.C. By the time John Heywood assembled his collection of proverbs (1546), this capacity for survival was figuratively ascribed to women as well ("A woman hath nine lives like a cat").

Longevity notwithstanding, a healthy octogenarian lady we know has regularly claimed, during her frequent bouts of imagined ill health, that she is *weak as a cat,* a saying dating back to at least 1840. O. Henry's version—"weak as a vegetarian cat"—sounds more plausible, as does Erle Stanley Gardner's "weak as a kitten." The word *kitten,* for a newborn or very young cat, has been around since the late 14th century. However, *to have kittens,* in the slang sense of becoming very upset, nervous, or angry, dates only from about 1900. The allusion is not very clear, since a cat in the throes of labor does not actually behave in this way.

Despite their attraction to the herb *catnip,* called *catmint* by the British, cats are carnivores and rely on meat and fish as staples of their diet. Hence *a cat among the pigeons* is sure to wreak havoc, and this term is sometimes used to describe a human being who incites a group to heated debate or even violence.

Cat Anatomy

> *The fog comes on little cat feet.*
> —Carl Sandburg, *The Fog* (1916)

The cat's stealthy tread not only inspired one of Sandburg's best-known poems but spawned *to pussyfoot,* which originally meant to tread softly and to lack forcefulness and assertiveness. By the early 1900s it took on additional figurative significance: that is, to act cautiously and noncommittally, in the way that politicians may hedge on controversial issues before an election. By the 1930s a *pussyfooter* was a coward plain and simple, a close cousin of the *scaredy-cat* and *fraidy-cat* of children's schoolyard taunts.

The cat's stealthy tread and agility probably gave rise to the term *cat burglar,* a thief who breaks in by climbing over roofs and through upper-story windows. And its fine sense of balance gave rise to *catwalk,* a narrow, high walkway above a construction site, over a theater's stage, outside a bridge's roadway, or the like.

A quite different portion of the cat's anatomy is alluded to in *catgut,* a resilient material used since the 16th century to string violins and other musical instruments. The origin of this usage is extremely puzzling, since the material is and always has been made from the dried intestines of sheep, never from cats. Word buffs can come up with fanciful reasons, and one has suggested that catgut is derived via *kit,* a tiny violin used by dancing masters in the 17th and 18th centuries. It was small enough to be carried in a pocket, and its strings may have been called "kit gut," which then became catgut.

A cat's eyes seem to glow in the dark, giving rise to the name *cat's-eye* for several semiprecious gemstones—especially chrysoberyl, which is yellow or green—that have a similar luster.

And finally we have *cat's-paw,* for a person who is easily duped. This expression comes from an ancient fable about a monkey who persuaded a cat to retrieve roasted chestnuts from a fire, thereby burning its paw. Some versions of this tale, told in numerous languages, use a dog, but it is the cat that has stuck in English.

Cats after Dark

In the night all cats are grey.
—Miguel de Cervantes,
Don Quixote (1615)

Cats are nocturnal beasts, and their sexual pursuits and proclivities have not been overlooked. *Tomcatting,* from the word simply meaning "male cat," has come to signify pursuing sexual lust and promiscuity. The word *cat* itself has been slang for a female prostitute since at least 1400, and thus *cathouse* came to mean a house of prostitution, particularly a cheap one (the term became current in the early 1900s but had been so used much longer).

The word *puss,* originally from Dutch and Low German and imitative of the spitting noise of a cat, became a call-name for cats in the 16th century and then, during the next hundred years, a slang word for girl or woman. About the same time, the diminutive *pussy* became a slang word for "vagina" and is still so used.

(The derivation of puss as slang for "face" is from the Gaelic *pus* and earlier *buss,* for "lip"; whence also *sourpuss,* for "a scowling expression," and by extension for a grouchy disposition.) In contrast, *pussycat* has no sexual connotations but is simply a colloquialism for a very amiable, likable person.

The 1920s gave us *the cat's meow* as a flattering superlative, and the jazz age gave us the equally admirable *cool cat* and *hep cat.* From about the same period comes the sobriquet *fat cat,* which originally denoted a rich person who makes a sizable contribution to a political campaign fund, often in exchange for special privileges of one kind or another, and was later extended to mean anyone who has great wealth and lives in lavish style.

There appears to be some linguistic ambivalence about the character and disposition of cats. No one admires the slavish imitator known as a *copycat* (dating from 1915 or so). A person given to malicious gossip and spiteful remarks has been termed *catty* since about 1885. An affectedly coy girl or woman is said to be *kittenish,* although this also can refer to the playfulness normal in young cats. But a *hellcat* is an out-and-out shrew. In the 16th century, however, a hellcat was a woman with evil magical powers, that is, a witch. This usage undoubtedly came from the medieval superstition that Satan often took the form of a *black cat,* a belief that led first to the notion that a black cat was the devil's familiar (slave or companion) and then that it was a witch's familiar—a personal, always available demon. In the witchcraft trials of 16th-century England and 17th-century Massachusetts such terms were frequently mentioned, and the presence of a black cat was even cited as "evidence." It is this association that gave rise to the idea that a black cat signifies bad luck and to such sayings as "Don't let a black cat cross your path."

The term *kitty* is another call-name for cat ("Here, kitty"). It also is used for a poker "pot" and, by extension, any pool or fund, but this usage has no feline connection; it comes from medieval Dutch *kitte* or *kit,* meaning "jug" or "vessel."

Let the Cat out of the Bag

> *I forgot, I was nigh letting the cat out*
> *of the bag again.*
>
> —Maria Edgeworth,
> *The Parent's Assistant* (1796)

Before the era of supermarkets or even the corner grocery, many households relied on a weekly farmers' market for their supplies. Especially prized and costly was a suckling pig, purchased for holiday fare and other special occasions. Sellers in olden times were not always above skullduggery, any more than they are today, and occasionally a farmer would put a worthless cat instead of the expected pig into the purchaser's bag, which was called a *poke*. The two animals weighed about the same, and unless buyers were cautious enough to check the contents, the substitution might not be discovered until they got home and *let the cat out of the bag*. And hence making a worthless purchase is described as *buying a pig in a poke*.

One of the earliest references to this practice dates from about 1350: "When one profereth ye pigge, opon the pogh." The same trick was reported in France, for in the 14th century John Wycliffe translated the French saying, *acheter chat en poche* ("buy a cat in a sack"), which was still current in the time of Montaigne (*chat en sac*). On the other side of the globe, the Chinese had a similar saying about a cat in a bag. In sum, this practice was so common that letting the cat out of the bag, in one way or another, survived, and it still means to reveal something prematurely, or to give away a secret.

Cheshire Cat

> *I didn't know that Cheshire cats*
> *always grinned; in fact, I didn't know*
> *that cats could grin.*
>
> —Lewis Carroll,
> *Alice's Adventures in Wonderland* (1865)

The origin of *grin like a Cheshire cat,* meaning to smile inscrutably, has never been satisfactorily determined. The saying was popular long before Carroll wrote *Alice,* in which the Cat slowly disappeared until all that was left of it was its grin. Most explanations involve the traditional cheese of the English county of Cheshire. One holds that the cheese, today sold in the shape of a wheel, was once so molded that it resembled a grinning cat's face; another claims that the cheese was imprinted with a local nobleman's coat of arms bearing a lion so poorly drawn that it resembled a grinning cat. Or, suggests still another, it has nothing to do with cats or cheese but is an abbreviation for a fierce forest ranger named Caterling who frightened poachers in his native Cheshire with his skilled swordsmanship and hideous grin.

Another proper name figures in *fight like the cats of Kilkenny,* meaning to fight virtually to the death. Among the earliest printed references to it is one in a nursery rhyme of about 1700:

> There were two cats at Kilkenny
> Each thought there was one too many;
> So they quarreled and they fit,
> They scratched and they bit,
> Till excepting their nails
> And the tips of their tails,
> Instead of two cats there weren't any.

One section of the town of Kilkenny, in Ireland, was called Irishtown and inhabited mainly by the Irish, while Englishtown, another section situated across a little stream, had mainly English inhabitants. Strife between the two, which nearly destroyed them both, appears to be the origin of the legend of the Kilkenny cats, who ate each other up.

As beloved by children as the Alice stories is the game of *cat's cradle,* in which two players take turns fashioning a loop of string into various intricate designs. It, however, has nothing to do with cats. The name is generally thought to be a corruption of *cratch-cradle,* cratch meaning "crèche" or "manger"—especially the manger in which the infant Jesus was laid—and to refer to the cradle-like designs that can be formed with the string. Eventually "cratch" dropped out of the language and the similar-sounding and more familiar word "cat's" was substituted.

Raining Cats and Dogs

> At last I went to Ireland,
> 'Twas raining cats and dogs:
> I found no music in the glens
> Nor purple in the bogs.
> —George Bernard Shaw (1931)

The British origin of this expression for a heavy downpour makes perfectly good sense, given that country's notorious reputation for rainfall. Two centuries before Shaw composed his concluding refrain to an Irish song, Jonathan Swift had written, "I know Sir John will go, though he was sure it would rain cats and dogs" (1738), using a term that was already a cliché. The expression's origin is cloudy. One writer says it comes from North European myth, where cats supposedly have great influence on weather and the dog is a symbol of wind; hence the cat denotes heavy rain and the dog strong wind gusts. Another suggests the analogy of a raging storm to the hubbub of a cat-and-dog fight. Still another says it is a corruption of the French *catedupe,* for the French describe a downpour as "raining like a waterfall." Perhaps a more literal meaning is the true source. In 17th-century Britain, after a cloudburst the gutters and ditches would overflow with a filthy torrent that included dead animals, as well as sewage and other debris. Whatever the source, the phrase calls up an image picturesque enough to have persisted and been passed down to the present.

A Dog's
Life

Dog may be man's best friend, but our language does not show the converse to be true. More often than not, terms involving dogs are negative or demeaning. A person unlucky enough to be called *a dog,* from Middle English *dogge,* is being described as unsuccessful, unattractive, and generally unlikable. Although this judgment occasionally is mitigated, as in *lucky dog,* meaning fortunate person, and *gay dog,* a man with an active social life, a *dirty dog* is mean, despicable, and in Victorian terms, a true cad or rotter. To be called a *cur,* from Old Norse and German terms for growling and now signifying a mean dog of unspecific parentage, is considerably worse, even without the commonly added modifier *mangy* (meaning literally "afflicted with mange" and figuratively "contemptible"). A similar allusion is evoked by *He who lies down with dogs will rise with fleas,* a proverb about the consequences of keeping bad company that was first recorded by John Florio in *First Fruites* (1578). And *It shouldn't happen to a dog,* an expression of commiseration for someone's misfortune, implies a fate that is too awful even for a lowly dog.

In mid-19th-century America a *dog* was an informer, one who betrayed his associates, and *to turn dog* meant to become a snitch. This meaning persists in Australia, where a *dogbox* is a special security area in prisons set up to protect inmates who are police informers. In vulgar slang, *dog* has meant "penis" since about 1600, a usage preserved in the 20th-century *beat the dog,* meaning to masturbate.

To *lead a dog's life,* which may derive from the 17th-century proverb "It's a dog's life, hunger and ease," is to live miserably, to be harried, nagged, and never left in peace. Even Erasmus said, in 1542, that a dog's life is a miserable life. And if living like a dog is bad, *to die like a dog* is no better. "He lyved lyke a lyon and dyed lyke a dogge," observed John Rastell in 1529, and four centuries later Ernest Hemingway said that in modern war "you will die like a dog for no good reason" (*Notes on the Next War,* 1935).

However, even though the dog often has been a symbol of misery, not all of the sayings about it are negative or pessimistic. Since ancient times, it has been pointed out, *Better a live dog than a dead lion,* a proverb with a Biblical antecedent (Ecclesiastes 9:4) that reminds us that there is always hope for the living—even for a lowly dog—but none for the dead. Similar thinking has given us *Every dog will have his day,* a proverb first recorded in Plutarch's *Moralia* (c. A.D. 95), where it is put as "Even a dog gets his revenge." According to Erasmus, the saying alludes to the death of Euripides, the famed Greek playwright who in 405 B.C. was killed by a dogpack set upon him by a rival. Nevertheless, for most dogs it may well be *a dog's age,* or a very long time, before their day comes. This phrase may rest on the mistaken belief that dogs are very long-lived; it dates from the 1830s.

Still other expressions use *dog* to indicate or intensify unpleasant conditions. Since the early 1800s, to be *dog-tired* has meant to be utterly weary, and *sick as a dog* means miserably sick, usually to one's stomach, a saying that has been traced to the Bible ("A dog returneth to his vomit," Proverbs 26:11). Some of that illness might be ascribed to *a dog's breakfast,* a 20th-century term now signifying a hastily prepared, random mixture of castoff foods. Since dogs don't normally consume a human-style breakfast, the expression presumably alludes to a dog's picking at bones and other debris as found in garbage cans.

Poets of scant skill write *doggerel,* mentioned by Chaucer in the 14th century as *rym dogerel,* and actors try out new shows in unimportant little *dog towns.*

Going to the Dogs

> *My granddad, viewing Earth's*
> *worn cogs,*
> *Said things were going to the dogs.*
>   —Author unknown (c. 1900)

According to Agis II, King of Sparta (c. 402 B.C.), who is described in Plutarch's *Lives, gone to the dogs* simply means that things are topsy-turvy. Only much later did this saying mean to come to a bad end. Robert Harris wrote, in 1619: "One is coloured, one is foxt, and a third is gone to the dogs" (*The Drunkard's Cup*). Eventually it came to signify being ruined. Thus, writing about the proposed British Reform Bill that would give further voting privileges to the working classes, Leslie Stephen reported that "an elderly Tory added that we are all going to the dogs in consequence of that."

Similarly, being *in the doghouse* signifies a state of disgrace, though usually more temporary in nature. The dog that misbehaves indoors is relegated to its outdoor kennel. In like manner Mr. Darling in James Barrie's *Peter Pan* lives in a dog kennel until his children return, in penance for his harsh treatment of the family dog, Nana. Although the saying today is associated mainly with wives who are angry with their husbands and figuratively "put" them in the doghouse, it was not always so. Charles Dickens's Mr. Harris, who was "dreadfully timid," went and stopped his ears in an empty dog kennel while his wife was in labor with their first baby "and never took his hands away or come out once till he was showed the baby" (*Martin Chuzzlewit*, 1843).

My Aching Dogs

Eric Partridge, in his *Dictionary of Catch Phrases*, maintains that *My dogs are barking*, meaning "My feet are hurting badly," is an American expression that originated some time before World War II and was quickly adopted by the rest of the English-speaking world. The *Oxford English Dictionary*, on the other hand, holds that *dogs* for

"feet" originated in rhyming slang—*dogs' meat* rhyming with *feet*—and quotes this usage by P. G. Wodehouse in 1924. The latter origin seems more plausible, and chances are that the term started in Britain, crossed the Atlantic, was embellished with "barking," and returned to the old country. In America it is not heard much any more, "My feet are killing me" being more common (and certainly more direct).

Dog Days

> *Mad dogs and Englishmen go out in the midday sun.*
> —Noël Coward, *Mad Dogs and Englishmen* (1932)

The ancient Romans called the hottest days of summer *caniculares dies,* or "dog days." They believed that the *dog star* Sirius, the brightest star in the heavens, located in the constellation Canis Major ("Big Dog," so named for its shape), added to the heat while it was in its ascendancy. To the ancient Egyptians this star's rising was a sign of the beginning of the annual Nile flood. Noël Coward's poem poked fun at Englishmen living in the tropics who persist in habits more suitable to the British climate and disdain the sensible local custom of a noonday siesta; he likened them to dogs that, according to superstition, are frequently driven crazy by the heat. Another way to beat the dog days is to indulge in a *dog paddle,* a term used since about 1900 for treading water to stay afloat or for a beginner's version of the crawl stroke.

In the heyday of imperialism the British were famous for their *dogged* insistence on keeping up standards in the colonies, clinging to formal dress for dinner even in the jungle and *putting on the dog* for visiting dignitaries. Originally meaning "ill-conditioned" and "ill-favored," the adjective *dogged* later (15th century) meant simply "canine," but by the 1700s it had come to mean "pertinacious" or "persistent," just as a dog is in worrying a bone. The verb *to dog* carries a similar meaning, that is, to follow closely and persistently, as a dog follows its master's footsteps or, in hunting, a quarry's tracks and scent.

Putting on the dog, however, is an American term dating from about the time of the Civil War, when it became slang for putting on a flashy display and dressing up, or, as Lyman H. Bagg put it about 1869, "to cut a swell" (*Four Years at Yale*). One writer believes it came from the practice of the nouveau riche of displaying their wealth not only in clothes, jewelry, and houses, but by keeping extravagantly pampered lapdogs, which therefore became a symbol of putting on a showy display. This turn of phrase is still current, but we rarely hear of someone looking like *a dog's dinner,* which had much the same meaning—that is, wearing glaringly smart attire and putting on airs. A still later expression is a *dog-and-pony show,* signifying an elaborate presentation designed to gain approval for a product or policy. It dates from the mid-20th century and alludes to a traveling variety show.

Love Me, Love My Dog

> *Old dog Tray's ever faithful;*
> *Grief cannot drive him away;*
> *He is gentle, he is kind—*
> *I'll never never find*
> *A better friend than old dog Tray.*
>   —Stephen Foster, Old Dog Tray (1853)

Certainly one trait widely attributed to dogs is their faithfulness to their owners, which has made them valued companions. Stephen Foster's paean to "old dog Tray" expresses a widely accepted sentiment, and indeed it has become a folk song. And *Fido,* presumably based on the Latin *fides* for "faithful," was long a very popular name for pet dogs. All the more puzzling, then, is the late 20th-century teenage slang expression, *doggin',* for cheating on one's partner.

As long ago as 1150 or so the learned St. Bernard of Clairvaux said, "Qui me amat, amat et canem meam"— or "Love me, love my dog"—an expression of unconditional affection that crops up in numerous languages. Incidentally, the St. Bernard breed of dog is named not for this French monk but for an Italian churchman, St. Bernard of Menthon, who spent his life working in the Val d'Aosta in northwest Italy and founded an Alpine hospice on the Great St. Bernard Pass (also named for him), where these big shaggy dogs were bred for Alpine rescue work.

Dogs originally were domesticated for their usefulness in hunting, herding, and keeping watch. From the first pursuit, considered a natural one for canines, we have the Southern expression *That dog won't hunt,* meaning that an idea won't work. Dogs still are used for these and other special jobs, such as guiding the blind and sniffing out illegal drugs.

It may be *hard to teach an old dog new tricks,* or so proverbs have said since the early 17th century, but in fact dogs have been trained to perform highly skilled tasks. One such job was to turn the spit holding meat over an open fire, an important culinary assignment from early times. To do this work manually is tedious and time-consuming. Therefore someone in the 16th century devised a wheel-cage mounted at one end of the roasting spit and put a dog inside it; the dog would run around and around the wheel, making the spit turn so that the meat cooked evenly. If the dog's efforts flagged, a live coal might be put inside the wheel to revive its ardor. The Abergavenny Town Museum in Wales displays a picture of a *turnspit,* a small dog bred just for this purpose. It had a long body, short legs, and a stumpy tail, a shape quite suitable for being put inside the wheel-cage. In this instance the name of the mechanism became the name of the dog's breed. In time, however, the turnspit was replaced with a clockwork mechanism to turn the spit (also pictured in the museum), and the dog part of the name somehow attached itself to andirons (about 1800), which were called *firedogs*. Possibly the name was first used for andirons shaped like dogs and eventually extended to mean any andiron.

Hair of the Dog

> *I pray thee let me and my fellow have*
> *a haire of the dog that bit us last night.*
> —John Heywood, *Proverbs* (1546)

The *hair of the dog*, an ancient recipe for curing a hangover that consists of having a little of the same intoxicating drink the next morning, comes from the even older folk remedy of placing the burnt hair of a dog that had bitten someone on the wound. Allegedly this was the best antidote to the aftereffects of dogbite. No doubt it cured rabies about as effectively as liquor cures the aftereffects of a drinking spree.

One side effect of alcoholic overindulgence is urinary frequency, causing the imbiber to *see a man about a dog* fairly often. This euphemism for excusing oneself to go to the toilet became common in the 1860s in both America and Britain.

Another consequence of a spree can be guilt feelings, especially if drinking loosened normal inhibitions enough to make one say or do something embarrassing. The result may be a *hangdog* look, meaning an extremely shamefaced one. In medieval and Renaissance England each large country house had a pack of dogs, and some of the dogs inevitably turned out to be incorrigible sinners. They might be guilty of worrying the barnyard fowl, biting family members or guests, digging up the garden, or similar misdeeds, and it was common practice to get rid of them by hanging them. Shakespeare mentions the hanging of dogs in half a dozen of his plays, and a ballad from about

1660 says, "Why rings all these bells? What dog is a-hanging?" The term in its present meaning of looking guilty is thought to come from the characteristic appearance of either the official hangman of dogs or the cowering, terrified look of a dog about to meet this fate.

Two other terms connected to canine looks are *dog-eared,* used since about 1650 for the corner of a page folded over and so resembling the ear found in many dog breeds, and the *dogtooth violet (Erythronium americanum)*, a wildflower so named because its long, sharply reflexed petals resemble canine teeth. In humans the four cuspid teeth, on either side of the incisors, also are called *canines* for their resemblance to the four prominent, pointed teeth on either side of a dog's jaw.

The derogatory epithet *dogface,* for an ugly person, may well be objected to by dog-owners who regard their animals as beautiful. Nevertheless, it began to be used derisively for humans in the mid-1800s. A century or so later it acquired a military meaning, a low-ranking enlisted man, and this usage coexists with the earlier one.

The names of man-made canine equipment have also been transferred to human uses. Pet dogs usually wear a collar bearing a tag identifying the owner. Consequently the name *dog collar* has been transferred to objects such as a lady's tight-fitting, wide necklace, also called a choker, or, somewhat irreverently, the high stiff collar worn by priests and other clergymen. The former usage dates from about 1915, the latter from about 1860. And sometime during World War I the name *dogtag* began to be applied to the identification tag worn by military personnel.

Dogs of War

> *Cry "Havoc," and let slip the dogs*
> *of war.*
>
> —William Shakespeare, *Julius Caesar*

Shakespeare's metaphor occurs in Mark Antony's soliloquy, in which he sadly predicts that Caesar's legacy will unloose the ghastly horrors of war on all of Italy. The fierceness of dogs fighting each other, an entertainment as old and popular as cockfighting, is referred to in *dogfight,* a World War I term for a violent engagement among fighter planes. The loser of a dogfight (between dogs) was called the *underdog,* a term later (late 19th century) extended to competitors in politics, sports, and other activities who were expected to lose. Fans frequently root for underdogs, both because they want them to win and because they want to see the upset of the odds-on favorite, or *top dog.* One theory holds that *underdog* and *top dog* come from the lumber industry. In premechanized times, logs from felled trees were placed over a pit dug in the ground, and two men used a long saw to cut the timber. One man, the bottom sawyer, stood in the pit and, since he had the worse job of the two, becoming covered in sawdust, was called "the underdog." The other, the top sawyer, stood at ground level and guided the saw, and so was called "top dog."

Ruthless competition in which no quarter is given is sometimes described as *dog eat dog,* a saying that dates from the 16th century and became current in the United States in the early 1800s. A much older observation, however, is that dogs are *not* by nature cannibals and do not usually devour their own kind; it was made by the Roman

man of letters Marcus Terentius Varro in 43 B.C. ("Canis caninam non est") and became a proverb.

Even older is the proverbial *dog in the manger,* from Aesop's fable (c. 570 B.C.) about a snarling dog that prevents the horses from eating their corn, even though the dog itself does not want it. The term is still used for an individual who, out of sheer meanness, takes or keeps something desired by another.

Given their potential fierceness, it was long ago concluded that it is safer to *let sleeping dogs lie,* that is, not to rouse a sleeping watchdog but to leave well enough alone. Rabelais quotes this 13th-century proverb, as did Chaucer in *Troilus and Cressida*: "It is nought good a sleping hound to wake, nor yeve a wight a cause to devyne" (It is not good to wake a sleeping hound, nor give a person a reason to speculate).

Sailors call either of two suppertime watches the *dog-watch*—that is, a bad watch because it causes them to miss a meal. However, a very experienced sailor will sometimes be called a *seadog,* usually regarded as a compliment. The first term dates from about 1700; the second arose about 1590, when it meant "pirate" or "privateer" and only later signified "highly experienced."

Hot Dog

> *"Hot dog," whispered Hydrangea.*
> —Elliott Paul, *Mayhem in B-flat* (1940)

Some would argue that not even apple pie is as American as *hot dogs,* which came upon the scene in the late 1800s. Hot sausages in rolls had been consumed for many years, and sometimes were even sold by street vendors in the 19th century. Supposedly it was Harry Mozely Stevens, owner of the food concession at the Polo Grounds (home of the New York Giants baseball team), who first sold sausages in heated buns with mustard and relish. Several sources hold that because of their resemblance to the short-legged, long-bodied dachshund, he called them

"dachshund sausages." Allegedly the famous sports cartoonist T. A. Dorgan, who signed his work TAD, could not spell the German breed name and so coined the name *hot dog*.

It was long alleged that meat for sausages came from dogs (the idea was cited in a New York newspaper in 1836). According to several language historians, in the mid-1890s Yale University students began to call the sausages "dogs," and the October 19, 1895, issue of the *Yale Record* referred to students munching "hot dogs."

Indeed, the notion that sausage might be made from dog meat was occasionally a problem, and in 1913 the Coney Island Chamber of Commerce ruled that the name "hot dog" could not be used on the boardwalk for this reason. Fortunately the hot dog lived down this undeserved slander, and a restaurant on Coney Island, Nathan's, became the most famous and successful purveyor of hot dogs.

As a food item the hot dog has remained immensely popular both in and out of ballparks, a staple of the backyard barbecue, carnival, circus, parade ground, and fast-food restaurant. Variations such as the *chili dog*, featuring spicier condiments, have been developed but have not displaced the classic hot dog.

Since a hot dog is generally regarded as a good thing, by extension the slang expression *Hot dog!* came to be an exclamation of excellence or approval, much like "Oh, boy!" or "Great!" In the second half of the 20th century a new meaning surfaced in the world of sports. A *hot dog* now was a winner who crowed over a loser, and *to hot dog* meant to show off, at first referring to athletic feats but soon extending to any kind of bravura display.

The hot dog is one food item not likely to be taken home in a *doggy bag,* a term dating from the latter part of the 20th century. Whether it was the result of restaurants' doling out larger portions or of diners' appetites shrinking, the practice of packing up a patron's leftover food became very widespread. It is so termed for the alleged provisioning of the patron's pet, which is largely fictional since the leftovers most often enter human mouths.

A different kind of fiction is the *shaggy-dog story,* a seemingly endless anecdote with an unexpected ending, so called because it features a shaggy (and talking) animal. It dates from about 1940, when comic routines often included such a tale.

Tail Wagging

> *What are little boys made of?*
> *Snips and snails and puppy dogs' tails;*
> *That's what little boys are made of.*
> —Nursery rhyme

Most dogs show friendliness by wagging their tails. A frightened dog, on the other hand, is apt to tuck in its tail, whence we have the locution *with one's tail tucked between one's legs,* to describe the retreat of a cowardly person. The word *coward* itself is derived from Latin *coda* or *cauda,* for "tail."

Whether pointed up or down, however, the dog's tail is its hindmost part. Consequently *the tail wagging the dog,* a term dating from about 1900, is a picturesque description of role reversal, akin to *putting the cart before the horse* (see HORSE).

Hound

Before the word *dog* entered the language, sometime before 1050, this animal was generally called *hund,* which became *hound.* Then *dog* displaced it, and by the 13th century a hound was generally a dog kept for hunting, and *riding to hounds* still means taking part in a hunt, usually a fox hunt. Technically the term *hound* is applied to any of several breeds of dog trained to pursue game either by scent or by sight. The beagle, for example, is a scent hound and is particularly adept at hunting rabbits. The sight hounds are the fastest of all dogs. They include the greyhound, used in dog racing (in which dogs chase a mechanical rabbit); its name was adopted by the largest American intercity bus company, *Greyhound* (whose speed, however, is considerably less than legendary). In the southern United States *hound dog,* the title of a song made extremely popular by Elvis Presley in the 1950s (more than two million disks sold), can mean any kind of dog, or it can mean a dog used primarily for hunting. The verb *to hound* means to pursue relentlessly, as hunting dogs are trained to do, as well as to persecute and pester, much as dogs worry their quarry.

Dogs have a far more sensitive sense of smell than humans do. The *bloodhound,* which has an exceptionally acute sense—allegedly one million times stronger than a human's—is a breed trained to track down escaped prisoners and other human quarry. Indeed, according to zoologist Warren D. Thomas, it is the only animal whose "testimony" can be used as evidence in U.S. courts. So occasionally the name is applied to a detective who is intent on tracking down some criminal. Similarly, the *autograph hound* chases down celebrities for their signatures, the *rock hound* is an eager geologically minded collector, and so on. The pattern on fabrics called *houndstooth check,* consisting of broken or jagged checks, presumably reminded someone of something roughly torn apart by hounds.

Puppy

In the 15th century *pup* and *puppy* referred to a breed of dog that no longer exists. By the 16th century the words meant any young dog, as they do today. The terms also were used contemptuously of a person, as in "that young pup," with the implication that the person was too empty-headed to be taken seriously. The same connotation survives in *puppy love,* young love that is more short-lived infatuation than serious romance.

Young lovers might be small or limber enough to fit into a *pup tent,* an American term from about 1860 for a small, A-shaped military shelter consisting basically of two sheets of canvas buttoned or roped together. Its proper name was "shelter tent," but it earned the derogatory nickname *dog tent,* and later pup tent, because it was thought to be better suited to small animals than grown men.

The same, many northerners believe, is true of the *hush puppy* of the American South, a small cornmeal cake fried in deep fat that probably derives its name from being fed to a hungry dog to quiet it (with the admonition, "Hush, puppy!"), but which became a staple of the human diet in the years immediately after the Civil War, when food was scarce. It survived into more prosperous times, and is usually served with fried fish or fried chicken. One American etymologist suggests that the first hush puppy may have been a salamander, also called *mud puppy, water puppy,* or *water dog,* which in hard times was disguised in corn batter and fried up along with fish, but this theory lacks sufficient corroboration.

His Bark Was Worse Than His Bite

> *Cowardly dog, the worse he barks*
> *the less he bites.*
>
> —Quintus Curtius Rufus (A.D. 50)

The old adage notwithstanding, loud and persistent barking can frighten off burglars as well as letter carriers, meter readers, and other legitimate strangers. Our friends' dog, a large and extremely amiable mutt, spends most days tied up in front of their house while they are at work, and is so delighted at the prospect of company that he greets all visitors with ecstasies of barking. As a result, their neighbors must take in nearly all their deliveries since most strangers won't go near their front door. Although an ancient adage has it that *barking dogs do not bite,* another states that *dogs bark as they are bred,* meaning they cannot change their essential nature.

In England *barker* has meant "loud troublemaker" since the late 15th century; in 19th-century America it came to be used for the person who stood outside a carnival, circus, or other public performance to shout out its attractions to passersby. From the same period (the 1820s) comes *to bark up the wrong tree,* from hunting dogs that crowd around a tree, barking loudly, in the mistaken belief they have treed a raccoon that in reality has taken a quite different route. The term is still used to mean wasting one's energy or efforts by pursuing the wrong object or path.

Bitch

> *Th'olde bitche biteth sorer and more,*
> *not with teeth (she has none) but*
> *with hir toung.*
>
> —John Heywood, *Proverbs* (1546)

The word *bitch* (in Old English spelled *bicce*) has meant female dog since before the 10th century, but in the 15th century it began to be used for an immoral woman, and *son of a bitch* has meant a despicable man since about 1700. Today these terms, along with the adjective *bitchy,* are rather rude insults, applied to either female or male individuals who are thereby accused of being malicious and nasty rather than lewd.

The verb *to bitch* meant "to curse" in 17th-century Britain, but today it usually means "to complain." The

noun form also can mean a difficult task or problem, as in "Fixing that gutter is a bitch," a usage dating from World War I.

Bulldog

The sport of setting dogs upon a bull in an arena became popular in the 12th century or earlier. Such fights were so popular that dogs were specially bred for the events. The bulldog has a low-slung body that prevents a tethered bull from placing its horns under the dog and injuring it. It also has short but muscular legs, a big head and short neck that cannot be easily snapped when jerked upward by the bull, and a nose curved upward so it can bite and breathe at the same time. Most of all, bulldogs had to be tenacious, attacking the enraged bull again and again. In the 1830s bull-baiting was outlawed, but the breed survived as a pet, and its name continues to be used for any stubborn, relentless individual. In the 1930s and 1940s a popular American radio serial featured a detective named Bulldog Drummond, who was so persistent that he always caught his man.

The name also is used as a verb, *to bulldog,* meaning "to attack or fight tenaciously." In the American West, the verb means to throw a steer to the ground by grabbing its horns and twisting its neck.

Red Dog, Yellow Dog

> *A good dog, like a good candidate,*
> *cannot be of a bad colour.*
> —Peter Beckford (1740–1811), *Thoughts*
> *upon Hare and Fox Hunting*

No dog is actually bright red in color, but the term *red dog* crops up in finance, football, and cards. In 19th-century America several kinds of bank note were called *red dog,* all of them stamped with red ink. In the 1950s and 1960s, a gridiron play in which defensive players rush the quarterback for a quick tackle was called a *red dog;* today it is more often called a "blitz." And finally, a card game in which each player holds five cards and bets, for a pool, that he or she holds a higher card than the top card of the remaining pack is called *red dog;* it is also known by the less colorful name of "high card pool."

The *yellow-dog contract* was one of several practices used by American employers to fight labor unions, until it was outlawed by the Norris-LaGuardia Act of 1937. Such a contract required an employee to agree not to join a union, under penalty of being dismissed if the agreement was violated. Whether it was the employer or the worker who was being called a *yellow dog,* in the sense of "cowardly cur," is now buried in the annals of American labor history.

Barnyard Fowl

Although today *fowl* refers mainly to domesticated birds such as the chicken, duck, goose, and turkey, it originally came from Old English and Old German words for hunting wild fowl, a meaning that persists in the verb *to fowl,* as well as in *fowler,* a hunter of fowl, and *fowling piece,* the gun used for this purpose. For a time it meant any bird, for in Old English *brid* (and in Middle English, *byrde*) denoted only the young of *foul* (also spelled *foule* or *fowell*). The King James Version of the Bible (1611) still refers to *dominion over the fish of the sea and over the fowl of the air,* a rule that obtains for barnyard birds more nearly than birds in the wild.

▼ Chicken

> *She's no chicken; she's on the wrong side of thirty.*
>
> —Jonathan Swift (c. 1738)

The modern name for "young hen" is derived from Old English *cícen* and late West Saxon *cýcen* and was occasionally shortened to *chick* as long ago as the 14th century. No one quite agrees as to when it was first applied to a young woman. H. L. Mencken held it meant a young foolish girl in the 19th century, when it replaced the use of *filly* (young horse) of the 18th century, but the term was current in Britain long before that. In 1711 Richard Steele wrote in *The Spectator*, "You ought to consider you are now past a chicken," and Jonathan Swift's usage, quoted above, occurred in *Polite Conversation*. In America a woman no longer young was described as *no chicken* as early as 1827, a description amplified to *she's no spring chicken* by about 1900. Another writer suggests that in America about 1860 *chicken* was used for a girl of "easy familiarity," not quite of easy virtue but not altogether respectable. In jazz-age slang *chick* meant simply a girl, and a sophisticated young woman of the late 1930s and early 1940s might be termed a *hip chick* or *slick chick*. This usage is preserved in the more recent *chick with a stick,* sports slang for a female hockey player.

Even before *chicken* was being used to mean young girl or woman, it began to denote "cowardice" or "faint-heartedness." Young chickens are timid creatures and tend to run to their mother at the slightest alarm. In 1633 Sir Thomas Stafford wrote, "Not finding the defendants to be chikins, to be afraid of every cloud or kite."

In mid-19th-century America we find *chicken-hearted* (used by John Bunyan in *Pilgrim's Progress* 200 years earlier) and, a little later, *chicken-livered,* also meaning cowardly, whereas in slangier 20th-century parlance one simply is said *to be chicken* or *to chicken out* (back out for fear). In the military, a *chicken switch* is a button or other control that aborts an operation, such as a space mission, or activates a pilot's ejection seat, or the like. This usage dates from the beginning of the space age, about 1960.

Playing chicken is a potentially lethal game in which two motorists drive at each other head-on to see who will be the first to *chicken out,* that is, swerve to avoid collision. Though the name originated in the mid-20th century, the game itself no doubt is much older, its equivalent probably having existed in the days of knights on horseback.

Still another meaning for *chicken* is "small" or "trivial." A *chicken lobster* is one that weighs less than a pound, and *chicken pox* is a mild disease compared to the smallpox it once was thought to resemble. *Chicken weed*

(15th century) or *chickweed* is a tiny wildflower, only a few inches high. In the 1830s in America *chicken feed* meant small change, or a small amount of money, stemming from the fact that chickens can be fed corn and wheat grains too small for other uses. The less polite *chicken shit* originated in the military, probably during World War I. During World War II it was widely used in complaint against petty, disagreeable military rules. Also from World War I we have *chicken colonel,* for a full colonel, whose insignia is an eagle, as opposed to a lieutenant colonel, whose insignia is a silver oak leaf.

Despite these largely derogatory associations, owning and eating chickens has long denoted wealth, as in an old fable's warning, *"Don't count your chickens before they hatch."* In the fable, a milkmaid carrying a full pail of milk on her head fantasizes about selling the milk for eggs that would hatch into chickens and make her so rich that she would toss her head at offers of marriage; whereupon she tosses her head and spills the milk. Cervantes's Sancho Panza echoed the moral many centuries later: "Many count their chickens before they are hatched, and where they expect bacon meet with broken bones." It is still commonly used today to warn those who want to spend or profit from something they have not yet earned.

In the U.S. presidential campaign of 1928 the Republicans urged voters to keep in power the party that had put *a chicken in every pot.* Their ad men may have gotten the slogan from the Scottish poet Alexander Smith (1830–1867), who said that if men of letters ruled the world, every man "would have his hen in the pot." But he did not originate it either, for when Henry IV of France was crowned in 1589, he said, "I wish that on Sunday every peasant may have a chicken in his pot."

As reliably as salmon swim upriver to spawn, chickens are said to come home to rest and sleep. The English poet Robert Southey is credited with being the first to use this observation metaphorically when he wrote, "Curses are like young chickens, they always come home to roost"

(*The Curse of Kehama*, 1810). The saying is still used to mean that the consequences of doing wrong always return to haunt the wrongdoer.

At least one would-be miscreant gave himself away, calling out, "*There's nobody here but us chickens.*" Allegedly this saying originated as the response of a chicken thief to a suspicious farmer who, investigating nighttime noises in his chicken coop, asked, "Is anyone there?" The retort, presumably first uttered in the United States in the late 19th century, became a jocular catch phrase, used, for example, when fewer people than were expected showed up at a gathering.

▼Hen

> *O! ye lords of ladies intellectual,*
> *Inform us truly, have they not*
> *hen-peck'd you all?*
> —Lord Byron, *Don Juan* (1818)

The word *hen,* derived from Old English *hen* or *henn,* for the adult female domestic fowl, has also denoted the female of other birds since the 14th century. Further, it has been a slang word for "woman" since the early 17th century. The motherly, nurturing aspect of hens is recorded in the King James Bible ("even as a hen gathereth her chickens under her wings," Matthew 23:37). We still call a maternal woman a *mother hen*, although as often as not it is meant as a criticism of her overprotectiveness.

Members of *Sempervivum,* a widespread genus of garden plants, are commonly called *hens-and-chicks,* or *hens-and-chickens,* because they take the form of rosettes that quickly multiply to produce new rosettes all around their perimeter and so resemble a mother hen surrounded by her chicks.

The *hen party,* a term used in the United States since at least the 1880s, is a social gathering including only women or girls; it is the female counterpart of the stag party (see STAG).

Like most birds, hens use their beaks as weapons. Byron was by no means the first (or last) writer to apply the analogy to women. Richard Steele, in *The Spectator* in 1712, described Socrates as "by all accounts undoubted head of the sect of the hen-pecked," referring to the Greek philosopher's reputedly shrewish wife, Xanthippe. There are numerous examples throughout literature where the henpecked husband is more a figure of derision than pity. One might wonder why pecking hens are said to confine themselves to the male of the species. Do hens peck only at roosters and never at other hens or chicks? Perhaps the truth here has been bent to accommodate a traditional stereotype.

The source of that colorful hyperbole, *scarcer than hen's teeth,* usually spoken in complaining tones, is not known, other than that it is American. Edmund Kirke, in *Southern Friends* (1863), wrote, "horses are scarcer than hen's teeth around here," and the term reappeared in a Southern historical novel, *Where the Battle Was Fought* (1884), as "sometimes clients get as scarce as hen's teeth." Hens, of course, have no teeth, so the expression uses a total lack to emphasize extreme scarcity. Earlier similes of rarity include birds' milk (Aristophanes), chickens' milk (Pliny), and black swans (numerous writers, from the Roman satirist Juvenal to Dickens and others). A less valid comparison is called up in *mad as* or *madder than a wet hen,* which surfaces in several popular novels of the 1930s and 1940s but has been traced to early 19th-century America. The domestic chicken is not a waterfowl, but it is not necessarily upset by the presence of water. Nevertheless, whoever first came up with this expression clearly believed that a farmer tossing a bucket of water at hens could expect them to flap about in a furious uproar.

▼ Cock

> *Better be a cock for a day than a hen*
> *for a year.*
> —James Howell, *English Proverbs* (1659)

The word *cock,* from Middle English *cok* and Old English *cocc,* has been used for the male domestic fowl since the 14th century. In succeeding centuries it was transferred in a number of ways, all of which preserved the male symbolism: in the 15th century to mean "spout" or "tap"; in the 16th century, "the discharging mechanism of a firearm"; in the 17th century, as a verb (*to cock*) meaning "to set up" or "to stick up assertively"; and since about the same period, a vulgar slang word for "penis." The synonym *rooster,* from the verb *to roost,* is of American origin and dates from the late 18th century; it has not been similarly transferred.

The proud strut of the cock about the barnyard, as he asserts his *rule of the roost* over the hens and chicks, is reflected in such terms as *cocky,* which has meant arrogantly sure of oneself since the 18th century, and *cock of the walk,* for a conceited, domineering leader. Only slightly further removed is *cockade,* originally from the French, a rosette worn proudly on one's hat as an indication of military rank or high office. "A cockade, a lapell'd coat, and a feather are irresistible by a female heart," wrote Royall Tyler in his play *Contrast* (1787). Similarly we have *coxcomb,* from "cock's comb," the showy crest on a cock's head. In the Middle Ages it denoted a badge worn on jesters' caps, and it then came to mean a silly or vain fellow. The *shuttlecock* of badminton also is named for the cock's comb, which its feathered top resembles.

In contrast, *cocksure,* now meaning very confident, in the 16th century meant very secure or very certain. Shakespeare likened it to the sureness of the cock on a firearm (in *Henry IV,* Part I), so named for its resemblance to the bird or its head or comb, and one etymologist traces it to *stopcock,* a device that kept liquid securely inside a barrel.

Similarly removed—that is, derived from the verb *to cock,* which in turn comes from the noun *cock*—is *cockeyed,* which first (18th century) meant "squinting" or "cross-eyed" (from cocking, or tipping up, an eye) and since has acquired a number of other meanings, among them twisted or askew ("that picture is cockeyed"), foolish or completely wrong ("what a cockeyed argument"), and drunk ("two beers and she's cockeyed").

The source of *cock-a-hoop,* used since the 16th century to mean jubilant or exultant, is disputed. Some say it comes from a cock's triumphant crowing; others hold that it refers to removing the cock (spigot) from a barrel of beer and laying it on the hoop, resulting in extreme jollity from the free-flowing beer.

In Victorian times, both in Britain and in the United States, the use of *cock* as a synonym for "penis" was considered so vulgar that various linguistic substitutions began to be made in otherwise innocent words. Thus the nautical *coxswain* (actually originating from different linguistic roots) temporarily became "roosterswain," the *cockchafer* beetle a simple "chafer," the *haycock* a "haystack," the *weathercock* a "weather vane," the *cockhorse* a "rocking horse," and the *woodcock* a "timberdoodle." Further, the utterance *cockeyed* in the sense of "drunk" was forbidden in all vaudeville shows controlled by the Keith booking office. Many of these euphemisms, if they can even be called that, were short-lived, but some, such as rocking horse and haystack, have remained the preferred usage.

The case of the *weathercock* is an interesting one. The earliest weather vanes—the name *weather vane* dates from the early 1700s but the practice of mounting them dates from Roman times—were usually in the form of a banner. However, by about 1300 the figure of a cock must have been used, since the word *wedercok* appears in a manuscript of that time. One writer suggests that the figure of the cock was used to represent the cock that crowed after the disciple Peter denied Jesus, but there is no firm evidence for this theory.

Cock and Bull Story

> Said my mother, "What is this story
> all about?"—"A Cock and a Bull,"
> said Yorick. "And one of the best of
> its kind."
>
> —Laurence Sterne,
> *Tristram Shandy* (1767)

So ends Sterne's book, which is indeed long and rambling, in the true tradition of the picaresque novel, but unlike a *cock-and-bull story*, which is far-fetched and intended to deceive, it is reasonably credible. No one knows the exact origin of the expression, which has been around since about 1600. Some say it came from a fable or folktale involving a cock and a bull. Others say it is named for an English coaching inn, a wayside stop for travelers, where such tales were often told. The French call such a yarn *coq-à-l'âne,* that is, "cock to donkey," which in Scotland became a *cockalayne.* By the 18th century the term had come to mean an incredible tale or an elaborate lie—in other words, a tall tale. This certainly is what is meant when Jack Point and Wilfred the Jailer, of Gilbert and

Sullivan's *The Yeomen of the Guard,* concoct a story about the hero's fictitious death, singing:

> Tell a tale of cock and bull,
> Of convincing detail full.
> Tale tremendous, Heaven defend us!
> What a tale of cock and bull!

The listener to a cock-and-bull story might well say *Poppycock!* This expression, now no ruder an expletive than "Oh nonsense," came from the Dutch word *papekak,* for "soft dung," and originally was the equivalent of the present-day "bullshit." Or one might describe it as a *cockamamie* story—that is, a ridiculous or absurd story—a term perhaps derived from *poppycock* and dating from about 1940.

Cockpit

> *Can this cockpit hold the vasty fields*
> *of France?*
>
> —William Shakespeare, *Henry V*

Staging *cockfights,* in which game cocks, usually fitted with metal spurs, are set against one another and allowed to fight to the death, may have originated in ancient China. It was popular with the ancient Greeks and Romans. The fierceness of the cock was also acknowledged by the Goths, who used its image on their ensigns. In Britain, where it was introduced by the Romans, the training and breeding of fighting cocks became an important industry by the 1700s and from there spread to the British colonies. Today cockfighting has been outlawed in most Western countries (except Spain and the Latin American nations), but it is sometimes carried on in secret.

The fiercest game cocks are a variety known as *bantam cocks.* Although quite small, they are known to be able to defeat much larger opponents. Their name, which comes from a small Javanese village where they are thought to have originated, is sometimes applied to a small, feisty human, known as a *bantam*. It is also used for one of the lightest weight classifications in boxing; a *bantamweight* weighs less than 118 pounds.

The name *cockpit,* for the enclosure in which game cocks fight, originated in the 16th century. In the 17th century it also was used as a figure of speech for any scene of fighting, as by Shakespeare in the quotation above. James Howell wrote, in 1642, "The Netherlandes have been for many yeares . . . the very Cockpit of Christendome, the Schoole of Arms, and the Rendezvous of all adventurous Spirits" (*Instructions for Foreign Travel*), and two centuries later another travel writer said, "The part of Belgium through which our route lies has been called the Cockpit of Europe" (Murray, *Handbook to Northern Germany,* 1843). Indeed, from Ramillies (1706) to Waterloo (1815) to Mons and Ypres and the German invasion of World War II, Belgium has been a traditional and tragic battleground.

During World War I, fighter pilots called the narrow section of their planes the *cockpit,* and this usage carried over to peacetime aviation. Today the word is used not only for the place where pilot, copilot, and instruments are housed, but also for the helmsman's place, usually an open sunken area, in boats and other small vessels, as well as for the driver's seat in racing cars and some sports cars.

Cocktail

> There was a young lady of Kent,
> Who said that she knew what it meant
> When men asked her to dine,
> Gave her cocktails, and wine,
> She knew what it meant—but she went!

> —Author unknown

Why a mixed drink should resemble a rooster's hind feathers is anyone's guess, and many have tried. The most famous of early references to this term, which most people agree is American in origin, is in Washington Irving's *Knickerbocker History* (1809). Among the theories put forth are that it comes from the African Creole dialect word *kaktel,* for "scorpion," and refers to the "sharp bite" of a mixed drink; that a mixed drink was invented in the 1790s by a New Orleans druggist who dispensed tonics of cognac and bitters in an egg cup called a *coquetier,* a name first applied to its contents and then distorted into "cocktail"; that an Aztec nobleman sent his daughter, *Xochitl,* to the emperor with a drink of cactus juice, and the emperor liked it so much that he married the daughter and her name became attached to the drink; that it comes from a mixture the British fed to their fighting cocks, consisting of stale beer or ale, gin, herbs, and bread, which men also drank, and which was called *cockbread ale* or *cockale,* which became "cocktail"; or that after one or two strong mixed drinks one feels ready for a race, just like a horse with a *cocked tail.* However, the word *cocked* here may not mean "turned up" but "short," signifying that such a horse was of mixed parentage rather than thoroughbred—and of course a cocktail is a mixed drink.

As if these were not enough, H. L. Mencken lists still more possible etymologies: that it comes from *coquetel,* a mixed drink known in Bordeaux and introduced to America by French officers during the Revolution; or from *cock ale,* a mixture of ale and the essence of a boiled fowl, drunk in England during the 17th century; or it is an abbreviation of *cock tailings,* the remains from a variety of liquors, thrown together in a large container and sold cheaply; or from the practice of toasting the winning cock after a cockfight with a drink containing the same number of ingredients as the number of feathers left in his tail. As the evidence for none of these is very convincing, we might as well settle for the most colorful. The word *cocktail* itself has been adopted worldwide, even into Japanese.

▼Duck

*With a quack-quack here, and a
quack-quack there . . .*
 —*Old MacDonald,* children's song

The name of both the wild and the domestic waterfowl,
and the verb *to duck,* meaning to stoop or bend down
suddenly, come from Old English *dūke,* meaning "diver."
(*Duck cloth,* a lightweight canvas, is derived from the
Dutch word *doek,* for "cloth.") Ducks are primarily
aquatic birds, but they also are excellent fliers, and wild
ducks migrate great distances at high speed. They are
hunted and raised domestically mainly for their meat, but
one kind, the *eider duck,* is valued for its fine down feathers (called *eiderdown*).

Duck hunting is a time-honored sport, since these
birds can present quite a challenge. However, a *sitting
duck*—one that is resting on the water surface rather than
in flight—is an easy target. Dating from the first half of
the 20th century, this term is often applied to other kinds
of easy target, as in "Always eager to make money fast,
he's a sitting duck for unscrupulous brokers." To make
their sport somewhat easier, hunters may use *decoy
ducks*—painted wooden birds—to attract wild ducks
within gunshot. Possibly it is this practice that gave rise to
getting one's ducks in a row, an expression used since
about 1960 for becoming fully prepared or getting one's
affairs in order. Or perhaps it alludes to the targets in a
fairground shooting gallery. The precise origin is not clear.

Some ducks are raised for their eggs. In Britain, *duck-
egg* is a colloquial term for "zero," the counterpart of
goose-egg in America.

Adept in water and air, ducks do less well on land. Their
walk is awkward because their legs are quite short and
placed far back on the body. Hence *duck-legged* has, since
the 17th century, described a person with short legs and a
waddling gait. To do the *duckwalk* is to walk with legs apart
and feet turned outward; it is imitated by bending over,

grasping one's ankles, and then attempting to walk. This position is called for in a number of children's racing games and also has been used as a punishment for prisoners and in the military. The *ducktail,* on the other hand, is a style of haircut that was popular among American teenagers in the 1950s; the front hair is slicked back and the back hair tapered into a point resembling the duck's tail feathers.

In America *ducky* has been slang for "marvelous" or "wonderful" since about 1830. In Britain, a *ducky* is a "sweetheart" or "dear," usually a woman; in Shakespeare's time, however, it was a slang word for the female breast.

Strictly speaking, *duck* means not just a kind of bird but also the female of the species, the male being called a *drake.* Playing *ducks and drakes,* a game of skipping stones over water, has been popular for at least four centuries; it may be so named from the resemblance of the skipping stones to birds taking off from the water. John Higgins defined it in 1583 as "a kind of sport or play with an oister shell or stone throwne into the water," and in 1605 George Chapman wrote, "Make ducks and drakes with shillings." To *play ducks and drakes* also has meant to play fast and loose or to throw something away carelessly, a meaning that dates back to the same period.

The affinity of ducks to water has given rise to a number of common expressions. A person with a particular attraction to something is said to *take to it like a duck to water.* Something that has no effect on a person, such as a vain warning, is said to roll off that person *like water off a duck's back.*

Since the early 19th century *a fine day for ducks* has described very wet weather, and from late in the century comes *Can a duck swim?*—the equivalent of "Is the Pope Catholic?"—meaning "certainly, obviously, yes." A similar expression of certainty is *If it looks like a duck, walks like a duck and quacks like a duck, it's a duck.* Often shortened to *If it looks like a duck,* this expression was first used in the 1950s, in the heyday of the infamous McCarthy investigations, by union leader Walter Reuther as a "test" to determine if a person was a Communist. It has since been used in numerous other and less hostile contexts.

The analogy in *duck soup,* American slang since about 1910 for "very easy to do," is baffling. Is duck soup easy to make? easy to eat? Whatever, it became the title of one of the Marx Brothers' most famous zany comedies, and is still used as the equivalent of "it's a cinch."

Lame Duck

> *I'll have no lame duck's daughter in my family.*
>
> —William Makepeace Thackeray,
> *Vanity Fair* (1848)

Like most migratory birds, ducks fly together, and an injured bird may not be able to keep up with the rest. In 18th-century Britain, a stock exchange jobber who could not or would not meet his debts was called, from about 1760 on, a *lame duck;* he was struck from the members' list and had to waddle away from the Exchange. ("Frauds of which a lame duck on the stock exchange would be ashamed," wrote Thomas Macaulay in 1841.)

A century later in the United States the term was applied to a congressman who failed to be reelected but

whose term of office had not yet expired. The Twentieth Amendment to the Constitution, called the *Lame Duck Amendment* and passed in 1934, calls for Congress and each new president to take office in January instead of March, as before, and therefore eliminates the *lame-duck session* of Congress. However, the Twenty-second Amendment, limiting the president to two terms of office, made it possible to be a *lame-duck president,* a description now used of presidents during their second term of office but usually not until the latter half of that term.

A different sort of derangement is conjured up by the expression *ruptured duck,* one of which actually resides among our family's attic treasures. A lapel button that was given to World War II veterans along with their honorable discharge, it actually bears the image of an eagle but was given its jocular nickname by veterans. It is also called a *screaming eagle.*

The original meaning of *dead duck,* used from about 1867 for a person whose political influence has declined, may have derived from *lame duck.* Today it generally refers to someone who has been defeated or is without hope of succeeding. In marked contrast is the *lucky duck,* the fortunate winner, a term that no doubt owes its origin to its rhyming sound.

The *ugly duckling* comes from Hans Christian Andersen's version of the Cinderella story, in which a baby cygnet, hatched with a brood of ducklings, is despised by both mother and siblings for its clumsiness until it grows up and becomes a graceful swan. In like manner, the homeliest or most awkward child may grow up into the most beautiful or talented member of the family.

The cry of the duck has been called a *quack,* an imitative (of the sound) word, since the 17th century, and since about the same time a *quack* has also been an ignorant or fraudulent pretender to medical knowledge or skill. The latter usage is a shortening of *quacksalver,* a 16th-century word from a Dutch term that meant "puffer of salves," that is, a vendor who exaggerated the benefits of medicines and salves he was selling. Today *quack* has been extended to mean any kind of charlatan.

▼ Goose

> *The goose is a silly bird—too much for one to eat, and not enough for two.*
> —Charles Poole, *Archaic Words* (1880)

Geese are no longer as important to the poultry industry as they were in Europe in earlier times, when no prosperous farm was without a good-sized flock. *Goose,* from Old English *gōs,* has also meant a foolish or silly person since the 16th century, perhaps because the bird was thought to be quite stupid, and we still call such a person a *goose* or *silly goose.* To be *a goose among the swans* is to be out of place and usually quite inferior to the others in a group. This saying dates from Roman times, when Virgil wrote, "He gabbles like a goose among melodious swans" (*Eclogues,* 37 B.C.).

In 19th-century America *goosey* (or *goosy*) was a synonym for "silly" or "dumb," and *You ain't got the brains God gave a goose,* meaning you are exceptionally stupid, was a common phrase. *Goosey* also meant "nervous" or "touchy," probably from the verb *to goose,* which meant, in America in the 1850s, to hiss or boo a public performance (a play or actor so treated was said to *get the goose*). Somewhat later, in the early 1890s, the verb acquired the more vulgar present-day meaning of poking or pinching someone between or on the buttocks in order to startle them. The origin of this usage is obscure. One theory is that it makes the victim hiss or cry out like a goose. H. L. Mencken believed it came from the fact that geese, pugnacious birds, sometimes attack human beings by biting at them, and that, given their size, this is the anatomical part they most often reach. Another theory is that the term comes from the farmer's custom of examining a goose

before it was turned out to feed in a field; he felt its bottom for an egg about to be laid, and if an egg was there, the goose was kept penned up until it had laid.

The expression *loose as a goose,* dating from the mid-20th century, was originally vulgar, meaning "promiscuous." Later it came to mean "very relaxed" (as in *hang loose*).

Perhaps the best-known reference to *goose eggs* comes to us from Aesop's fable about the goose that laid golden eggs. The farmer who owned the goose tried to get the mass of gold he thought must be inside her, so he cut her open and she died. Aesop's moral, that one should be content with what one has and not be greedy for more, is now enshrined in the proverb, *Don't kill the goose that lays the golden eggs.* The American use of *goose-egg* for "zero" (the British say *duck-egg*) dates from the 1850s and became common in baseball from about 1866 on. It may perhaps have led credence to the popular belief, which is discounted by most etymologists, that the term for "zero" in tennis, *love,* came from the French word for egg, *l'oeuf.*

Mother Goose became synonymous with nursery rhymes about 1760, when a collection was published in London entitled *Mother Goose's Melody.*

Like duck, *goose* is the name for both the species and the female, the male goose being called *gander.* Proverbially, however, there is no great difference between the two, one of the older English sayings being, *What's sauce for the goose is sauce for the gander.* It appeared in John Ray's collection of proverbs of 1670 (to it he appended the note, "This is a woman's Proverb") and means, basically, equity for one and all.

The verb *to gander* has meant "to wander aimlessly," as the male goose often does, since the late 1600s. Possibly it is the source of the expression *to take a gander,* meaning to take a long look at something or someone, which originated early in the 20th century. One writer suggests this term comes from *gander month,* an obsolete term for the time of a woman's confinement for child-birth, during which her husband, called a *gandermooner,* was apt to wander about much as a gander does while the goose sits on her eggs. More probably, however, it alludes to the long-necked bird looking about as it wanders. (Hence perhaps also the nursery rhyme, "Goosey goosey gander, whither shall I wander? Upstairs and downstairs, and into my lady's chamber.") The same part of goose anatomy is alluded to in *gooseneck,* a word applied to anything resembling the bird's long, curved neck, such as the flexible, long-shafted *gooseneck lamp.*

Another portion of goose anatomy that has been sin-gled out is *gooseflesh,* a word dating from about 1400. In the Middle Ages geese were plucked several times a year, their feathers being highly valued for stuffing pillows, bed coverings, and the like. With its downy covering removed, the naked goose's reaction to any drop in temperature was very obvious, as its skin contracted to form little bumps. The same condition in human beings, induced by cold or fear, thus was called *gooseflesh,* and later also *goose pimples* or *goose bumps.*

The stiff-legged walk of geese gave rise to the name *goose step,* a military gait in which the legs are moved with knees rigid, from the hip, each leg swinging as high as possible. In Germany this gait was used from the time of Frederick the Great (1712–86). In Britain it was used from 1800 on as a marking-time exercise in calisthenics. In a similar exercise a recruit would stand on one leg and swing the other back and forth. Such exercises eventually were used by most of the European armies during the 19th century. By 1900, however, the *goose step* had become a slow, straight-legged marching step. It was used by Mussolini's and Hitler's troops in the 1930s, and ever since has been associated with fascism and despotism.

Cook Your Goose

> *This business . . . may cook his goose good and proper.*
> —Agatha Christie, *Tuesday Club Murders*
> (1933)

How the British got from roasting their festive holiday goose to saying *Your goose is cooked,* meaning "You're done for," is not clear. Several etymologists quote a picturesque story about the inhabitants of a besieged town in the 16th century who hung out a goose to show the besiegers they were not starving. This show of defiance so angered the attacking leader, Eric the Mad of Sweden, that he burned down the town and thereby cooked their goose, literally and figuratively. Another writer suggests it comes from the fable about killing the goose that lays the golden eggs (see above), where the farmer was left with nothing but a goose to cook. The only verifiable things about this expression are its meaning and that it appears in a street song published in 1851 expressing opposition to Pope Pius IX and his appointment of Nicholas, Cardinal Wiseman, as Archbishop of Westminster:

> If they come here we'll cook their goose,
> The Pope and Cardinal Wiseman.

In America a couple of decades earlier there was a similar saying, *gone goose,* meaning "done for," which first appeared about 1830. John Bartlett's *Dictionary of Americanisms* (1848) explains that *It's a gone goose with him* meant he was lost beyond recovery, and that it was a New England form of speech, whereas in New York one would say *He's a gone gander.*

Wild Goose Chase

*A pursuit of something as unlikely to
be caught as a wild goose.*

—Samuel Johnson (1775)

Dr. Johnson's definition of a *wild goose chase* as a "vain pursuit" is how we use the term today, but its original meaning is different and much older. In Elizabethan England there was a popular game of follow-the-leader on horseback that was called a wild goose chase because geese fly in similar formation, evenly spaced behind a leader. Shakespeare referred to the game: "If thy wits run the wild-goose chase, I have done" (*Romeo and Juliet*), meaning that "My mind will not be able to keep up with yours." This sense apparently was forgotten by the time of Samuel Johnson, whose meaning Charles Dickens took in the 19th century when he wrote, "The disappointed coachmaker had sent me on a wild-goose errand" (*The Uncommercial Traveler*, 1868).

▽Turkey

*Here he comes, swelling like a
turkey cock.*

—William Shakespeare, *Henry V*

The very name of this fowl is a misnomer. The original turkey was the guinea fowl, named *turkey* about 1550 by the British, probably because it was brought to western Europe by Portuguese traders from Africa via Turkey. A century later they confused it with the native American bird—a different species but somewhat similar in appearance— which most Americans eat at Thanksgiving and most Britishers at Christmas. This accounts for its mention by Shakespeare and others before there was a major English settlement on North American soil.

Native Americans introduced the hungry Pilgrims to the American bird, and it is an Indian anecdote that supposedly gave rise to the term *talk turkey,* or speak plainly and to the point, which dates from about 1830. As with most such tales, several versions exist. According to one, an Indian and a white man went hunting together and afterward sat down to divide the spoils. The white man proposed, "Either I'll take the turkey and you the buzzard, or you the buzzard and I the turkey." The Indian, however, replied, "You never once talk turkey to me." In the latter half of the 19th century this term sometimes became *to talk cold turkey,* meaning to face the facts and speak bluntly, even (or especially) if this would be unpleasant, and by about 1920 *cold turkey* had come to mean an abrupt (blunt and usually painful) withdrawal from drugs, alcohol, or another addictive substance.

Given its festive nature at the dinner table, it seems odd that the bird's name in slang usage also means a loser, a failure, a dud. Since the 1920s it has been applied in this sense to individuals and, even more often, to a failed theatrical production, a flop. Turkeys also are rather stupid beasts, so applying the name to a stupid or inept person seems more logical. This last usage is newer, dating from about 1950.

In the barnyard the turkey has a distinctive, stiff-legged gait ("Strut like a turkey-cock," wrote Thomas Shadwell in 1689). During the first half of the 19th century this gait gave rise to the name *turkey trot* for a round dance in which the steps resembled a straight-legged springy walk. In the early 1900s the same name was used for a new ragtime dance in which the dancers took springing steps on the balls of their feet while jerking their shoulders up and down.

Farm Animals:
In Barn
and
Meadow

The word *cattle* comes from the same Latin root as the words *chattel* and *capital,* signifying they were regarded as important property from very early on. *Cattle* comes from Anglo-Norman *catel,* which in the Middle Ages meant movable property of any kind. Later it was restricted to mean livestock, and in the 19th century to mean bovine beasts exclusively—bull, cow, calf, ox, and steer. (*Bovine* itself comes from Latin *bōs,* for "cow.") Valued for milk, meat, and hides since prehistory, these animals are firmly entrenched in our language as well.

Cattle tend to keep together in a group called a *herd,* a word also applied to large groups of humans, but usually in a disparaging way. Even less flattering is *the herd,* a term for "the common people" or "rabble." And then we also have *the herd instinct,* a term invented about 1900 to describe an innate tendency to think and act as one of a crowd.

On the range, cattle still move on their own, but when they are shipped to market they generally are herded into *cattle cars.* For a time in the 1860s this term was a slangy usage for a railroad passenger car providing scant comfort, and during World War II it acquired a more sinister meaning. The Nazis used cattle cars to transport hundreds of thousands of Jews, under worse than bestial conditions, to concentration camps.

▼Bull

> *He bellows like a bull whose throat*
> *has just been cut.*
> —Aeschylus (c. 458 B.C.)

The male of the species is a large, formidable and loud-voiced creature. Its name comes from Middle English *bule* and Old English *bula,* and is virtually synonymous with sexual potency. (A castrated bull is called a *bullock, ox,* or *steer.*)

In the 17th century, *bull* also meant a jest ("And swear he is the father of all bulls since Adam; if all fail he has a project to print his jests.—His bulls, you mean." James Shirley, *The Gamester*). This meaning is now obsolete, but some etymologists believe that a version of it survives in the 20th-century slang meaning of *bull* as "exaggerated nonsense." Others hold the modern term to be a polite shortening of *bullshit,* which apparently started out as military slang for excessive spit and polish and then came to mean anything pretentious, boastful, or downright false.

A *bull session* has meant, since the 1920s, an informal gossip fest for men, where they are said to *shoot* (or *sling* or *throw*) *the bull,* that is, freely express their views about anything and everything, including sexual prowess, backed up by as much or as little experience and knowledge as they might have.

The bull's appearance and other qualities gave rise to such words as *bullfinch,* a bird named in the 14th century for its large head and squat form; *bulldog,* a similarly large-headed and prominently muscular dog, originally bred for the sport of *bull-baiting* (see under BULLDOG); *bull-headed,* meaning "obstinate," since bulls are not quick to adapt to changing conditions but tend to forge ahead (*bull their way*) regardless of circumstances; *bull-necked,* having a short, thick neck; *bullhorn,* a high-powered megaphone or loudspeaker, reminiscent of the bull's loud bellow; and, also alluding to the animal's noisiness, *bull-roarer,* a wooden slat that produces a roaring sound when whirled around on the end of a thong or string and that is used either as a toy or, in some cultures, in religious ceremonies.

Architects call a rounded or obtuse exterior angle a *bull-nose,* which it resembles, and sharpshooters aim for the black target center called, since the early 19th century, the *bull's-eye.* The latter was also, in the early 19th century, a nickname for a British coin, the crown, and one writer suggests that the target was named for the coin, which in turn was named for a common bet made in bull-baiting, where those backing the bull put their crown on the "bull's eye," just as one might bet on a "horse's nose." He supports this theory by saying that the coin and target center were of similar size. However, the *Oxford English Dictionary* quotes a cavalry regulations manual of 1833 that specifies "A bull's-eye of eight inches diameter," and not even in Great Britain's most glorious days were its coins as large as that.

Bull in a China Shop

The earliest recorded use of this simile for extremely clumsy, inappropriate, or even violent behavior is in Frederick Marryat's *Jacob Faithful* (1834): "Whatever it is that smashes, Mrs. T. always swears it was the most valuable thing in the room. I'm like a bull in a china-shop." Vivid as the image is, it is unlikely that it was based on any real-life event. Charles Earle Funk suggested it originated in Aesop's fable about the ass in the potter's shop that breaks the earthen pots, and that a British cartoonist of the early 19th century took this theme to caricature *John Bull* and his awkward dealings with China (the East India Company's monopoly on trade with China having been terminated in 1834). And the cartoon in turn inspired Marryat's turn of phrase, which has since been used by many others. However ingenious and plausible this explanation is, there is no evidence for it. The usage *John Bull* for the English nation or the typical Englishman comes from the Scottish satirist John Arbuthnot's 1712 allegory, *The History of John Bull*, which considerably predates the British China trade.

Take the Bull by the Horns

> *He had not, as the phrase goes, taken the bull by the horns.*
>
> —Sir Walter Scott, *Old Mortality* (1816)

This expression for meeting a problem head-on rather than evading it probably comes from bullfighting, and possibly in an ancient form. In the classic present-day *bullfight,* the banderilleros plant darts in the bull and then jump on its back and seize it by the horns. In another version, it is the matador who tires the bull in various ways and then seizes it by the horns in order to wrestle it to the ground. The sport has been depicted somewhat differently on Cretan pottery. In ancient Crete a number of young athletes would approach the bull from the front, grasp him by the horns, and vault over his head, landing either on his flank or behind him. The object in all these sports, of course, is to avoid being gored. Animal horns, and a bull's in particular, have been a symbol for cuckoldry since

ancient times and were so regarded by Chaucer, Shakespeare, and numerous later writers. This meaning, however, is not involved in *take the bull by the horns*, which simply means to face up to a difficult situation.

A similar term comes from the American West, where *bulldogging* a steer means to get a grip on his horns and twist his head so he is forced to the ground. It is a favorite event in rodeos.

Bullpen

Another term from American ranching is *bullpen*, for an enclosure for steers. In the early 19th century it came to mean a similar log enclosure for human prisoners, which was extended to mean a prison cell, guardhouse, or similar small place of confinement. The idea of being crowded, as bulls certainly are inside a pen, caused the term to be used also for a dormitory or bunkhouse for cowboys, lumberjacks, and the like. Of these meanings, only the original—an enclosure for animals—has survived.

Around 1910, the area where relief pitchers warm up during a baseball game began to be called the *bullpen*. This term, however, may have had a quite different origin. In those days ballparks often had huge advertising billboards looming over the fences. One of the chief advertisers of the time was Bull Durham Tobacco, whose ads pictured an enormous, brightly colored bull. In a master stroke of publicity, the company offered any batter who hit a ball into one of its signs $50 and two bags of Bull Durham tobacco. Because the relief pitchers often practiced near or under the shade cast by this billboard, their area was called the *bullpen*. Although this etymology, recounted by Stuart Flexner, may be fanciful, it commemorates a colorful aspect of American social history.

Bulldozer

The name of this earth-moving tractor comes from a less lighthearted phase of history. It probably originated in *bull-dose,* a dose of punishment (a thrashing) for a bull. Drovers used a *bullwhip,* a long leather lash, to keep cattle from straying. In the American South after the Civil War, white bullies also sometimes used a bullwhip to intimidate black voters, threatening them with "a dose of the bull" if they voted for the wrong candidate (or voted at all). In the last quarter of the 19th century, therefore, *bulldozing* came to mean violent coercion. With the invention, about 1925, of a machine that could clear away trees and knock down buildings with sheer force, it seemed quite natural to call it a *bulldozer.* (Incidentally, the word *bully,* for "tyrant," comes from Middle Dutch and German words quite unrelated to the animal.) See also BEARS AND BULLS.

Cow

> *The cow is of the bovine ilk,*
> *One end is moo, the other milk.*
> —Ogden Nash, *The Cow* (1930)

The name of the female domestic bovine animal comes from Old English *cū.* Despite the cow's obvious value and importance for its milk, meat, and hide, its name most often has derogatory connotations. Calling a woman a *cow* is distinctly offensive, implying that she is large, fat, placid, not too bright, and/or overly fecund. Describing a place as a *cow town* or *cow college* is equally unflattering, suggesting that it is unimportant, dull, and provincial in the worst sense. In the 1830s in America a *cowcatcher* was a triangular frame set in front of a locomotive in order to clear the railroad track of obstructions, such as cattle. A century later it became a slang term for a brief commercial placed at the beginning of a radio program, designed to catch the attention of unsophisticated listeners (rural "hicks"). Even that charming wildflower, the *cowslip,* a primrose abundant in British pastures, is so called because the plant thrives on cow manure (Old

English *cuislyppe,* from "cow" + "slime or dung"). Shakespeare mentioned it in *The Tempest:* "Where the bee sucks, there suck I, In a cowslip's bell I lie."

Also from Shakespeare's time is the saying, *Not until the cows come home,* meaning not for a long time. Probably it refers to the time when cows return to the barn for milking, which actually may not be all that long an interval, depending on how it is applied. However, Beaumont and Fletcher, in their play *The Scornful Lady* (1610), wrote, "Kiss till the cows come home," which here did signify a long embrace.

Cowboy

> *I'm an old cowhand, from the Rio Grande,*
> *And my legs ain't bowed, and my skin ain't tanned.*
> *I'm a cowboy who never saw a cow,*
> *Never roped a steer 'cause I don't know how,*
> *And I ain't a-fixin' to start in now,*
> *Yippee—ai—oh—ky—ay.*
>
> —Folk song

Around that romantic figure of the American West, the *cowboy,* grew an elaborate vocabulary, wardrobe, and set of customs. His skills in riding, herding, roping, and branding cattle today survive mainly in the rodeo, still an extremely popular form of entertainment in the western United States. In the latter part of the 19th century a cowboy also might be called a *cowhand,* meaning simply a worker on a cattle ranch, or a *cowpoke* or *cowpuncher,* for the prod (metal-tipped pole) he used at roundup time to goad the cattle into pens or stock cars. Because he was admired especially for his skill and daring on horseback, *cowboy* became a slang term for a wild, very fast automobile driver or for an individual who performs a delicate task recklessly.

The word *cowboy* originated about 1720, but during the American Revolution it acquired a quite different meaning. The *cowboys* then were a band of Tory (pro-British) guerrillas who fought between the American and British lines north of New York City in what is now Westchester County, plundering the local populace. According to one source, they were so called because they hid in the brush and tinkled cowbells in order to lure American soldiers, who, hoping to find a cow, instead found themselves ambushed.

A coinage attributed to cartoonist T. A. Dorgan (who signed himself TAD) is *drugstore cowboy,* an idler who hangs around drugstore soda fountains, often with the purpose of meeting young women. It was first recorded in 1923. With the demise of drugstore soda fountains, the term was broadened to include would-be cowboys and actors who portray cowboys, this usage being equally pejorative.

Cowlick

Since the late 19th century the word *cowlick* has referred to a tuft of hair that sticks up because it grows in a different direction from the others, presumably looking as though it had been licked askew by a cow. Close observers note that most cows have a section in their hide where the hairs, growing in a different direction, meet and form a projecting ridge. Supposedly the animal licks this section, making it stick up even more.

A better-documented bovine habit is that of *chewing the cud,* shared by sheep, bison, buffalo, and goat, as well as domestic cattle. Technically all these animals are *ruminants* (from Latin *ruminatus,* meaning "chewed over and over"), which means they bring up food in a cud that is chewed and swallowed again. While engaged in this practice cows tend to look intensely preoccupied, giving rise to a second meaning for *ruminate,* to meditate, muse, or ponder. Human beings described as chewing the cud are similarly said to be deep in thought.

Cash Cow

The world of high finance recalls the milk-producing ability of cows in the term *cash cow*, signifying a highly profitable division or company of a business concern. Frequently the cash cow is an old, well-established producer of a popular product that continues to sell reliably well without requiring additional expenditures on advertising or costly marketing strategies. In other words, it yields "milk" (that is, profits) year after year, and its proceeds can be relied on to enable investing in riskier areas of the business.

Sacred Cow

The Hindu religion regards all life as sacred, but the most important living creature to Hindus is the cow, considered a symbol of God's generosity to humanity. Cows may never be slaughtered, and their flesh never consumed. From these beliefs the British in India came up with the term *sacred cow*, a metaphor for any person, group, or belief that may not be attacked or criticized; it became current in the early 20th century.

The important status conferred on cows is not uniquely Indian. A number of African peoples, among them the Masai of Tanzania and Kenya, regard cattle as sacred and raise them mainly for the prestige they confer on their owners. The Masai drink cattle blood mixed with milk in many important ceremonies, thereby indicating their blood brotherhood with the beasts, and they use cattle in place of money to pay fines and taxes, as compensation for injuries, and as payment for wives. Cows are killed only for sacrifice at certain ceremonies, such as a chief's funeral, and since the Masai themselves are not permitted to slaughter cattle, they ask members of neighboring tribes to do it for them. The meat, which may be taken only from an animal killed in sacrifice, may not be eaten inside the village; it must be cooked and served in a secluded spot. In recent decades these traditional customs have been changing, but the idea of the sacred cow persists, despite the efforts of modern agronomists and even in lands ravaged by drought and famine.

▼ *Calf*

For more than 1,000 years the young of the cow has been called a *calf*, from Old English *cealf*. The other *calf*, signifying the fleshy part of the human leg below the knee, has been around only since about 1300, and is traced to Old Norse for that part of anatomy, *kalfi*. One writer suggests that the identical English word came to be used because this portion of human bodies bears a close resemblance to the prominent leg musculature of bovine calves, called *kalfr* in Old Norse. The resemblance is certainly there, both in muscle and name, but the exact connection is more an educated guess than a documented fact.

According to an ancient proverb, *A bellowing cow soon forgets her calf.* Rather than berating the animal for short-lived affection, it merely points out that excessive grief doesn't last long. The saying first appeared about 1330, cited in Thomas Wright's *Political Songs*. Translated into modern English, it was:

> It is not for the calf that the cow loweth,
> But for the green grass that in the meadow groweth.

The modern form of the proverb appeared in the mid-1500s.

The Fatted Calf

> *And bring hither the fatted calf and*
> *kill it; and let us eat, and be merry.*
> —Luke 15:23

The ancient Hebrews made animal sacrifices and had no scruples about killing a sacred cow. On the contrary, killing a calf especially fattened for a gala celebration was the norm. In the Biblical parable of the prodigal son as recorded by St. Luke, the father celebrated his son's return with just such a feast, and ever since, *to kill the fatted calf* has meant to welcome a guest by presenting him or her with the best of everything.

The *golden calf* predates the fatted one by many centuries. In Exodus, the second book of the Old Testament, the Hebrews' high priest, Aaron, fashions a golden calf and builds an altar before it. God then tells Moses, who brought the Israelites out of Egypt, that his people have corrupted themselves by worshiping a golden calf instead of their Lord God. Moses takes the calf and burns it, grinds it into powder, mixes the powder with water, and makes the people drink it. Ever since, the term *golden calf* has signified crass materialism, that is, the worship and pursuit of riches instead of higher things.

Mooncalf and Dumb Ox

> *I hid me under the moon-calf's gaber-*
> *dine for fear of the storm.*
> —William Shakespeare, *The Tempest*

Medical knowledge during the 16th century was a combination of fact, fancy, and superstition. A deformed and aborted fetus, unable to support life, was thought to result from having been conceived during an unfavorable phase of the moon and so was called a *mooncalf*. This precise meaning became obsolete, but perhaps because many premature babies who survived proved to be mentally retarded, *mooncalf* in the 17th century came to signify a dolt or a born fool, and later, an inveterate daydreamer. These meanings have persisted to the present. (There is an equivalent German term, *Mondkalb,* which some say gave rise to the last meaning.)

A low opinion of bovine intelligence is also perpetuated in *dumb ox,* which according to Ebenezer Brewer is what Albertus Magnus reportedly called his pupil, Thomas Aquinas ("a dumb ox who will one day fill the world with his lowing"—1248). In fact, St. Thomas was his favorite pupil and his teacher probably was jesting. But oxen are still not considered very bright, and *dumb ox* has remained in the language.

▽ *Ass, Donkey, and Mule*

> *What, you ass! Must I begin to teach you your letters? For that I shall need not words but a cudgel.*
> —Cicero (c. 55 B.C.)

From the Latin *asinus*—and taxonomists call the domestic ass *Equus asinus*—we have the English words *ass* and *asinine,* for "stupid person" and "stupid." This long-eared, patient domestic beast of burden was considered synonymous with stupidity not only by the ancient Romans; Cicero was quoting a still older Greek proverb. The ass figures in a number of Aesop's fables and rarely comes off as anything but a dullard. For example, it puts on a lion's skin in order to frighten a fox but betrays itself by braying loudly. Hence we say *make an ass of oneself* for acting foolish. In addition to folly, asses are credited with conceit in the proverb *Every ass likes to hear himself bray,* first recorded in 1732.

Dim-witted it may be, but the ass has been valuable since prehistoric times for carrying loads. More sure-footed than the horse, it can move easily over steep and narrow mountain paths and rough roads. It can go without food and water for long periods and work twice as hard as a horse with little or no care. Asses were employed to haul the heavy stones used to build the Egyptian pyramids and for similar work in Babylonia and ancient Greece. Nevertheless, at least since the 15th century, an unmitigated fool has been called an *ass* or a *jackass,* the latter meaning "male ass." (For some reason human stupidity has not been attached to the female *jenny ass,* or *jennet.*)

The word *ass* also is a vulgar term for "buttocks" or "rectum," which until about the year A.D. 1000 was called *arse* (and in Britain still is). This meaning gave rise to the even more vulgar *asshole,* for "anus," and vulgar slang for "a stupid or contemptible person."

Sometime in the 18th century the word *ass* began to be replaced with *donkey.* Originally pronounced to rhyme with monkey, the name was thought to come from the dun color of the animal. One writer suggests it was a euphemism for ass, which fell into disfavor because of its secondary sense, so that by the later 19th century "donkey" was in exclusive use in polite society. Calling a person a *donkey,* however, is the same as calling one a fool or stupid, and *donkey work* is uninteresting, repetitive drudgery, much like what donkeys are used for.

The origin of *donkey's years,* meaning a very long time, is disputed. Some say it is a rhyming term for "donkey's ears," which are quite long; others say it alludes to the fact that donkeys are very long-lived. The latter idea is borne out by the Scottish equivalent, *a donkey's age,* also meaning a long time.

Since 1874, a year of hotly disputed congressional elections, the donkey has been the symbol of America's Democratic Party. It, like the Republican Party elephant (see ELEPHANT) and the Tammany Hall tiger, was established through the clever and forceful political cartoons of Thomas Nast, published in *Harper's Weekly.* Nast first drew an ass in a lion's skin to represent the *New York Herald* frightening off people from voting Republican, and before long the ass, now a donkey, symbolized the Republicans' chief opponent, the Democratic Party. The symbol survived, despite a later comparison of the party to a mule.

"The Democratic Party is like a mule," said the 19th-century Populist leader Ignatius Donnelly before the Minnesota State Legislature, "without pride of ancestry or hope of posterity." The comparison was not wholly original, since John O'Connor Power was quoted by H. H. Asquith in his memoirs as saying the same of "the mules of politics." It probably was originated by the great 19th-century political orator Robert Ingersoll: "A mule has neither pride of ancestry nor hope of posterity." The reference, of course, is to the fact that a mule is the sterile offspring of a male ass (jackass) and female horse (mare) and hence cannot reproduce itself. As Josh Billings put it, "The mule is half horse and half jackass, and then comes to a full stop, nature discovering her mistake."

The English word *mule* comes from Latin *mulus*. The animal has long been bred for its strength and endurance. Mules can be trained to march in single file in orderly fashion for long distances with heavy loads, and they were at one time so used by the United States Army. Since the 1920s, the word *mule* also has been slang for a person who smuggles contraband, especially illicit drugs.

Despite their usefulness, mules have a legendary reputation for stubbornness, and when we call someone *muleheaded* or *mulish*, we are referring to that particular characteristic.

▼ Goat

> *And he shall separate them one from another, as a shepherd divideth his sheep from the goats; and he shall set the sheep on his right hand, but the goats on the left.*
>
> —Matthew 25:32

Even in Biblical times, goats were less valuable than sheep. Since they can survive on the scrubbiest pasture land, eating vegetation no self-respecting sheep will touch, they are often confined to the upper reaches of steep, rock-strewn mountainsides and kept out of grasslands suitable for sheep. (In Britain today, however, sheep and goats frequently graze side by side.) Separating the sheep from the goats thus means dividing the worthy from the unworthy, or the good from the evil.

The word *goat* comes from Old English *gāt* for the female goat (she-goat); Old English for male goat was *bucca,* which became the modern *buck.* Although biologists and naturalists call the male of numerous species, including the goat, a *buck* (and the female a *doe),* the more common colloquial terms are *billy goat,* from the diminutive for William and dating from the 18th century, and *nanny goat,* from the diminutive for Anne and dating from at least the late 18th century. A young goat, less than a year old, is a *kid,* which in the 19th century became an informal word for a human youngster.

Billy goats are popularly thought to be randy creatures, so that calling a man a *goat* is an informal and not altogether disapproving way of calling him licentious or lecherous; the adjective *goatish* means the same thing. It is not clear just how long this usage has been current, but it is applied exclusively to boys and men. An *old goat* has been, since the 1940s, an offensive old person, usually but not always a man and sometimes but not always implying a lecherous bent.

Both male and female goats are bearded, giving rise to *goatee* for a carefully trimmed chin beard that resembles the goat's tufts of hair. This term surfaced about 1840 in America, where the style was quite popular until after the Civil War. It first appeared on a picture of Uncle Sam in 1868. Around 1870 fuller whiskers became the fashion, and today a goatee looks distinctly dated.

An old proverb, recorded in Thomas Fuller's *Gnomologia* (1732), has it: *An old goat is never the more revered for his beard*; in more modern locution it is: *If beards were all, then goats would preach.* In other words, old age does not necessarily betoken wisdom.

Get One's Goat

> *[He] stopped at third with a mocking*
> *smile on his face which would have*
> *gotten the late Job's goat.*
> —Christy Mathewson, *Pitching in a Pinch*
> (1912)

The origin of *getting one's goat,* for making someone lose their temper or become annoyed and frustrated, is not totally documented. The expression definitely is American and was generally known by the time Christy Mathewson used it. H. L. Mencken was told that it came from the practice of putting a goat inside a skittish racehorse's stall because it supposedly had a calming influence. A gambler might then persuade a stableboy to remove the goat shortly before the race, thereby upsetting the horse and reducing its chances of winning (and improving the gambler's odds). Hence, *getting its goat* meant annoying the horse. It also has been suggested that the term has some connection with *scapegoat* or with the verb *to goad.*

Scapegoat

> *But the goat on which the lot fell to*
> *be the scapegoat shall be presented*
> *alive before the Lord, to make an*
> *atonement with him, and to let him*
> *go for a scapegoat into the wilderness.*
> —Leviticus 16:10

The *scapegoat*—the innocent person who shoulders the blame for others—was originally the *escape-goat,* the one that escaped (the New American Catholic Edition of the Bible calls it the "emissary goat"). According to the law of Moses, the ritual for the Hebrew Day of Atonement, Yom Kippur, involved two goats. One, the Lord's goat, was sacrificed as a "sin offering." The other, the scapegoat to which the high priest Aaron transferred the sins of his people, was taken to the wilderness and let go, taking the Israelites' sins away with it.

While the concept is very old, the word *scapegoat* entered the language only in 1525, when William Tyndale translated the Bible from Hebrew and so rendered the word *azazel.*

▼ Horse

Among the most useful of animals, horses have been employed since prehistoric times to carry people and burdens in both peacetime and wartime, to pull carts and other wheeled vehicles, and for racing. The word *horse* comes from Old English *hors.* In the 20th century *horse* also became slang for "heroin."

When steam engines began to replace horses in the 19th century, the steam locomotive was for a time called an *iron horse.* Today we still rate the capacity of automobile and other engines in terms of *horsepower,* a measure fixed around 1800 by James Watt for his steam engine as equivalent to lifting a weight of 33,000 pounds by one foot in one minute's time. Watt based it on the estimate that a strong horse working at a cotton gin for eight hours a day averaged 22,000 foot-pounds per minute, and this amount was increased by fifty percent to take into account the greater power of an engine. To *work like a horse* or to be a *workhorse* has been used to describe a tireless human worker since the 16th century.

Anyone who has ever ridden will testify to the fact that a rider must assert some mastery or the horse will stop to graze on tempting greenery, refuse to move at all, or go in whatever direction suits it. *You can take a horse to water but you can't make it drink* is the proverbial expression of the determined self-will horses often display; it is quoted in John Heywood's collection of proverbs (1546) and many other places, and is frequently applied to stubborn human behavior.

Do horses have a sense of humor? It is unlikely, but *horse laugh,* which amounts to a loud snort by the animal, is the term that has been applied to a loud, vulgar human noise since the early 18th century. Back in 1713 Richard Steele called it "a distinguishing characteristic of the rural hoyden." Horses may not understand a good joke, but they can, especially if young, be playful and frolicsome. From this comes *horseplay,* a late 16th-century expression for rough play, and the more recent *to horse around,* for indulging in such play.

Horses are eminently trainable, but there is some dispute as to their intelligence. Nevertheless, from America of the 1820s comes *horse sense,* for "practical wisdom." Its exact origin is not known but it almost certainly came from the West, where horses were of paramount importance. One writer suggests it comes from the fact that horses were so adept at herding cattle and finding their way home without guidance. H. L. Mencken disagrees, claiming that horses are in reality stupid and that "sense" refers to the smartness of *horse traders,* whose well-known shrewdness made *horse-trading* synonymous with clever bargaining (and, sometimes, sharp practices).

Horsehair, from the mane and tail of horses, was used from about 1300 on to stuff mattresses and cushions, and was largely replaced by synthetic materials only in the mid-20th century. Given that the winged horse, *Pegasus,* was strictly a mythical creature created from the blood of the equally mythical Medusa, one might wonder where we get *horsefeathers,* an emphatic interjection meaning "Bunk!" or "Nonsense!" or "Rubbish!" One etymologist suggests that because horses obviously cannot fly, it expresses the equal absurdity of any silly statement. But lexicographer Charles Earle Funk, who entitled his last book *Horsefeathers,* believed it was an old term from the building trades in New England and New York for a particular pattern of clapboards laid to provide a flat surface for roofing. It consisted of laying butt edges against butt edges, a method also called "feathering strips," and possibly because the pieces were so much larger than any bird's feathers they were called "horsefeathers"; or, John Ciardi suggested, the term is an alteration of "house feathers." A more likely explanation, however, is that the present meaning of the expression ("nonsense") evolved as a euphemism for *horseshit,* an impolite way of saying the same thing.

High Horse

> *He was determined to ride the high horse.*
> —Frederick Marryat, Mr. *Midshipman Easy* (1836)

"Altogether upon the high horse," wrote John Brown to actor David Garrick in 1865, referring to someone who was putting on grand airs. About 500 years earlier John Wycliffe described a royal pageant in which high-ranking personages were mounted on high horses, or chargers, and these mounts became symbols of their superiority and arrogance. Certainly mounted knights were superior to foot soldiers, and even in 19th-century armies the cavalry regarded itself as superior to the infantry. Ever since, to *get on one's high horse* has meant to "behave arrogantly," with or without justification.

Since the mid-17th century a military charger experienced in battle has been called a *warhorse.* In time the term began to be used for a highly experienced military leader, and, in the 19th century, usually together with *old,* for an old campaigner, a veteran of political struggles and other controversies. In this usage the term could be affectionate and admiring or contemptuous and derogatory. In the 20th century, however, it began to be used also for a play, composition, motion picture, or other work that, because of its reliable public appeal, has been performed so often it has become hackneyed.

The 19th-century *horse marine,* originally a marine on horseback or a cavalry soldier assigned to a ship, soon became a derisive term, a mounted sailor being considered a man out of his element, and *tell it to the horse marines* became an expression of incredulity. The term originated in Great Britain and was spread and perpetuated by means of an immensely popular song:

> I'm Captain Jinks of the Horse Marines,
> I give my horse good corn and beans;
> Of course, it's quite beyond my means,
> Tho' a Captain in the army . . .

This ditty about a smooth army officer who lived well and was always in debt was composed about 1860 by T. Maclagen and popularized by the comic artist William Horace Lingard, who brought it to the United States in the 1860s and made it equally popular there.

Put the Cart Before the Horse

> *Excuse me that the Muses force*
> *The cart to stand before the horse.*
>
> —Edward Ward,
> *Hudibras Redivivius* (1705)

To *set* (or *put*) *the cart before the horse,* meaning to reverse the natural order of things, has probably been said in one way or another ever since horses first were used to draw wheeled vehicles. Cicero so accused Homer in 61 B.C., complaining that the Greek poet stated the moral of a story before telling the story. From the 16th century on numerous English writers used the same turn of speech, among them Richard Whittinton (c. 1520), Sir Thomas More, William Shakespeare ("May not an ass know when the cart draws the horse?"—*King Lear*), and Charles Kingsley. Perhaps the most amusing version is playwright George Kaufman's turnabout concerning a college student who left school to elope: "She put the heart before the course."

"He locked the stable door while they were putting the cart before the horse," quipped Stanley Walker in *The*

Uncanny Knacks of Mr. Doherty (1941). It alludes to one of the oldest adages attesting to the value of horses and the danger of horse thieves, *to shut the barn* (or *stable*) *door after the horse is stolen.* First recorded in a French proverb collection from about 1190 (in English it appeared in the Douce Manuscript, c. 1350), it is still used today to criticize precautions taken too late.

Of much more recent vintage is the admonition to *hold your horses,* believed to have originated in America in the 1840s. "Hold your hosses, boy—she'll come out directly," wrote John S. Robb in *Streaks of Squatter Life* (1844). Simply derived from instructing a driver to hold back his team, it became a gentle instruction to be patient and is still so used.

A couple of decades later President Abraham Lincoln, upon learning that the National Union League was backing his renomination for a second term, said: "I do not allow myself to suppose that either the convention or the League have concluded to decide that I am either the greatest or the best man in America, but rather they have concluded that it is not best to swap horses while crossing the river" (June 9, 1864). Several versions of this speech were recorded, and the key phrase, which actually may have originated earlier, has survived in slightly altered form as *don't swap* (or *change*) *horses in midstream.* The meaning remains the same: don't change methods or leaders in the midst of a crisis.

That it makes no sense to *flog a dead horse* was pointed out in 195 B.C. by the Roman playwright Plautus. Presumably no rider or coachman would actually take a whip to a horse known to be dead, and the figurative meaning has been clear for centuries: it is pointless to carry on or try to revive interest in an issue or cause that has proved hopeless. The expression appears often in the political arena for issues that no longer interest voters or their representatives. The British statesman John Bright said it to his friend, Richard Cobden, who was trying to get Parliament to reduce spending. Though Bright himself favored this course of action, he told Cobden that persuading Parliament to act on it was *flogging a dead horse.*

The early use by Plautus notwithstanding, John Ciardi cited a quite different origin for the expression. On late 18th-century British merchant vessels, sailors often were paid in advance when they signed on. Many of them spent this sum, usually a month's wages, before their ship actually sailed. The advance pay was called a *dead horse,* and they could draw no more pay until they had worked off that amount, that is, until "the dead horse was flogged." This theory is further borne out by the naval use of *dead horse* for an unpaid debt.

A badly injured horse is traditionally put out of its misery by being shot. This practice gave rise to the expression, *They shoot horses, don't they?* meaning sometimes one must be cruel to be kind. Its first recorded use was as the title of a 1935 novel by Horace McCoy, and it gained currency with a 1969 motion picture based on the novel and with the same title. The plot concerns a marathon dancer, a hopeless derelict, who is finally murdered by her dance partner.

Don't Look a Gift Horse in the Mouth

> *A gyuen hors may not be loked in
> the tethe.*
>
> —John Stanbridge, *Vulgaria* (c. 1520)

The first person on record for issuing this warning to accept a gift in good faith was St. Jerome, who stated it in Latin about A.D. 420, in his commentary on St. Paul's Epistle to the Ephesians. Jerome was replying to critics of his writings and telling them not to find fault with free-will offerings. The metaphor rests on the fact that a horse's age is revealed by its teeth, and as the identical phrase appears in French, German, Italian, Spanish, and Portuguese, the concept obviously has international endorsement. On the other hand, H. L. Mencken, in his essay on popular fallacies, pointed out: "Some people

have a knack of putting upon you gifts of no real value, to engage you to substantial gratitude." His countryman, William Allingham, put it even more emphatically, holding that the policy of not looking a gift horse in the mouth "may easily be carried too far." Indeed, the gift may be a WHITE ELEPHANT.

From the 1920s comes yet another term, *straight from the horse's mouth,* referring to information that comes from the best authority, just as the age of a horse can be told fairly precisely by looking in its mouth. A horse's permanent teeth appear in succession, the first pair at the age of two and one-half, the second pair at three and one-half, and the third pair between ages four and five. Thus the shrewdest horse trader cannot really fool a knowledgeable buyer as to the age of a race horse, although its other qualities might well be open to fulsome exaggeration.

Horse Races

> It is difference of opinion that makes horse-races.
>
> —Mark Twain,
> *Pudd'nhead Wilson* (1893)

The sport of horse racing is said to date from ancient Egyptian times. Presumably even then horse owners would make bets as to whose horse was fastest. The ancient Olympic games of Greece included what are thought to be the first public horse races, and harness-horse racing began some years later when horses were set to pulling chariots. The Romans preferred the chariot race above all others. Organized horse racing dates from 12th-century Britain, when royalty encouraged this pastime, and horse racing is still called "the sport of kings." Betting—both informal and formal—is an integral part of the racing scene, and unfortunately many individuals find themselves *backing the wrong horse,* a saying for making the wrong decision that has been extended to various causes and candidates since about 1860. "We all put our money upon the wrong horse," said the Marquis of Salisbury before Parliament in 1897, discussing some fine point of foreign policy.

Another saying from the racing scene is *horses for courses*—that is, horses suitable for a race course—which originated in Britain about 1860. By the end of the century it was being used for other kinds of suitability, such as a suitable match (as opposed to a misalliance). And eventually it came to mean just about anything that is appropriate in given circumstances. Despite its rhyming appeal, it is not heard much in America but remains current in Britain.

Occasionally one may, in placing a bet, confuse one horse with another. Probably from some such occurrence comes a *horse of another color,* meaning a matter quite different from the one at hand. In Shakespeare's *Twelfth Night* Maria says, "My purpose is, indeed, a horse of that colour," meaning, Yes, that is precisely what I intend. The current sense—that is the *opposite* of what I intend—is believed to have originated in the United States in the late 18th century and subsequently adopted in Britain. It was stated by Anthony Trollope in *The Last Chronicles of Barset* (1867): "What did you think of his wife? That's a horse of another colour altogether."

Dark Horse

> . . . and a dark horse which had never
> been thought of . . . rushed past the
> grandstand in sweeping triumph.
>
> —Benjamin Disraeli, *The Young Duke*
> (1831)

In racing terminology a horse is called "dark" when its history is unknown and the racing form sheets shed no light on it. One writer suggests a more nefarious reason: the owner of a well-known steed would sometimes dye its hair in order to disguise it and so get better odds. Such a horse would necessarily be darker, since hair cannot be lightened just with dye. Another theory traces the expression to a Tennessee horse trader who owned an extremely fast black stallion. He made a practice of riding the horse into a strange town as though it were an ordinary saddle horse and then persuading the locals to set up a horse race. Not knowing they were up against a proven winner, the townspeople usually lost, and the trader's *dark horse* became legendary.

Neither origin has been verified, but the expression *dark horse* was known in the early 19th century. It was extended from racing, where it is also still used, to politics when James Polk, who had not even been mentioned at the Democratic Convention in 1844 until the eighth ballot, won the national election and became the eleventh president of the United States. Ever since, the term has been applied to a political candidate or other contender who is little known but who, possibly owing to excellent qualities that have been deliberately kept secret, has a good chance of winning. Disraeli himself, who wrote the novel quoted above before he entered Parliament (he was to stand for election four times before he won), was something of a dark horse when he became leader of the Tory Party and eventually prime minister.

A *white horse*, on the other hand, is considered by some—opinion on this issue is divided—to be a fortunate omen. And the symbolic *knight on a white horse* represents the romantic figure of a rescuer.

The *horseshoe* is a time-honored good luck charm. Legend has it that Saint Dunstan (c. A.D. 910–988), who numbered blacksmithy among his talents, was asked to shoe the devil's cloven hoof. In complying he so hurt the devil that he exacted a promise from him: the devil would never enter a house that displayed a horseshoe. In the Middle Ages horseshoes were often hammered above doorways to ward off evil and bring good luck.

One-Horse Town

> *A little one-horse town.*
> —Mark Twain, *Huckleberry Finn* (1884)

Given the importance of horses in the American West, the presence of but a single horse signifies very small size, extreme impoverishment, or just plain inferiority. The term *one-horse* used in other than its literal sense (as in *one-horse carriage,* a vehicle drawn by a single horse) dates from the mid-19th century and has been applied not only to places (*one-horse town*) but to professionals (*one-horse lawyer*) as a synonym for "smalltime."

Similarly disparaging is *horse opera,* originally (1850s) any Western entertainment featuring local color, especially cowboys, and not necessarily any music whatever. Later it was extended to radio and television programs and motion pictures with Western themes, featuring cowboys, gunmen, Indians, stagecoaches, prospectors, and the like.

By the mid-1930s horses had little commercial use, especially in the eastern United States. In 1935, President Franklin D. Roosevelt attacked an Interstate Commerce Commission clause at a press conference, saying, "The country was in the horse-and-buggy age when that clause was written." Ever since, *horse-and-buggy* has meant old-fashioned and outmoded.

Horse Latitudes

In the days of sailing ships, nothing was so important to sailors as wind. From the 18th century the latitudes forming the edges of the trade wind belts, one north and one south (approximately 30 degrees north and south latitude) were called the *horse latitudes*. There are several theories as to why. The most likely is that the term comes from the Spanish *Golfo de las yeguas,* or Gulf of Mares, an area between Spain and the Canary Islands whose tricky winds sailors likened to the movements of capricious mares (see also under MARE'S NEST). Another theory is that when ships were becalmed in these latitudes, as they often were for weeks on end, the hot muggy climate was fatal to horses aboard the ships. And finally, someone has suggested that the term referred to advance pay sailors received while on shore leave; it was called *dead horse pay* because it had to be worked off on-board, which usually took as long as it took to reach the so-called horse latitudes (see also FLOG A DEAD HORSE).

Charley Horse

Baseball players are not the only sufferers from muscle aches and pains, but they were the first to call stiffness in an arm or leg muscle a *charley horse,* sometime in the late 1880s. Most likely the expression was first used by or for a player who limped like an old horse, Charley being the name of either the player or the horse. In those days groundskeepers used horses to drag the infield, so such an analogy could be observed close at hand. The name stuck, and today it is used by athletes and nonathletes alike for muscle pains resulting from overuse or a blow.

Stalking Horse

*He uses his folly like a stalking-horse
and under the presentation of that he
shoots his wit.*

—William Shakespeare, *As You Like It*

Riding to the hounds is not the only way hunters have used horses. In the 16th century they sometimes dismounted and, hiding behind their horses, stalked game on foot, advancing step by step until they were within shooting distance. From this sort of pursuit comes the current meaning of *stalking horse,* a means of concealing a secret plan, sometimes applied in politics to a candidate who is being used to hide the candidacy of some more important person.

Hiding behind a horse figured in Morris dancing as well, although here the "horse" was a representation made of wicker and held by the performer who acted the part of a horse. (Morris dancing is a ritual form of rural folk dance originating in northern England in the late Middle Ages, performed by men in costume who originally represented characters in the Robin Hood legend.) Later this *hobby horse,* as it was known, became less elaborate, consisting merely of a stick with a horse's head; as such it was a popular children's toy in the 16th and 17th centuries. Indeed, it was so popular that the term *hobby horse* was extended to mean one's favorite theory or scheme. "Almost every person hath some hobby horse or other wherein he prides himself," wrote Sir Matthew Hale in 1676; in a more serious vein, John Wesley warned in one of his sermons, "Hobby horses cost more than Arab steeds" (c. 1785). We still say of people pushing a pet project that they are *riding their hobby horse.* And the term also still refers to both the stick-horse toy and the horse figure mounted on rockers, more commonly called a *rocking horse.*

Another, less exact representation of a horse is the *sawhorse,* a movable frame used to support wood that is being sawed. Its only resemblance to a real horse is that it has four legs, so it might just as well be called a "sawpig" or "sawbull," but it has borne its present name since about 1775.

Mare's Nest

> *Nor stare in a man's face, as if he had spied a mare's nest.*
> —Robert Peterson, trans., *Galateo* (1576)

The mature male horse is called a *stallion,* and the mature female a *mare.* A newborn horse is a *foal,* and during the time of nursing its mother is called a *brood mare.* A female foal, from the time of weaning until about the age of four, is a *filly*—also an informal term for girl or young woman, largely replaced in Britain by *bird* and in America by *chick*—and a male is a *colt.* Colts frequently are playful and frolicsome, whence the adjective *coltish* for similar human behavior, and the saying *Young colts will canter,* meaning that children will act like children.

No matter how domestic their instincts, mares do not and never have made nests. The term *mare's nest* dates from the late 16th century, when it meant an illusory discovery, one that turned out to be worthless or fraudulent. Later it came to mean simply a hoax.

To *ride shank's mare* is an elaborate way of saying "to walk," that is, use one's own shanks (legs) instead of a horse. Originally a Scottish expression, it sometimes is put as *shank's pony.* The word *pony* itself originated in the 17th century from Scots *powney* for a young animal or foal, itself of uncertain origin. Today *pony* is applied to any small horse, as well as to at least two totally unrelated objects: (a) half a jigger, or three-quarters of an ounce, of a drink, or a beverage bottle that is smaller than the standard size—in both usages the reference is to small size; and (b) a translation of a foreign-language text that is used illicitly by students and is also known as a *trot.* This American student slang term may have derived from the translation so used having to be concealed and be small enough to be tucked into a pocket, inside another book, or the like, but this is a guess.

More straightforward are the origins of *ponytail,* a hairdo in which long hair is drawn back and tied at the nape or higher so it resembles a pony's tail; and *Pony Express,* the system of mail delivery used in the American West in the 19th century, which involved relays of riders on ponies.

▼Pig

> *Pigs are pigs.*
> —Charles Lamb, letter to Samuel Taylor
> Coleridge (1822)

The word *pig,* from Middle English *pigge,* originally meant only young swine, but it has come to be used interchangeably with *hog* for all domestic swine. Pigs actually are quite intelligent (some biologists say they are second only to the great apes in this respect). They also are extremely clean, but they wallow in mud to clean and cool themselves, a practice that has given them an undeserved reputation for filth. Further, farmers feed pigs liberally in order to fatten them, and they are able to digest almost anything, including kitchen refuse, so they have the reputation of gluttony. Calling a person a *pig,* therefore, is tantamount to an accusation of filth, greed, gluttony, and obesity, and *to pig it* is to wallow in filth. *To pig out* or *to be piggy* means to overeat, and persisting in this behavior will make one *fat as a pig.* A pig's abode, called *pigpen* or *pigsty,* likewise is assumed to be very dirty, and when either of these terms is applied to a room or house it means it is a miserable, filthy place.

The term *pig* has denoted a loathsome person since before 1600, and prior to that *swine* served the same purpose. In 19th-century Britain *pig* also was slang for a policeman or detective, a usage current in America from about 1840. It may have dropped out for a time but was

revived in the 1960s by the Black Panthers and other anti-establishment groups. Further, pigs are commonly thought to be as obstinate as mules, and *pigheaded* has meant "stubborn" since the early 17th century.

Given its reputation, it seems unlikely that anyone would wish to ride a pig, and indeed, *piggyback* does not mean doing so and never has. Rather, it is a corruption of *pick-a-back,* meaning to carry something or someone on one's back or shoulders like a pack, and dates from the 16th century. (Earlier forms were *pick-back* and *pick-pack.*)

To *bleed like a stuck pig* means to bleed copiously but has nothing to do with domestic pigs. It comes from the sport of hunting wild boar, usually on horseback and with a spear rather than a gun. The actual slaughter is called *pigsticking.*

Recent archaeologic research in Turkey revealed that the pig has been domesticated for more than 10,000 years and thus was the first animal actually raised for food—1,000 years earlier than domesticated sheep and goats. Today pigs still are raised mainly for their flesh and fat, producing pork, ham, bacon, numerous specialty meats, and lard. Their hide, called *pigskin,* makes a very good leather that is used for gloves, handbags, luggage, saddles, and other products. It also is used to cover

American footballs, and since the late 1890s a football itself has been called a *pigskin.*

Piggy Bank

Although inflation threatens to do away with it, the *piggy bank,* a money box in the shape of a pig, is still a favorite repository for children's coins. There are several theories as to the term's origin. One claims the name comes from the 15th-century word *pygg,* for earthenware pitcher or jar, a term that survived only in local dialects. Housewives would keep spare coins in it, so that the pygg (or diminutive *piggy*) came to be considered the family vault, giving rise years later to the practice of making pig-shaped pottery coin containers for children. Another source holds that the term comes from a traditional pig-shaped money box that was given, with one or more coins inside it, to apprentices on Boxing Day during Tudor times (1485–1603). On the other hand, one major American dictionary holds that the term *piggy bank* dates only from about 1940 or so, and the *Oxford English Dictionary* agrees.

A full piggy bank may have you living *like pigs in clover,* a term occasionally used to describe human prosperity. Although pigs may be indiscriminate gourmands, they presumably would love to feed happily in a field of clover.

Reaching that field of clover might not be too easily accomplished. Indeed, *if a pig had wings he might fly* is a 19th-century Scots proverb betokening an improbable state of affairs. It is this saying, also put as *pigs might fly,* that may in turn have given rise, via rhyming, to the expression *in a pig's eye,* meaning "never" or expressing incredulous doubt and disagreement. Eric Partridge, however, believed it originated as a euphemism for *in a pig's ass,* which in turn came from a bawdy song of the early 1900s.

As for eyesight, *blind pig* has long been the name for a tavern that sells liquor illegally or is open after the legal closing hour in its locale. Although it might seem to be associated with the era of Prohibition, it predates it by some years, the first recorded use being in 1886. The reason for the name is not known. See also BLIND TIGER.

Pig Iron

As long ago as the 1570s the names *sow* (female pig) and *pig* were used for lumps of cast iron. In the 17th century the molten metal that is tapped from the hearth of a blast furnace was called *pig iron*. The main channel of the grid of sand into which the metal is poured is called the *sow*, and the ingots of iron formed in short connecting channels are called *pigs*. Possibly these names came to be used because pig iron is crude and unrefined, and requires further processing to be made into cast iron, steel, or wrought iron, but that is speculation.

Pig Latin: Igpay Atinlay

A language devised by school children, *pig Latin* consists simply of transposing the first consonant of an English word to the end of the word and adding the sound *ay* to it. Spoken rapidly, it sounds like gibberish and effectively makes one's conversation unintelligible to the uninitiated, such as teachers, which of course was the point. One source traces the name to England in the early 1900s, when Latin was still a basic part of the curriculum, but it is safe to guess that resourceful youngsters invented it much earlier than that.

Pigtail

In the 17th century a *pigtail* was tobacco twisted into a thin rope, which resembled the animal's tail. In the 18th century the name was attached to a plait of twisted hair worn by sailors, who were probably imitating a Chinese style. When the Manchu invaded and conquered China in the 17th century, they made the Chinese wear queues, or *pigtails,* as a sign of servitude. English sailors and also some soldiers adopted this hairstyle until the early 19th century. By then it was being worn by young girls as well. Strictly speaking, *pigtail* means a single plait of hair, but the term also is used in the plural, for a pair of braids.

▼Hog

Originally a hog, from Old English *hogg,* was a male swine that was castrated, raised for its meat, and slaughtered young. Like *pig,* with which it often is used interchangeably (see PIG), the term *hog* applied to a person means a coarse, filthy, gluttonous individual, a definition current since the 15th century. *To hog it* is the same as *to pig it,* that is, to eat or drink greedily and sloppily. Also, since about 1887 in the United States, *to hog* has meant to take more than one's fair share of something, and *hoggish* calls up the beast's selfishness as well. From this last sense comes the slang use of *hog* for a large, extravagantly luxurious automobile or motorcycle, and the related *road hog,* used since the 1890s for a driver who takes up more than his or her fair share of the road. Disapproval of such rudeness was registered long ago in the expression, *What can you expect from a hog but a grunt?* First recorded in 1731, the saying was widely quoted until about 1900 but is rarely heard today.

Of quite mysterious origin but used since about 1350 is *hogshead,* a large cask holding 63 to 140 gallons of liquid, and also the name of a liquid measure equivalent to 52.5 imperial gallons (63 U.S. gallons, or 238 liters). The name comes from Middle English *hoggeshed,* meaning "head of a hog." Possibly the shape of such a cask resembled the animal's head, but no authoritative explanation survives. A *hogback,* however, so called since the mid-1600s, is a long, sharply crested mountain ridge that does resemble the animal's back.

Pigs being taken away for slaughter are not apt to go willingly. Farmers therefore would tie their feet—all four together—which gave rise to the expression *hog-tied,* a term first appearing in *Harper's Magazine* in 1894. Whether their struggles are manic enough to warrant such a description or the term betokens some other mysterious animal enthusiasm, *to go hog-wild* is an Americanism dating from about 1905 for being extremely excited or enthusiastic about something.

High Off the Hog

Because the choicest cuts of ham and bacon are taken from high up on the animal's sides, *to eat high off the hog* became a colloquial term for living well and prospering. It originated in the American South in the 19th century and is also expressed as *living high off the hog's back.* What hogs themselves eat, however, was called *hogwash,* a synonym for kitchen swill since the 15th century, and also for bad liquor (rotgut) in the 18th century and for cheap journalism from about 1880. Today hogwash is yet another synonym for the interjection "Nonsense!"

The Whole Hog

> *I reckon Squire Lawrie may go the*
> *whole hog with her.*
> —John Galt, *Laurie Todd* (1830)

During Andrew Jackson's campaign for the U.S. Presidency in 1828, he was touted as a *whole-hogger* who would see things through to the end and "damn the consequences." What exactly *the whole hog* originally meant and where it came from are not known. Charles Earle Funk thought it came from a poem by William Cowper (1731–1800), *The Love of the World Reproved, or Hypocrisy Detected,* in which, concerning the Islamic prohibition against eating pork, he wrote, "But for one piece they thought it hard From the whole hog to be debar'd." A more likely source, however, is the Irish slang word *hog* for various coins, among them the British shilling and American ten-cent piece, or dime. Thus *going the whole hog* would mean spending the entire shilling or dime at once, and today the term still means going the whole distance, that is, doing something thoroughly.

A curious expression that Funk used as the title of one of his best books is *a hog on ice.* Although rarely if ever heard today, it is odd enough to warrant investigation. Funk found it used in two ways: to mean as "clumsy" as a hog on ice, and by extension "awkward" and "helpless"; and as "independent" as a hog on ice, meaning "supremely self-assured." The former seems self-evident, as the animal's feet have smooth pads that make it impossible for it to gain a footing on ice. The latter is more puzzling, and Funk believed he had found its origin in the sport of curling, where *hog* refers to a stone that impedes play. Possibly, however, it simply meant "independent" in the sense of "alone," for what sensible hog would want to join another that was trapped on ice?

Swine and Sow

> Neither cast ye your pearls before
> swine, lest they trample them under
> their feet.
>
> —Matthew 7:6

Do not *cast pearls before swine,* that is, do not waste precious words or deeds on the undeserving, a saying quoted in numerous proverbs through the ages, was said by Jesus in his Sermon on the Mount.

Further, you can't *make a silk purse from a sow's ear,* that is, you cannot turn an undeserving creature or thing into one of great worth. This proverb was frequently repeated from the early 17th century on, although the valuable material cited varied from cheverill to satin to velvet before it finally became silk.

Sheep

All we like sheep have gone astray.
—Charles Jennens, Handel's *Messiah*
(1742)

The outstanding characteristic of sheep, from Old English *scēap,* which have been raised domestically for their wool and meat for an estimated 9,000 years, is that they are sociable beasts, tending to flock together and more or less blindly follow one another. When one walks up to a sheep in the meadow, to take its photograph or pat its head or simply observe it more closely, it generally turns and bolts away, along with its fellows. Therefore, shy, bashful, and awkward behavior is described as *sheepish,* a term so used since the 12th century. Although most sheep do behave in this way, we once encountered a small flock, including a ewe and her very young lamb, on a Welsh mountaintop, and the sheep literally nosed their way into our laps as we sat on the rocks eating our lunch. Another hiker there called them "carnivorous sheep," and they were indeed trying to share our ham sandwiches. Nor did pushes, shoves, or even kicks dissuade them. They kept at it until we got up and left.

For separating sheep from goats, see under GOAT.

Sheep's Eyes

She casts many a sheep's eye at thee.
—Robert Greene, *Never Too Late* (1590)

To cast sheep's eyes at someone has meant to flirt, or to look amorously or longingly at someone, since the early 16th century. An early use of the term was in 1529 by poet John Skelton ("When ye kyst a sheeps ie . . . [At] mastres Andelby"), who was probably writing tongue-in-cheek. In reality sheep's eyes are not especially romantic in appearance.

Sheep hides, on the other hand, have been important from early times for making clothing as well as leather and, later, parchment. Until the advent of printing, parchment was the principal material of book pages, and even after paper of good quality became abundant and cheap, parchment continued to be used for very important documents, such as land deeds and university diplomas. Although most diplomas today are no longer handwritten in Latin on genuine parchment but are simply printed on heavy paper, the name *sheepskin*, a slang word for "diploma" originated by American students, has stuck.

Black Sheep

> Indeed a black sheep is a perilous beast.
>
> —John Lyly, *Endimion* (1591)

Black sheep long were considered less valuable than white ones because their wool could not be readily dyed. Happily, they were rare anyway, as most domestic sheep range in color from white to light brown. By the late 18th century, *black sheep* had come to mean a person out of favor, someone oddly different and therefore a renegade. Sir Walter Scott wrote, "The curates know best the black sheep of the flock" (*Old Mortality*, 1816). Today we still speak of a family's or other group's *black sheep*, meaning its least successful or least admirable member.

▼ Lamb

> As good be hang'd for an old sheep as a young lamb.
>
> —John Ray, *English Proverbs* (1678)

The word *lamb* for "young sheep" comes from Old English and has been part of the language since at least A.D. 900. Young lambs are gentle animals, and a person being called a *lamb* is being characterized as gentle and mild. Indeed, *gentle as a lamb* appears as far back as the mid-14th century in William Langland's *Piers Ploughman,* and *meek* and *innocent* are two other words frequently used in connection with the animal.

The New Testament characterizes Jesus as the *Lamb of God* (*Agnus Dei* in Latin), words that are an integral part of the Roman Catholic Mass, and in Christian iconography the lamb is a symbol of Jesus.

Lambs also are playful creatures and move remarkably fast. Hence *in two shakes of a lamb's tail* means "very quickly" or "very soon," and has done so since at least 1840 in America (and possibly much longer). Mark Twain rephrased it to "In three shakes of a sheep's tail" (*Huckleberry Finn,* 1884), and it is often shortened to *in two shakes.*

Although the meat from a lamb is more tender and its wool is softer, one gets considerably less of both than from a grown sheep. In Britain and elsewhere both animals were considered valuable enough commodities that the theft of either was punishable by death until as late as the 1820s in some places. Hence the saying, *as good be hanged for a sheep as for a lamb,* a well-known proverb by 1678, indicating that one might as well steal the object of greater value if the punishment would be the same anyway. The saying has survived, advising one not to stop at half-measures but to enjoy a forbidden enterprise to the hilt.

▼Ram

> *Who plays at butting with a ram*
> *Will quick a broken forehead rue.*
> —Sadi, *Gulistan* (c. 1258)

The male sheep, called a *ram* in Middle and Old English as well as in the modern variety, has been known for its assertive head-butting behavior since antiquity. In Roman times it gave its name—*aries* in Latin—to a military machine that had been used to batter down city walls since Assyrian times (10th century B.C.) and continued to be used until the invention of gunpowder. Originally this *battering ram* probably consisted simply of a swinging log hand-operated by a few soldiers, but soon it was elaborated into a long, heavy beam hung by chains from a wooden frame. About 100 feet long and with an iron-shod head, the beam was operated by 100 or more soldiers. Sometimes the head was fashioned in the form of a ram's head. In its most elaborate form, the battering ram consisted of an instrument mounted in a wooden tower that was roofed and shielded in front with metal plates, and which moved on six wheels. Under the roof was a platform for archers, who picked off the defenders on the city walls.

The verb *to ram,* also so called from the butting behavior of male sheep, comes from Middle English *rammen,* derived from the noun, and means to drive into with great force, or to dash violently against. With the development of more sophisticated firearms in the 18th century came the *ramrod,* a device for pushing (tamping down) the charge of a muzzle-loading firearm. Because it was necessarily stiff and strong, *ramrod* came to be used figuratively for a strict disciplinarian, and as an adjective for very stiff and straight. It also came into use as a verb, meaning to push through, as for example, *to ramrod* a measure through the legislature.

The Wild:
In Field
and
Forest

▼Badger

This burrowing member of the weasel family most probably was named for the white badge on its forehead; the
name, dating from the 16th century, came from *badgeard*
(*badge* + *ard*). Although very useful in settled regions
because it lives on undesirable rodents and thus controls
their numbers, the badger in medieval times was made the
object of a cruel sport called *badger-baiting*. The animal
was put in a box or tub and dogs would be set on it to
drag it out. It would be allowed to return to safety for a
period of recovery, and then the process would be
repeated. Badgers are fierce fighters, relying on their formidable teeth, strong jaws, and remarkably long claws.
Their loose-fitting hide makes them appear larger than
their actual size, and when an attacker grabs a badger by
the scruff of the neck, the animal has so much room in its
loose skin that it can actually turn around inside it and
attack the other animal from below. Nevertheless, they are
far too small to cope with a pack of dogs, so the odds in
badger-baiting were hardly equal. From this pastime
comes the verb *to badger,* meaning "to harass" or "pester
unmercifully."

A human version of badger-baiting was the *badger game,* so named in the late 19th century but almost certainly a much older practice. In this blackmailing con game, a prostitute entices a client to bed, only to be "discovered" there by an accomplice posing as her irate husband. The victim then must pay handsomely in order to be allowed to leave in safety, having been trapped like a badger in a box.

Wisconsin acquired its nickname, the *Badger State,* not because of a plethora of these animals but from a practice linked to an early industry. In the 1840s lead was mined in the southwestern part of the state. Because of a shortage of timber in the area, the miners built their houses into hillsides, burrowing into the dirt like badgers.

▼ Bat

> *It's a case of bats in the belfry on that one subject.*
> —R. D. Saunders, *Colonel Todhunter*
> (1911)

The only flying mammal of modern times was named *bat* in the 16th century, replacing the Middle English name *bakke.* Because some bats are considered quite ugly and their behavior is poorly understood, many superstitions about them have arisen. Among them is the unfounded belief that they cannot see, giving rise to the simile *blind as a bat;* "the weakey'd bat," wrote William Collins in his *Ode to Evening* (1747). Bats actually can see quite well, although being largely nocturnal they depend on senses other than sight.

The bat's power of flight is equaled only by that of birds, but its course tends to be darting rather than smooth. No doubt this dashing about accounts for the expression *like a bat out of hell,* for very fast flight or movement, which originated in the Air Force during World War I. Bats generally move about only at night, and show remarkable skill at avoiding obstacles in the dark. While in flight the bat keeps up a constant, high-pitched

twitter that bounces back from obstacles; its ears pick up
the echoes of the sound, thus enabling the animal to detect
solid objects in its path. It is this remarkable natural
sonar, called echolocation, that accounts for the animal's
seemingly erratic flight. It also gave rise to the expression
to have bats in one's belfry for "crazy" or "very eccentric," since bats might well fly wildly about in the confines
of a church bell tower, just as peculiar ideas seem to fly
about in a slightly deranged person's head. From this also
comes the related adjective *batty,* meaning "crazy." Both
locutions are American in origin and date from the early
20th century.

In the 1970s the American television situation comedy *All in the Family* portrayed Archie Bunker as a work-
ing-class man who responds to social pressure with self-
righteous bigotry. In this role he popularized *dingbat,* his
favorite opprobrious name for his wife, Edith. In the
United States a dingbat is a silly, empty-headed, stupid
person. In Australia, however, a dingbat is eccentric or
slightly mad, much the same as one who is batty. There
are several theories as to the origin of this word, which
dates from the mid- or late 19th century. One is that it
combines *bat,* in the sense of "eccentric," with the Dutch

ding, meaning "thing," which also became *dingus* (for "whatchamacallit" or "thingamajig"). Another is that it was an Australian colloquialism for delirium tremens, whence the idea of craziness. At any rate, by about 1940 it designated a stupid person, especially a stupid female, and it was this meaning that Archie Bunker perpetuated.

▼ Bear

> *The captain was as savage as a bear*
> *with a sore head.*
>
> —Frederick Marryat,
> *The King's Own* (1830)

There is considerable ambivalence in our views of bears and their dispositions. We call a gruff, surly person *a bear* and term such behavior *bearish.* We accuse someone of being *cross as a bear,* and have done so since the 18th century ("He grumbled like a bear with a sore ear"—Grose's *Dictionary,* 1785). This last simile is also put as *like a bear with a sore paw* or *head* (as in the quotation above). On the other hand, a *bear hug* is an affectionate, if sometimes overwhelming, embrace. Further, bears have long been used in circuses and, even earlier, by wandering entertainers—"No dancing bear was so genteel, or half so degagé," wrote William Cowper in *Of Himself* (c. 1782)—and scores of children have been entertained by that Bear of Very Little Brain but enormous charm, Winnie the Pooh, not to mention the beloved stuffed TEDDY BEAR.

The bear, whose name comes from Middle English *beare* and *bere* and Old English *bera,* is a formidable beast, especially when cornered. Hence we have the slang usage of *bear* for a formidable or difficult task. A mother bear will fiercely protect her young, called *cubs.* This name has been transferred to young and inexperienced humans, as in *Cub Scout,* the youngest category of the Boy Scouts, and *cub reporter,* a beginning journalist. Long ago newborn bear cubs were thought to be shapeless creatures that were carefully licked by the mother. It may be from this or similar behavior in other creatures that we have the expression *lick into shape,* meaning to arrange something or someone properly.

In the Middle Ages *bear-baiting,* which consisted of setting dogs on a captive bear, was a popular pastime for bloodthirsty spectators.

Bears are associated with cold and wild terrain, such as is found in Alaska and Siberia. By the 16th century the bear was a symbol of Russia; Shakespeare wrote of "the rugged Russian bear" in *Macbeth.* Bear-hunting was long a popular if dangerous sport, and being *loaded for bear,* an expression taken from the hunt, means to be ready and eager for a fight. Theodore Roosevelt loved bear-hunting, yet he was not only an ardent sportsman but a dedicated conservationist. Allegedly, during a hunt in 1902 his dogs found a very young bear cub, and Roosevelt insisted on letting it go. Soon afterward someone thought of calling a stuffed toy bear *teddy* (short for Theodore) *bear* after him and thus began the popular phenomenon that persists to the present day.

A similar event occurred in 1950, when game warden and conservationist Elliott Barker sent a singed and frightened bear cub, rescued from a forest fire, to Washington, D.C., to represent the U.S. Forest Service. The cub, christened *Smokey Bear,* became a living national symbol for fire prevention and remained a beloved inhabitant of the National Zoological Park in Washington until his death in 1976. His image still appears in national and state parks throughout the country, accompanied by a warning about extinguishing campfires and preventing forest fires.

Bears and Bulls

> *He has nothing of the bear but his skin.*
> —Oliver Goldsmith (c. 1773)

The wild beasts of Wall Street—*bears* and *bulls*—are said to take their name from an old story about a man who sold a bear's skin before he had actually trapped the bear. From this came, in the 16th century or even earlier, the term *bearskin jobber,* a broker who gambled on his belief that the market would fall (prices would drop) and behaved accordingly (sold his holdings while he could still get a high price). This term was easily shortened to *bear.* The bear's counterpart, the *bull,* believes prices are going to rise and therefore buys while they are still low. The source for this kind of bull is less clear. Some believe it comes from the bull's tossing objects up with his horns; others believe that bull-baiting was more or less a companion sport to bear-baiting. Whichever the case, both the concept and the terms have stuck, and we still speak of a *bullish* or *bearish* investor, described as optimistic or pessimistic, respectively, and a *bull market* or *bear market,* in which one or the other type of investor prevails.

▼Beaver

The beaver, a large aquatic rodent valued for its fur, weighs only thirty to fifty pounds but is able to gnaw so well that it can cut down trees up to three feet in diameter. It also digs enormous canals, 2 feet wide and deep, and 1,000 or more feet long. The animal floats logs and branches down the canals to a dam site, where it builds an underwater lodge for the female to bear young. It also uses the canals to adjust the water level in the pond formed behind the dam. When danger is near, the beaver signals its family by slapping its broad tail on the water surface, sending a warning into the underwater den.

Owing to all this labor-intensive activity, the beaver has been synonymous with ambition and hard work since the 17th century or longer. We therefore say someone is *busy as a beaver* or *works like a beaver,* and we call an ambitious person an *eager beaver.*

Beaver fur was long used to make men's top hats, which therefore acquired the name *beaver.* Also, the word, derived from Middle English *bever* and Old English *beofor* or *befor*, was used for other objects resembling the animal's fur, including a kind of soft, warm cloth with a thick nap, and, in vulgar slang, a woman's pubic hair.

▼Buck

A large assembly of young fellows
whom they call bucks.
  —Henry Fielding, *Amelia* (1751)

Little has entered the language concerning the female deer, or *doe*, other than *doeskin*, the soft, pliable skin of a doe, and *doe-eyed*, for human eyes resembling the large, limpid eyes of a doe. With regard to the male, or *buck*, however, we have another story entirely. Technically, *buck*, from Old English *bucca* for he-goat and *bucc* for male deer, means the male of several animal species—deer, antelope, rabbit, sheep, goat. However, most of the terms evolving from buck refer to the male deer.

One of the first transfers was to the male of the human species, and *buck* has meant "a young man" since the 18th century. In 19th-century Britain it sometimes had the connotation of a young dandy or man-about-town. In the military, *buck* has, since about 1870, denoted the lowest of the noncommissioned ranks with the same name; thus a *buck private* is a plain private, as opposed to a private first class, and a *buck sergeant* is a sergeant, as opposed to a staff sergeant, first sergeant, or master sergeant. Presumably the designation *buck* here means simply "male," without any other special status, although of course today it applies to women soldiers as well.

Many of the terms relate to deer hunting, where in terms of both sport and commerce a buck is far more valuable than a doe. A nervous, inexperienced hunter is said to have *buck fever*, a term also applied to any nervous anticipation of a new experience; it originated in America in the 1830s. *Buckshot*, a large size of lead shot used in

hunting game, dates from the early days of firearms and has been so called since about 1400. One writer suggests it gave rise to *pass the buck*—that is, to shift responsibility or blame to someone else—from putting a counter consisting of a piece of buckshot in front of the dealer in a poker game and passing it on to the next person who was to deal. Another source suggests the object so passed originally was a *buckhorn,* a type of knife so named because its handle was made from a buck's antlers. Whichever is true, the expression originated in the United States in the latter half of the 19th century and was made famous after 1949 by President Harry S Truman, who kept a sign on his desk in the White House that said, "The buck stops here" (that is, I'll take full responsibility).

A male deer's antlers are a hunter's source of pride, but another feature of his head is considered less attractive. *Buck teeth,* so called for their resemblance to the deer's protruding dentition, have enriched many an orthodontist and impoverished many a parent.

The verb *to buck,* usually referring to the vertical jumping of a horse with its back arched and feet drawn together, most likely comes from the abrupt leaps and plunges of deer in the forest. In the sense of offering strong resistance (as in "he bucked a trend") or proceeding against an obstacle ("the plane bucked strong headwinds"), it probably comes from the butting of bucks with their antlers. To *buck for* something, on the other hand, is slang for striving fervently for a particular goal; it first gained currency in the military but then acquired wider use. The origin of to *buck up,* meaning to "cheer up" or "hurry up," is less clear; it dates from the 1840s and may be related to the cheerful aspect of the gay, dashing human buck.

The slang term *buck* for "dollar" comes from abbreviating *buckskin,* which was a valuable item of Native American trade that sometimes served as money. Buckskins were used to clothe first the Indians and then the American settlers. Although deerskin is no longer much used for this purpose, various imitations, made from sheepskin or from cloth, are still manufactured and are also called *buckskin.* A style of white leather shoe that became the collegiate rage in the 1940s was called *white bucks,* and wearing them signaled that one belonged to the "in" group.

Stag

> *Paulina her first husband made*
> *a stag.*
>
> —Thomas Pecke,
> *Parnassi Puerperium* (1659)

The adult male deer is called a *stag,* from Middle English *stagge* and Old English *stagga.* In the 12th century *stag* meant mainly the male red deer, and in northern Britain in the 14th century it meant a young horse. Soon afterward the word came into its present meaning but acquired a variety of connotations. In the early 17th century, *to go in stag* meant to go naked. Since the 1920s, however, the adjective *buck-naked* has been the preferred term for "stark naked." Further, to *wear a stag's crest* or *be made a stag* meant to be made a cuckold, as *giving [a man] horns* had meant since about A.D. 100.

Today the principal informal meaning of *stag* is a male without female companionship. As long ago as 1854 a *stag party* was a bachelors' gathering, and by 1900 it implied a gathering with entertainment unsuitable for polite female eyes and ears, featuring strippers and the like. Such antics traditionally characterized the traditional *stag dinner* given a bridegroom by his male friends just before his wedding, representing a last fling of freedom before entering the bonds of matrimony. Today such goings-on may be becoming as archaic as the *stag line* at a dance, formed by men who had come without a date. And today *stag movie,* a term for a pornographic film intended mainly for a male audience, has been largely replaced by the so-called adult film.

▼Buffalo

Americans tend to think of the buffalo, whose image once appeared on the five-cent coin (*buffalo nickel*), as quintessentially American. In fact the name *buffalo,* from the Spanish *búfalo* (in turn from Latin *bubalus* and Greek *boubalos,* for an African antelope), came into use in the 16th century, before European settlers had had much contact with the American *bison.* At that time the name was used for the Indian or African ox, today generally called *Cape buffalo* or *water buffalo.* Later it was applied to the native American bison, and *bison* is the term used in zoology for this beast. It is the *buffalo* that fires the imagination with images of the Great Plains.

Buffalo used to range the North American continent in vast herds containing millions of individuals. They were invaluable to both Native Americans and early Western settlers, who relied on them for food and hides. Among the famous figures of the American West was William Frederick Cody (1846–1917), internationally known as *Buffalo Bill.* He won his famous nickname for supplying fresh buffalo meat to laborers building the Kansas Pacific

Railroad. It is said that he killed 4,862 buffalo in one season, and 69 in a single day. After a career as a Pony Express rider, an army scout (during the Civil War), and Indian fighter, he entered show business and in 1883 organized his own Wild West Show, which toured the United States with Indians, cowboys, stagecoaches, and other relics of the vanishing frontier. The show won him a fortune and made him an international celebrity. (Cody, Wyoming, was founded and named in his honor.)

Fortunes also were built on the sale of buffalo hides. Their name was shortened to *buff*, and they made a thick, soft, light-yellow leather. The same word was later used for the skins of other animals, and *buff color* described their pale yellowish tan. Buffalo leather is now a rarity, since the encroachment of civilization has wiped out the herds, and today buffalo are found only in the refuges of national parks.

A massive animal with a huge head and powerful shaggy shoulders, the buffalo is the largest animal found in the present-day American wild. A full-grown bull (male) weighs up to 1,600 pounds and stands more than five feet high at the shoulders. Although they are gentle and shy in temperament, their very size makes buffalo look so formidable that the verb *to buffalo*, used since the 1890s in the United States, means both to intimidate or impress, and to confuse or mystify.

Somewhat earlier, immediately after the Civil War, the first African-American military regiments came into existence by virtue of an act of Congress. Their main job was to serve on the rapidly expanding Western frontier, and there the Native Americans called them *buffalo soldiers,* perhaps for their toughness and determination but more probably because they often wore buffalo robes for protection against the freezing cold of the Plains winters. The appellation survived and continued to be used for the African-American troops who served in the Spanish-American War, in the Philippines and in Cuba, in both World Wars, and in the Korean War—until the armed forces were desegregated.

The city of Buffalo, New York, is named not for the animal but for *beau fleuve,* French for "beautiful river," which is the name a Belgian explorer, Père Louis Hennepin, gave to the Niagara River and its falls. The Indians pronounced this name *bouf-flo,* and English settlers assumed they meant the buffalo, even though there is no record of buffalo ever having been found so far east.

▼ Camel

> *The last straw breaks the laden camel's back.*
>
> —Charles Dickens,
> *Dombey & Son* (1848)

The desert's beast of burden has been known since ancient times. The English name for it comes from Greek *kamelos* and is also similar to Hebrew *gamal.* The animal has been used for thousands of years to carry people and goods, as well as for its milk and flesh, and its hair, which makes a fine wool cloth. Unlike domesticated cattle and horses, camels can get along perfectly well without human help. They tolerate broiling sun and freezing cold, and can go without food or water for quite long periods. They also can carry prodigious weights. It is this characteristic that is referred to in *the straw that broke the camel's back* and the related term, *the last straw.* Even the strongest camel eventually can be overburdened and collapse if too much is required of it, a concept readily transferred to human beings. This idea has been stated in numerous expressions: "not the last drop that empties the water-clock but all that has previously flowed out" (Seneca, A.D. 60); "the cord breaketh at the last by the weakest pull" (Sir Francis Bacon, 1608); "the last feather breaks the horse's back" (John Bramhall, 1677). But it is the camel's *last straw* that survives today, appearing again and again.

In the New Testament, the Gospel of Matthew (23:24)

quotes Jesus as scolding the scribes and Pharisees, saying: "Ye blind guides, which strain at a gnat and swallow a camel." In other words, it is wrong to fuss over trivia (symbolized by the tiny gnat) and agree too quickly to important matters (symbolized by the camel). Today such behavior is still described as *to strain at a gnat and swallow a camel.*

Coyote

Oh bury me out on the prairie,
Where the coyotes may roar o'er
my grave.

—Anonymous, cowboy song

The coyote, also called a *prairie wolf,* is a well-known feature of the vast prairies and plains of the American West. Its name comes from Spanish *coyote,* which in turn comes from Nahuatl *coyōtl.* The coyote's call, an eerie sound usually heard at night, is a warning to ranchers and farmers that marauders are near, since the coyote is a wise and wily predator of sheep, poultry, and young cattle. It also is a scavenger, devouring carcasses and scraps from dead bodies, and it destroys many jack rabbits and some rodent pests.

Because the animal is for the most part hated and feared, the name *coyote* always seems to retain negative connotations. In the 1870s it was transferred first to a contemptible person, especially a greedy or dishonest one, and in the 1920s, to a person who smuggles illegal immigrants into the United States from Mexico, usually for a high fee and often robbing or assaulting them in the process. The former slang usage seems to be dying out, but in the 1980s *coyote* also became slang for an extremely homely woman, termed *coyote ugly.* And about the same time *coyote* began to be used for a roving firefighter who is sent, often for long periods, to remote forest fires. It is too soon to say if these last two usages will survive.

▼ Elephant

Women and elephants never forget.
—Saki, *Reginald on Besetting Sins* (1910)

Elephants have been known in the Western world since ancient Greek times—the word *elephant* comes from Greek *elephas*—but the Greeks regarded the giant pachyderm as a stupid beast and gave the camel credit for a prodigious memory. Today we say that *Elephants never forget,* but when and why this transfer took place has indeed been forgotten.

Elephants are the largest of modern animals that live on land. The giant of the three modern species is the African elephant. A full-grown adult stands more than 10 feet high and weighs more than six tons; it needs 600 to 700 pounds of food daily. From this we have the adjective *elephantine,* a synonym for "very large" (and from the elephant's ancestor, the *mammoth,* another adjective denoting large size). Also, the animal's ears are very large—especially in the African elephant—and *elephant ear* is the name of a large, flat pastry of similar shape.

Unless you live in Africa or on the Indian subcontinent, it isn't every day that you see an elephant. Consequently we have the expression *to see the elephant,* which according to slang historian J. E. Lighter has been used in several ways since it was first recorded in 1835. At first it meant having seen just about everything, or enough—in effect a synonym for "been there, done that." A decade or so later it was used to signify gaining considerable experience, and hence to see unusual sights. It was also used to mean seeing combat for the first time, and that usage survived as well.

African elephants are hard to tame and so are not often used in circuses. However, one of the most famous circus elephants was an African elephant named *Jumbo,* a huge animal bought by P. T. Barnum in 1882 from the London Zoo and brought to the United States. From it we have the adjective *jumbo,* for the largest size of any object or commodity, including *jumbo jet* and the oxymoron *jumbo shrimp* (see also SHRIMP).

In the United States the elephant is the symbol of the Republican Party, a connection originating about 1860 in a campaign poster for Abraham Lincoln showing an elephant wearing boots. It did not become firmly established until the appearance of a cartoon by Thomas Nast in *Harper's Weekly* on November 7, 1874, during a hotly contested congressional election. Nast drew an ass wearing a lion's skin—as in Aesop's fable (see under ASS, DONKEY, AND MULE)—to represent the *New York Herald,* a newspaper that was trying to create public alarm at the prospect of Ulysses S. Grant's seeking a third term as President, and an elephant, which was one of the animals being frightened, to represent the Republican vote. After the election, in which the Republicans fared poorly, Nast drew another cartoon connecting their party with the elephant, and the symbol caught on for good.

White Elephant

> The white elephant whereon the King
> of Siam was mounted.
>
> > —Henry Cogan, trans.,
> > *Pinto's Travels* (1663)

That standby of church bazaar and garage sale, the *white elephant,* owes its name to an apocryphal legend concerning an ancient custom of Siam (Thailand), where only the king was allowed to own an albino elephant, and consequently these rare animals were considered sacred. No one else might ride one, and certainly not kill one, without the king's consent. However, albino elephants have, like other elephants, an appetite appropriate to their size, and so they were expensive to keep. When the king was displeased with a courtier, he would present him with a white elephant and quietly wait until the high upkeep costs caused the man to be ruined. Charles Earle Funk reports that King Charles I received the gift of an elephant

from Siam at a time when he was battling a hostile Parliament and desperately trying to raise money. Allegedly the beast was so expensive to keep that his Queen had to put off her annual trip to Bath for want of funds.

Our modern *white elephant* tends to be an inanimate possession that is similarly unwanted and hard to get rid of, but too costly simply to throw out or abandon.

▼ Ferret

The ferret is a variety of polecat that has been domesticated in Europe to drive out rabbits, rats, and other destructive rodents from their burrows, and occasionally has been tamed enough to be a pet. Its name comes from Latin *furritus,* for "little thief," which probably alludes to the fact that ferrets like to steal hen's eggs. Its name also developed into a verb, *to ferret out,* meaning to dig out or bring something to light.

▼ Fox

An old fox need learn no craft.
—John Ray, *English Proverbs* (1670)

The fox and its cunning have fascinated writers for centuries. An extraordinary number of Aesop's fables involve foxes. Among the most famous are the story of *the fox and the crow,* in which the fox slyly flatters the crow into showing off its supposedly beautiful voice and causes it to drop a piece of cheese from its beak; and *the fox and the grapes,* in which the fox, unable to reach the fruit on the vine, concludes it must be sour, giving rise to the saying *sour grapes,* for disdaining something one cannot attain. Despite being hunted for years, both in the wild for its fur and purely as a sport, as well as by farmers to stop its barnyard raids, the fox has managed to survive.

The word *fox* comes to us straight from Old English *fox* and has been transferred to human beings since about A.D. 1000 to mean a crafty or wily person. *Sly as a fox* is a time-honored simile, and *to fox* means to deceive. The brilliant German general Erwin Rommel earned the nickname *Desert Fox* for his eminently clever campaign with the Afrika Korps in North Africa during World War II, and was elevated to the rank of field marshal. Years earlier Marshal Soult, who distinguished himself as Napoleon's commander of the Peninsular War (1803–13), was called the *Old Fox* for his outstanding strategy. And still earlier, American Revolutionary General Francis Marion (c. 1732–1795) was called the *Swamp Fox* for his guerrilla tactics, which involved retreating into and attacking from the South Carolina swamps when his forces were badly outnumbered by the British.

We also call someone who is especially clever in a sneaky way *crazy like a fox;* the American humorist S. J. Perelman used this phrase as a book title in 1944, spurning the more grammatical *crazy as a fox*. The verb *to fox,* dating only from about 1960, means to deceive or to trick, but also since about 1960 both the noun *fox* and the adjective *foxy* acquired meanings other than "sly" and "wily." *Foxy* has signified "sexually appealing" and/or "stylish," especially as applied to a young woman, and *fox* has similarly meant a very attractive young man or woman. At one time *foxy* also meant strong-smelling—Shakespeare used it in this way in *Twelfth Night* ("rank as a fox")—but this usage is rare today.

The female fox in Old English was *fyxe,* whence the modern *vixen* for both a female fox and an ill-tempered, shrewish woman. Nor are young foxes exempt from evil. The Bible's Song of Solomon has *"little foxes that spoil the vines,"* presumably an allusion to their greed. Also alluding to greed is the title of one of Lillian Hellman's best plays, *The Little Foxes* (1939), about greed and corruption bringing down an old Southern family.

Foxfire is an eerie phosphorescent light caused by the presence of fungi on decaying wood. It has been so called since the 15th century, probably for its resemblance to silvery fox fur.

The name *foxglove,* for the garden flower botanically named *Digitalis,* comes from Old English *foxesglofa* and is thought to allude to the fact that its drooping, tubular blossoms resemble the empty fingers of a glove; its association with the animal has never been explained satisfactorily.

The *foxhole,* a battle shelter for one or two soldiers consisting of a hole dug in the ground, was so named during World War I, when it was first widely used. Foxes are not genuine burrowing animals, but like their close relatives, dogs, they scratch relatively shallow holes in the ground. Presumably this habit accounts for the term.

Fox Trot

Before the name was used for a popular dance, the *fox trot* was a horse's gait of short, broken steps, intermediate between a trot and a walk; it was so called because it resembles the gait of the short-legged fox. The ballroom dance called *fox trot,* also consisting of short rhythmic steps, originated in the United States about 1912. It is in duple meter, either 2/4 or 4/4, and can be either slow or fast. The 2/4 version is also called the *two-step*.

In the series *Able-Baker-Charlie*-etc., used to communicate clearly the letters of the alphabet over imperfect communications lines, *fox* at first was used for the letter *F*, but it was later replaced by the even clearer *Fox trot*.

▽ Groundhog

> *How much wood would a wood-*
> *chuck chuck if a woodchuck could*
> *chuck wood?*
>
> —Anonymous, tongue-twister

The groundhog, also known as a *woodchuck*, is a fat, lazy, clumsy rodent that works only when it must burrow and build an underground home. It spends its time sleeping and foraging for food, and is a nuisance to farmers, for it loves leafy green plants (lettuce, cabbage, and the like), and its burrows in pasture can cause injury to livestock that stumble into the burrow holes.

Groundhogs hibernate in their burrows from late autumn until February or March. According to legend, after this long winter sleep the animal emerges on February 2, called *Groundhog Day*, to survey conditions above ground. If the day is sunny, it will see its shadow and scurry back underground; this means there will be six more weeks of cold winter weather. If the day is cold and cloudy, there will be no such shadow, supposedly signifying that winter is almost over and spring is on the way.

▽ Guinea Pig

The name of this small South American rodent is a case of either mistaken origin or convoluted derivation. It first came to Europe in the 17th century from South America and was either misnamed *guinea* (Guinea being in West

Africa) for Guiana, in South America, or it was named for the Guineamen, slave traders who took blacks from Guinea to the West Indies and then conveyed a variety of goods from the Indies and North America to Britain. (Actually, another etymologist suggests that *guinea* originally meant "Africa" but then was extended to mean any distant land.)

In the 19th century *guinea pig* became British slang for a person of standing who allowed his name to be put on a company's roster of directors for a fee paid in guineas but who was not active in the company.

Because they are easily tamed and reproduce rapidly, guinea pigs came to be widely used in scientific and medical experiments, leading to the transfer of the name to the subject of any kind of experiment or trial.

▽ Jackal

They must not be like the Joecaul,
which provides food for the lyon.

—William de Britaine,
The Dutch Usurper (1672)

The jackal is an animal about the size of a fox and, like it, belongs to the dog family. It has been prevalent in the Near East since Biblical times, and the name seems to come from Persian *shagal*. It was once believed to hunt in troops in order to provide the lion with prey and then eat whatever the lion left behind. It thus was called the *lion's provider*. This myth survived, and today we use the name *jackal* for a person who does demeaning or dishonest tasks for someone else, that is, an individual who does another's dirty work.

▽ Kangaroo

Kangaroos are found only in Australia and Tasmania, and their name, brought to Europe in the 18th century by

Captain James Cook, is said to come from the aboriginal Australian language. Since that language was not a written one, the origin cannot be verified.

The term *kangaroo court,* however, is American, although the practice may have originated elsewhere, and it dates from the mid-19th century. The outstanding characteristic of kangaroos, other than the pouches in which they carry their young, is their fantastic jumping ability. The *kangaroo court,* a mock court of law conducted without regard to proper legal procedure among prisoners in a jail or among settlers in an outlying area, is thought to be so named because it "jumps" to conclusions and decisions, and administers so-called justice on this decidedly shaky basis. From it also comes the verb *to kangaroo,* meaning to convict on the basis of false evidence. A secondary meaning of *kangaroo court* is any court of law in which the rules are rigged so as to prevent a genuinely fair trial.

Two other characteristics of kangaroos have been linguistically transferred more recently. The newborn kangaroo, or *joey,* is quite immature at birth and must remain in the mother's pouch for a fairly long time. From this we have *kangaroo care,* a form of intensive care for premature human infants in which prolonged skin-to-skin contact with the mother (such as holding her baby close for up to six hours) serves as a substitute for life-sustaining technologies like incubators, respirators, feeding tubes, and the like. This form of care, developed in Colombia about 1980, is practiced mainly in countries where more technologically advanced treatment for newborns is not available, but it also has been found to reduce the length of hospitalization for premature babies in countries with modern medical resources.

The kangaroo's remarkable jumping ability is due in large measure to its powerfully muscled rump. From this we have *kangaroo ticket,* for a political ticket in which the running mate is stronger than the primary candidate. The term may date from 1932, William Safire suggests, when the Democratic vice-presidential nominee, John Garner, was thought by some to be more appealing than presidential candidate Franklin D. Roosevelt. It was revived in 1971 when

Treasury secretary John Connally allegedly said he would agree to be President Richard Nixon's running mate provided that their partnership be announced as a kangaroo ticket. And again in 1992, one reporter described the Clinton–Gore ticket as a potential kangaroo ticket, "stronger in the hind legs."

▼ Leopard

Lions make leopards tame. Yea, but not change his spots.
—William Shakespeare, *Richard II*

The leopard, a fierce, handsome cat, is actually a panther. Its name comes from Greek *leopardus,* a combination of *leōn* ("lion") and *pardos* ("panther"), because the ancients believed it was a hybrid of these two animals. There are many color variations among these animals, and indeed, a jet-black leopard found in parts of Africa is more commonly called a *black panther.* However, it is the spotted leopard, tawny with black circular marks arranged in circles and rosettes, that gave rise to the most frequently quoted statement about the animal. It was first recorded in the Bible's Old Testament (Jeremiah 13:23, c. 700 B.C.): "Can the Ethiopian change his skin, or the leopard his spots?" It later became a Greek and then a Latin proverb, and today *a leopard cannot change its spots* remains a classic characterization of the unchangeability of one's intrinsic nature.

▼ Lion

There may come a time when the lion and the lamb will lie down together, but I am still betting on the lion.
—Josh Billings (1818–85)

Long called the *king of beasts* for its large size, majestic bearing, and ferocity, the lion is a serious hunter in the open plains of sub-Saharan Africa and Asia. Its name comes from Greek *leōn,* via Latin *leō.* Large and strong, it often stalks and preys on animals larger than itself, giving rise to the simile *brave as a lion.*

The lion has been the national emblem of Britain since the Middle Ages, and the British heraldic shield bears its image. Not only is Britain personified as a lion, but to *twist the lion's tail* means, in British terminology, to provoke or insult the British or their government. A number of coins, both British and of other nations, notably Scotland and France, have been called *lion* and borne the figure of a lion. In the Bible a *winged lion* is the emblem of St. Mark. Several monarchs have been called "lion," among them Sweden's King Gustavus Adolphus, hero of the Protestant side in the Thirty Years' War, and Haile Selassie, Emperor of Ethiopia, who called himself the *Lion of Judah.*

To be lion-hearted is to be exceedingly courageous, a sobriquet applied to Richard I, Coeur de Lion (*Richard the Lion-hearted*), King of England (1189–99); to *put on a lion's skin* is to pretend to such bravery (see THE LION'S SHARE).

Lionizing

> A lion is a man or woman one must
> have at one's parties.
>
> —William Makepeace Thackeray,
>   *Contributions to Punch* (1886)

One of the major attractions of the Tower of London in the 17th century was a menagerie that included lions, and Londoners often took out-of-town visitors to see it. (Indeed, Samuel Pepys wrote in his diary in 1662 that he had taken some friends there.) The menagerie was removed in 1834 and thereafter tourists had to content themselves with such Tower sights as the crown jewels and the Beefeaters, but by then to be a *lion* had become a figure of speech, attached to any fashionable object of special attraction or interest, or to any person of importance. Thus, *to lionize* at first meant to show someone the Tower lions, and by extension to make a fuss over a celebrity. Eventually people who sought out celebrities were called *lion hunters,* a term immortalized by Mrs. Leo Hunter in Charles Dickens's *Pickwick Papers.* The usage is by no means obsolete. The New York Public Library in 1981 began holding an annual *Literary Lions* dinner to honor famous authors (and to raise money).

Beard the Lion

> *Nothing less would satisfy her than to beard . . . the lion in his den, the arch-accuser, in the very court of judgment.*
>
> —R. D. Blackmore, *Perlycross* (1894)

One needs to be as brave as a lion in order to face one. According to the Old Testament, David took on a lion before he took on the giant Goliath. A good shepherd, he went after a lion that had stolen a lamb "and smote him, and delivered it out of his mouth: and when he arose against me, I caught him by his beard, and smote him, and slew him" (I Samuel 17:35). Nearly half a millennium later, the enemies of the prophet Daniel caused him to be thrown into a den of lions, which was then blocked up with a stone. Daniel had to spend the night there, but in the morning he was still alive, saying that God had sent his angel to shut the lions' mouths. Whereupon Daniel was released and his enemies were shut up in the den, where the lions promptly destroyed them (Daniel 6:16-24). Despite the 500-year time lag, the two stories were somehow combined into one saying, *to beard the lion in his den,* even though it was David who grasped the beard and Daniel who went into the den. Nevertheless, the term means to be unusually (if rashly) brave. It crops up in several versions of a Latin proverb quoted by, among others, Horace, Martial, and much later Erasmus, all of which involve a timid hare plucking a dead lion's beard (in contempt). The only good lion, it seems, is a dead one. Both

Thomas Kyd (*The Spanish Tragedy*, 1592) and William Shakespeare (*King John*, 1596) refer to it, and it continued to appear in the 18th and 19th centuries (Tobias Smollett, Sir Walter Scott) and remains current. It is now considered a cliché.

"Save me from the lion's mouth," says the Bible's Book of Psalms (22:21). To *put one's head in the lion's mouth* still betokens a foolhardy risk born of either true or false courage.

The Lion's Share

Might makes right, and intimidation will get you the lot. The *lion's share* used to mean just that—the whole prize— but today it is used in the sense of the greater part. The origin lies in another of Aesop's fables, in which a lion, ass, fox, and wolf hunt together and bring down a stag. The lion divides the prey into four equal parts but, just as the others are about to claim their shares, says he is entitled to one-fourth of the kill because of his prerogative, one-fourth for his superior bravery, and one-fourth for his dam and their cubs; and he is willing to fight them for the last fourth. In another version of the tale, a lion, ass, and fox kill a stag, and the ass is chosen to divide it. He does so, very equally, but the lion, enraged at not receiving the largest portion, attacks the ass and kills it. Thereupon the fox decides to play it safe, takes a small nibble, and gives the rest to the lion. In both versions, of course, the victor gets the spoils.

Although the preponderance of tales and sayings about lions portrays them as fierce, unfriendly creatures, Aesop's tale of the lion and the mouse suggests some redeeming qualities. A mouse hears a lion roar in the woods and runs to see what is happening. The lion has been trapped in a net. The mouse remembers it had fallen under the paw of a certain lion a short while before, and the lion had let her go. Looking closely, she recognizes the very same beast, now hopelessly trapped. So she gnaws through the net and frees him. The story was revived more than 2,000 years later by George Bernard Shaw in *Androcles and the Lion* (1913), a comedy about a Roman slave who helps a lion by removing a crippling thorn from its paws and then in turn is assisted by the lion.

▼Mole

> Too much amplifying thinges yt be
> but small, makyng mountaines of
> Molehils.
>
> —John Fox, *The Book of Martyrs* (1570)

The mole, a small, burrowing, insect-eating mammal whose name comes from Middle English *molle* and/or Middle Dutch and German *mol,* is one of the animal world's most effective diggers. With its broad forefeet and well-developed claws it digs underground, breeding and nesting in burrows called runs. Moles usually burrow in a hillside, making a central chamber from which several runs radiate in different directions. The runs look like slightly raised areas or ridges on the surface and so are called *molehills.* They are only a few inches high, giving rise, as early as the 16th century, to the saying, *to make mountains out of molehills,* meaning to exaggerate a small obstacle or minor problem.

Occasionally, however, molehills can be more than just a nuisance on the golf course or suburban lawn. According to popular belief, King William III (he of William-and-Mary and Glorious-Revolution fame), a singularly unloved monarch, was killed in a riding accident when his horse stumbled over a molehill in 1702. Sir Walter Scott referred to this incident (true or legendary, it is not known) when he wrote, "The little gentleman in black velvet who did such a service in 1702" (*Waverley,* 1814); the "gentleman" in question was, of course, the mole.

The mole's digging expertise made it the logical source for the name of a tunnel-boring machine developed in the

1960s. Guided through rock by a laser beam, this *mole* is capable of boring through sandstone and siltstone at the rate of twenty feet per hour.

A *mole* is also a spy who builds a legitimate reputation in a foreign country or intelligence organization over a period of years and does not actually engage in espionage until he or she is "activated," that is, called on for a specific important mission. Such a mole is also called a "sleeper," dormant until "awakened." The burrowing action here is figurative, consisting of digging oneself into an organization and then undermining it from within. This usage became popular through 1970s spy novels about the Cold War, especially those of the English writer John le Carré. However, there had been a much earlier use of *mole* for a spy by Sir Francis Bacon in his *History of the Reign of King Henry VII* (1622): "Hee was carefull and liberall to obtaine good Intelligence from all parts abroad. Hee had such Moles perpetually working and casting to undermine him." It is doubtful, however, that this 17th-century usage gave rise to the modern one.

The ancients respected moles because they were able to survive living underground, the traditional realm of the dead. They also were mistakenly thought to be blind, and *blind as a mole* was a popular simile until about 1750. In Europe the mole was thought to have curative powers (its blood and/or flesh were thought to cure disorders ranging from deafness, warts, and epilepsy to rheumatism), and it was used as an amulet to serve as protection against various illnesses.

▼ Monkey

Strictly speaking, *monkey*, a word that entered the language in the 16th century and may have come from Arabic *maimun* via Turkish and the Romance languages, is an appellation for all but the highest orders of primate—that is, all but the anthropoid apes and human beings.

However, it is generally used loosely to include all primates. More intelligent and closer to human beings in appearance and behavior than any other animal, monkeys always have had considerable appeal because of their playful antics and their ability to imitate human behavior. To call someone a *monkey,* therefore, is not necessarily an insult; rather, it is saying that the person is a skilled mimic or a performer of playful tricks. *Monkey see, monkey do,* an American catch phrase from about 1920, is another comment on the former. As for playful tricks, *more fun than a barrel of monkeys,* dating from about the same time, means "a great deal of fun indeed."

Calling a child a *little monkey* may imply he or she behaves mischievously, but it is not really pejorative. The same is true for *monkeyshines,* meaning "mischievous antics," which originated in America in the 1820s. *Monkeyshines Publications* of Greensboro, North Carolina, which since 1986 has been putting out a children's magazine and dozens of appealingly illustrated books on history, geography, science, and the arts, adopted the name because it "mischievously tricks" youngsters into reading about various serious subjects. Similarly, *to monkey with* and *to monkey around,* originating in the United States about 1880, mean to tamper with or to play mischievous tricks. *To make a monkey of someone,* however, is less flattering, since it means to make someone look ludicrous or stupid. It, too, is American, dating from about 1900. From somewhat earlier, the 1880s, comes *monkey business,* used in one of two ways: either for frivolous, lighthearted mischief, or for underhanded, not quite legal behavior.

I'll be a monkey's uncle, a simple expression of astonishment, dates from about 1926. It may have originated as an allusion to the famous Scopes trial of 1925, in which schoolteacher John T. Scopes was tried for violating a Tennessee law that prohibited teaching the theory of evolution. Prosecuted by William Jennings Bryan and defended by Clarence Darrow, Scopes was convicted but then acquitted on a technicality.

The organ grinder's monkey, dressed in a little jacket and given a hat in which to collect coins, was a familiar sight in the 18th and 19th centuries. About 1820 a close-fitting short jacket worn by British sailors was called a *monkey jacket* for its resemblance to that of the street musician's monkey, and toward the end of the 19th century in America this name came to be used for the jacket of a tuxedo or full-dress suit, which itself was called a *monkey suit.* In the armed services, however, a *monkey suit* was a full-dress uniform.

As popular as the potted palm in Victorian parlors was a little statuette group of three monkeys, sometimes called *the three wise monkeys.* They were often made of brass, and one monkey had its paws over its eyes, another over its ears, and a third over its mouth, portraying the saying, *See no evil, hear no evil, speak no evil.* Some believe that this familiar household decoration gave rise to the saying, *cold enough to freeze the balls off a brass monkey,* common throughout the English-speaking world since about 1825 for "very cold." In the United States *nuts* was usually substituted for *balls.* Because of the saying's obvious rudeness, several euphemistic forms exist, substituting "ears" or "tail" for the genitals. However, there is another totally different theory about the origin of the phrase. A 19th-century warship needed to carry cannonballs for the 100 or so heavy cannon and many smaller guns it bore. To save space, cannonballs were stacked in pyramids on brass trays called *monkeys.* In very cold weather the brass contracted, causing the balls to fall off the brass monkey.

To have *a monkey on one's back* long meant to be angry or annoyed, a sense that is now obsolete. Instead, in the United States about 1942 it came to mean to be addicted to a drug, the monkey representing the addiction; later it came to mean having any kind of burdensome affliction.

The origin of the name of that most useful of tools, the *monkey wrench,* is uncertain. One writer suggests that the name is a corruption of Charles Moncke, a

London blacksmith who devised such a tool, which consists of a wrench with a movable jaw adjusted by means of a screw. More likely, however, the sliding jaws reminded someone of a monkey's jaws, especially since the term originated in America in the 1850s; in Britain the tool is called an "adjustable spanner." *Monkey wrench* also acquired a figurative meaning, that is, an obstacle that interferes with proper functioning. In a short story by Philander Johnson in *Everybody's Magazine* (May 1920), a character said, "Don't throw a monkey wrench into the machinery," and this expression for sabotage has stuck.

A *grease monkey* is a mechanic. Originating about 1910, the term is used mainly for auto and airplane mechanics, and the origin is not clear, other than that such mechanics often must be quite agile (like monkeys) in order to work in awkward places, such as underneath an automobile.

In the United States in the mid-1960s *the monkey* was a dance descended from the twist and the frug, and like them enjoyed a brief period of discotheque popularity. It required the dancers to move their hands as though they were climbing a tree or pole, and to jerk their heads and shoulders back and forth.

Other Primates

> *Detraction is but baseness' varlet;*
> *And apes are apes, though clothed in*
> *scarlet.*
>
> —Ben Jonson, *The Poetaster* (1601)

Although calling someone a monkey is generally not too insulting, a similar use of *ape, baboon,* or *gorilla* constitutes abusive name-calling. Although *to ape* has meant to imitate since Chaucer's day, a human *ape* (from Old English *apa*) was a fool or worse even at that time: "And thus with feyned flaterye and japes, he made the person and the peple his apes" (Prologue to *The Canterbury Tales*). Today we use *ape* for a clumsy, unattractive person.

To go ape is 1960s slang for becoming violently emotional; *to go ape over* something similarly betokens violent enthusiasm, such as might be displayed by a crowd of fans at a rock concert.

The saying *The higher the ape goes the more he shows his tail,* meaning the more the lowly advance, the more their crudeness is exposed, was first recorded in Michel de Montaigne's essays (1580). In English it appeared a few years later, and it was frequently repeated until the mid-1700s but is rarely heard today.

The name *baboon,* from Middle English *baboyne,* meaning a grotesque figure or gargoyle, is even worse when applied to a person; it then signifies a coarse, brutish individual with low intelligence. It is often put as *big baboon.* Baboons are in truth quite ugly, with their long-muzzled, doglike faces and massive bodies, but they are considered the most intelligent of the primates after the anthropoid apes.

The largest anthropoid is the *gorilla,* a name adopted by the American missionary and naturalist Thomas Savage in 1847 as the specific name for that animal. It came from Greek *gorillai,* which supposedly was an ancient African name for a wild, hairy tribe and by extension came to be used for any savage people; in Britain in 1800 it still meant a hairy aborigine. Thus the gorilla is one of the very few animals whose name came from humankind and not vice versa. The name was soon transferred again, however. By the 1860s *gorilla* was slang for a hairy, tough man, and in 1920s parlance it meant a thug or hoodlum, especially in detective stories. Today it still carries associations with mobsters and organized crime.

▼Moose

I am strong as a bull moose.
—Theodore Roosevelt (1900)

The moose, largest member of the deer family, is a native of North America. Its name is derived from the

Algonquian language, where it means "he trims smoothly," alluding to the propensity of moose to strip and eat the bark from trees. Roosevelt's first recorded mention of the animal, which he enjoyed hunting, was in a letter to Mark Hanna at the opening of the 1900 presidential campaign, in which he was William McKinley's running mate. In 1912, after some years out of politics, Roosevelt traveled to the Republican convention in Chicago, and upon his arrival said he "felt like a bull moose." Roosevelt failed to get the Republican nomination, but he then became the nominee of the Progressive Party, which adopted the bull (male) moose as its emblem. During the height of the campaign, on October 14, 1912, an attempt was made to assassinate the candidate, and he was wounded in the chest. That same day he made a speech in Milwaukee and said, "It takes more than that to kill a bull moose." He recovered from the wound but lost the election to Woodrow Wilson.

About the same time, the Canadians were calling bootleg whiskey *moosemilk*. In the United States this name was later given to a cocktail made from rum and milk, popular on college campuses in the 1940s.

▼Mouse

He could invent the best mouse-trap.
—John Wesley, *Journal* (1772)

Mouse, from Old English *mūs,* is a general name for a large number of small rodents, none of which is especially friendly to human endeavors. The meadow or field mouse, also called a *vole,* is probably the most common mammal in all North America and more numerous than any other. It feeds on grain and is very destructive to fruit trees, voraciously gnawing their bark. The house mouse is only slightly less destructive than the rat, spreading disease and pestilence, spoiling grain, and damaging wooden interiors, clothing, and food. Certainly this behavior accounts for humankind's obsession with finding a more effective mousetrap. Ralph Waldo Emerson is credited with being the first to say, in a lecture, that if a man can write a better book, preach a better sermon, or *make a better mouse-trap* than his neighbor, the world will make a beaten path to his door.

Cats, of course, can serve as a considerable deterrent to the mouse population and have long been so valued. *When the cat's away the mice will play* was already an old-hat proverb by 1600 and is often applied to absent human authorities (bosses, teachers) and their underlings.

Perhaps because they are elusive, mice have been called shy, and we therefore call a quiet, bashful, timid individual *a mouse* or characterize him or her as *mousy*. The latter adjective also is used to describe a dull, nondescript, grayish color (as in "Her hair was best described as mousy"). Mice also are relatively noiseless, giving rise to the simile *quiet* (or *still*) *as a mouse.*

Since the 16th century, *Are you a man or a mouse?* has represented the contrast between bold and timid ("Fear not, she saith unto her spouse, A man or a mouse whether ye be"—*Scholehouse of Women,* author unknown, c. 1541). On the other hand, *mouse* has been a British colloquialism for "girl" (similar to "bird") since the 1950s, and no other special characteristic, such as femininity or modesty, is implied by it. In America, *a mouse* is also slang for a black eye (a bad bruise or swelling under the eye). And more recently, computer manufacturers adopted the name *mouse* for the device that controls the cursor on a monitor screen. It is small, like a mouse, and has a long "tail"—that is, a wire connecting it to the microprocessor.

Finally, we have that old saying, *poor as a church mouse,* whose origin has been forgotten but which means very poor indeed. Common conjecture says it comes from the fact that since a church normally has no food cupboard or pantry, at least not in the sanctuary, any mice inhabiting a house of worship would have a lean time of it.

Mickey Mouse

> *Girls bored me—they still do. I love
> Mickey Mouse more than any woman
> I've ever known.*
>
> —Walt Disney, quoted in W. Wagner,
> *You Must Remember This*

Walt Disney's most famous cartoon character was Mickey Mouse, who first appeared in *Steamboat Willie* (1928). His popularity was enhanced by a children's variety show, *Walt Disney's Mickey Mouse Club,* which featured child performers called the *Mouseketeers* wearing black "mouse-eared" caps. With his comical face and big black ears, the character still delights children at the various Disney parks.

Since his beginnings, however, the character's name has acquired an abundance of other meanings. During World War II, *Mickey Mouse* began to be used in the military to describe mindless, petty rules and regulations. Troops also used the term *Mickey Mouse money* for Japanese currency as well as for military scrip.

In civilian life after the war, *Mickey Mouse* was extended to anything ridiculous, trivial, or pointless. Subsequently a broad variety of expressions came into being, such as *Mickey Mouse music,* for trite, uninspired jazz resembling the background music of cartoon films, and *Mickey Mouse courses,* for college courses criticized as being oversimplified and childish. It even took verbal form, *to mickey mouse,* meaning to behave foolishly.

The actual Mickey Mouse character is a fairly benign individual, cheery if somewhat naïve. Why, then, are there so many negative meanings connected with his name? In the 1930s the Ingersoll Watch Company had begun marketing *Mickey Mouse watches,* cheap children's timepieces that pictured the cartoon character on their face. William Safire suggests that it is these rather junky items that gave rise to the many negative meanings of Mickey Mouse—trivial, corny, childish, simplistic—which persist to the present day.

▼Opossum

He is playing 'possum with you.
—Adiel Sherwood, *A Gazetteer of the*
State of Georgia (1829)

The opossum is the only marsupial (pouched mammal) native to North America. Its name originated in the 17th century from an Algonquian word meaning "white animal," and the North American opossum does have long thick hair that is light gray on the upper surface of the body and white on the underside. It hunts at night, eating roots, fruits, insects, and small mammals such as mice.

Opossums are not very intelligent, but they have managed to survive for two reasons. One is their high rate of reproduction: the female bears as many as twenty young a year. They are born only twelve or so days after fertilization but cannot survive in this stage of development. Rather, they must climb into the mother's pouch, attach themselves to one of her mammary glands, and take in milk and complete their development there, which takes another two months.

The second reason for their survival is their self-defense mechanism. The opossum is often attacked by other animals, such as foxes, and also is hunted by humans, since its flesh is quite tasty. When attacked or caught, the animal falls into a kind of coma and pretends to be dead. Whether it is actually paralyzed by fear or is genuinely pretending is not known. This behavior confuses animal predators, which usually skulk off. And from it comes the term *to play possum,* meaning to dissemble or to pretend to be dead or ignorant; it originated in the United States in the early 1820s, along with such variants as to *act possum* and *come possum.*

In Australia, where opossums and other marsupials are found in far greater numbers, one is said to be *like a possum up a gum tree* when one is completely happy or perfectly at home, since the gum tree (eucalyptus) is the opossum's favorite habitat and the leaves its favorite food.

▼Rabbit

In the 14th century *rabbit* referred to the young of the species, which we now colloquially call *bunny.* Technically, rabbits are related but not identical to *hares;* often, however, the words *rabbit* and *hare* are used interchangeably. Found in many climates and parts of the world, hares and rabbits have been bred and crossbred for domestic purposes, and hundreds of species and varieties have been developed. All the animals in this group are gentle and easy to maintain in captivity. They also produce offspring at a tremendous rate, which has made them extremely useful in biological and medical research, and gave rise to the expression *to breed like rabbits,* applied to various kinds of prolific output.

An early form of testing for a human pregnancy was called the *rabbit test,* developed about 1928. It involved the injection of the woman's urine into a rabbit, which, if the woman was pregnant, induced ovulation in the rabbit within 24 to 48 hours. However, the use of rabbits, which had to be killed to verify the result, was soon abandoned because it was too expensive.

In the wild, rabbits and hares breed so rapidly that they can become pests, competing with human beings for the plant food that both depend on. They eat their way through gardens, both suburban and commercial, where they will devour just about any leafy crop and vegetable. This propensity gave rise in the early 20th century to the term *rabbit food* for raw vegetables, especially those used in salads. The place where rabbits breed is called a *warren,* and with reference to the animal's fecundity, *rabbit warren* has, since the 18th century, referred to a crowded human abode, such as a tenement building.

Rabbits have been hunted for their fur and flesh for centuries. In America in the early 19th century, or perhaps even before, a *rabbit's foot* was carried about as a good-luck charm. This superstition is thought to date as far back as the 6th century B.C., and possibly even earlier.

Butchers generally stunned a rabbit with a blow to the head before cutting it up. From this practice came the name for *rabbit punch*, for an illegal chopping blow to the back of the head in boxing.

Both rabbits and hares are distinctive for their ears, which are quite long relative to their heads and bodies, and for their ability to jump and run quite fast. The former characteristic is referred to in *rabbit ears*, for a pair of indoor television aerials, and also a slang term for exceptional sensitivity to insults and gibes on the part of a professional athlete. The fleetness of rabbits is referred to in *rabbit ball*, baseball slang (since the 1920s) for an exceptionally lively baseball, as well as *rabbit* for a runner whose goal in a distance race is to set an extremely fast pace in order to wear out an opponent or help a teammate set a new record.

The *jackrabbit* is actually a hare. It was so named in the mid-1800s by combining *jack(ass)* and *rabbit*, the former word alluding to its extremely long ears. It also has very long legs, enabling it to move very fast. From this we have *jackrabbit start*, for a sudden rapid movement, especially by an automobile driver.

Because rabbits are tame and readily available, magicians often use them—particularly white ones—in their performances. One of the most familiar of magic tricks is that of producing a rabbit from a supposedly empty hat, whence the expression *to pull a rabbit out of a hat*, meaning to come up with a surprise, usually a pleasant one.

Magic tricks with rabbits find a ready-made audience among children, who also regard these animals as appealing pets. Authors have capitalized on this appeal since the last century, which gave us Joel Chandler Harris's *Br'er* (Brother) *Rabbit* in his Uncle Remus tales, Lewis Carroll's White Rabbit, down whose hole Alice fell to begin her adventures in Wonderland, and somewhat later Beatrix Potter's tales of

Peter Rabbit. The wonderful animated *Bugs Bunny* first appeared in cartoons produced for Warner Brothers by Leon Schlesinger in 1938. Bugs's principal creators included Friz Freleng, Tex Avery, and Chuck Jones, and his voice, with its trademark line "What's up, Doc?" was that of Mel Blanc. First seen in a Porky Pig film, *Porky's Hare Hunt,* the rabbit caught on and became the star of numerous subsequent films and later comic strips based on them.

Welsh Rabbit

Willful obscurantism temporarily cast dark clouds over the origin of *Welsh rabbit,* a dish of melted cheese mixed with ale or beer, mustard, and spices, and served over toast or crackers. What it basically meant was "poor man's rabbit"—an economical cheese dish for those who could not afford meat—and the "Welsh" alluded to the fact that Wales was poorer than England in the early 18th century, when the term first appeared.

Or, possibly, it may have been a joke, similar to, as food writer Craig Claiborne pointed out, calling codfish "Cape Cod turkey." That term originated when the lowly New England cod was less expensive than turkey. Either the joke was not understood or it was judged to be in poor taste, but somewhere along the line *rabbit* got changed to *rarebit,* making *Welsh rarebit,* a meaningless euphemism for a simple savory.

Bunny

Bunny, today an informal word for a very small or young rabbit, entered the language as a diminutive of *bun,* of Celtic origin and meaning a small stump of a tail. For a time bunny meant either a squirrel or a rabbit, and then it became a term of endearment for a woman or a child. It also can be a slang term for any person, male or female. Thus *dumb bunny* is a mild epithet for a somewhat silly individual.

The word is also slang for a young woman who appears to be engaged in some sport but in fact is present more for the social than the active life. For example, *snow bunny* identifies a woman who wears fashionable ski clothes and spends most of her time in the ski lodge rather than on the slopes, and a *beach bunny* is one who lounges about on beaches more for self-display than swimming or surfing.

Among the popular dances developed around 1910, along with the FOX TROT, was the *bunny hug,* danced to syncopated ragtime rhythms that made the dancers' steps resemble the skittish hops of a rabbit. Unlike many dances of this period, it survived into the jazz age, and its name still brings up associations of this period.

As in other species, the young of rabbits are thought to be more sprightly than their elders. Alluding to this propensity is *quick as a bunny,* meaning quite fast, although one writer believes it refers to the animal's rapid breeding habits.

Hare

The word *hare* is much older than rabbit, coming from Old English *hara,* which is related to various words for the color gray. Most hares are in fact gray or grayish brown.

A number of words allude to hares. Among them is *harelip,* a congenital deformity of the upper lip that resembles the cleft lip of a hare and has been so called since the 16th century. Another is *harebell,* at first (14th century) the wild hyacinth or bluebell and later (18th century) the campanula. All these flowers have bell-shaped blossoms and grow in meadows, fields, and other places frequented by hares.

Still another is *harebrained,* meaning giddy and foolhardy, and dating from the 16th century. It possibly is an offspring of the still older saying *mad as a March hare,* which dates from at least 1500 and possibly much earlier (about 1385 Chaucer wrote, "This somnour wood [mad] were as an hare. . . ."). The most colorfully crazy March Hare was the one that joined in the mad tea party in Lewis Carroll's *Alice's Adventures in Wonderland,* where it buttered the Mad

Hatter's watch to make it run again, then dipped it into his tea, and remarked, "It was the *best* butter, you know."

It was long believed that hares are unusually wild in March, during the rutting season. According to Erasmus, their behavior could be accounted for by the absence of hedges and other cover at that time of year; but Erasmus mistook the saying for "mad as a marsh hare," somehow confusing the month with a swamp. At any rate, during rutting season, it was reported, hares boxed one another's ears with their clublike forepaws and kicked at each other with their strong hind legs, exhibiting, it was concluded, normal mating behavior in which the males fight each other over females. In the 1970s some British naturalists undertook a study of hares in Somerset, using long-lens video cameras for night and day surveillance of a drove of hares. Their observations, published in the British journal *Nature,* yielded more accurate data. Mating among hares takes place at night, and not just in March, but from January through August. Before March, however, it grows dark too early to see it, and after March, the grass grows too high for good visibility. Moreover, the embattled hares are not males fighting against males, but females fighting against males, presumably to resist their advances. Since the females are generally bigger than the males, they often win these battles. Nor do the fighting partners end their battles in mating; the triumphant female simply hops away. From this behavior we could easily conclude that *mad as a March hare* means "angry" rather than "crazy."

Aesop was probably the first to mock the speed of rabbits in his oft-quoted fable of *the tortoise and the hare*. The hare, sure of winning a race against the slow tortoise, stops to take a nap, while the tortoise plods along at a steady pace and reaches the finish line just as the hare awakens. The moral today is still applied to compare the folly of hurrying humans, who are too hasty, to the virtue of careful plodders.

Rabbit hunting is the source of *hare and hounds*, an outdoor game so called since the mid-19th century but probably much older. In the game one team, the hares, has a few minutes' head start to scatter scraps of paper or other objects, which represent a "scent" trail. They then run as far away as they can from the other team, the hounds, who try to catch the hares before they can reach a predetermined place.

Since the mid-15th century people who try to take both sides in a conflict have been accused of *running with both hounds and hares*—that is, siding with both hunter and hunted. "Thou hast a crokyd tunge heldying with hownd and wyth hare," wrote the author of *Jacob's Well* about 1440, and by the time John Heywood assembled his proverb collection a century later, it was included:

> There is no such titifyls [knaves] in England's ground
> To holde with the hare, and run with the hound.
> Fire in the one hand, and water in the other.

▼ Raccoon

The raccoon, a nocturnal mammal common throughout North America and long hunted for its fur, was called *aroughcun* (or something like that) by the Algonquian Indians, who had no written language. Its English name dates from the 17th century, and by the 18th century it was frequently shortened to *coon*. By then frontier clothing had long included garments made of its fur, especially a *coonskin cap,* sporting the animal's tail.

In the U.S. presidential campaign of 1840 the Whig Party, which ran more on the basis of personalities than issues, characterized its candidate, General William Henry Harrison, the military hero of Tippecanoe, as a sturdy son of the frontier and a man of the people. In its "log cabin and cider" campaign (based on a sarcastic description of Harrison in an opposition newspaper, the *Baltimore Republican*), it used, along with campaign hats, floats, emblems, and the like, transportable log cabins furnished with coonskins and barrels of cider. Hence for a time *coon* became a nickname for Whig. Sometime in the 19th century *coon* became a disparaging word for a black person. This offensive usage is largely obsolete.

In the South hunting coons on moonlit nights has long been a favorite sport, and their meat is roasted and eaten. Dogs trained to hunt raccoons are still called *coon dogs.* In the North, raccoon skins were valued for sleigh robes and overcoats. In the early 20th century coats of raccoon fur, which is long-haired and a blend of black, brown, and gray, became very fashionable, and the *raccoon coat* remains a symbol of the "roaring twenties," although from time to time it has returned to fashion.

Although their fur is very durable, raccoons are not much longer-lived than related animals, but for some reason they were thought to be, and the expression *a coon's age,* which dates from the early 19th century, means a long, long time.

▼Rat

> *Yf they smell a ratt, they grisely chide and chatt.*
>
> —John Skelton,
> *Image of Hypocrisy* (c. 1550)

The rat, whose name comes from Old English *ræt,* is one of the worst animal pests. It destroys stored grain, young poultry, fruits, vegetables, and other food products; it gnaws through wood, plaster, and soft metal; and it can spread dreadful diseases, including bubonic plague. Perhaps its only value to human beings is its use for scientific experimentation, although white rats also have been used as pets.

For the most part, rats are hated and feared, and calling someone a *rat* has been an insult for centuries. At best you are calling the person a scoundrel, and at worst, a deserter, an informer, or simply a despicable individual.

The holds of sailing ships were routinely infested with rats, since these holds also served as the ship's larder. Actually, in the 17th and 18th centuries sailors on long voyages occasionally would eat the ship's rats. Rats would remain on board devouring stores until the ship foundered in a storm or ran into other severe difficulties; only then would the rats depart. Hence the expression *rats desert a sinking ship* has symbolized desertion since at least the 16th century, when Francis Bacon wrote, "It is the Wisdome of Rats that will be sure to leave a House somewhat before its fall" (*Essays,* 1597). Shakespeare echoed the sentiment: "A rotten carcass of a boat, . . . the very rats instinctively have quit it" (*The Tempest*).

Rats do not like water, and *wet as a drowned rat* has provided a picturesque image of utter bedragglement for nearly two thousand years; Petronius wrote, "It rained by the bucket and they came home wet as drowned rats" (*Satyricon,* A.D. 60). The adjective *ratty* means in terrible condition, very ragged or shabby, although in Britain it signifies irritable and ill-humored (that is, ratlike and fierce).

The presence of rats means trouble, and *to smell a rat* has meant to suspect big trouble, such as treason or other rottenness, since the mid-16th century. A ballad from 1533 includes the refrain, "For yf they smell a ratt," and the saying reappears unchanged in the works of Ben Jonson and Samuel Butler, as well as in the proverb collection of John Ray, and continues in use up to the present day. Other than being a term of general contempt, *rat* has specifically meant, at various times, the deserter of a political party (late 18th century), a strikebreaker or scab (19th century), a police spy (since 1850), and an informer. *To rat on* someone means to inform or betray. Sometimes the term has been embellished, as in *rat fink,* an American sobriquet for "traitor" from the 1960s; *you dirty rat,* attributed to James Cagney in the 1931 motion picture *Blonde Crazy;* and *you dirty double-crossing rat,* common in crime stories of the same period.

Given their hostile environment littered with traps, which have been used since at least the 17th century ("Welcome death, quoth the rat, when the trap fell down" is quoted in James Howell's *English Proverbs* of 1659), it is no wonder that rats are engaged in a relentless struggle for survival. It is this aspect of their existence that is expressed in *rat race,* an American term from about 1940 for the fierce competition one faces to get ahead and succeed in a profession or in commerce, especially in a hectic urban work environment.

One North American species of rodent of the genus *Neotoma,* commonly called the *pack rat,* is known for its habit of carrying off various small articles and bits of debris to store in its nest. Cigarette butts, bits of cloth, coins and other shiny objects—anything small is fair game for this animal. From this behavior we have applied the name *pack rat* to humans who collect, save, or hoard small useless items.

The expletive *Rats!*—originally an American contemptuous retort equivalent to "Bosh!" or "Nonsense!"—now is a mild oath, used as an expression of disappointment or annoyance, and is more common in Britain than in the United States.

▼ *Shrew*

> *There is but one shrewde wyfe in the worlde but . . . euery man weneth he hath her.*
>
> —Sir Thomas More, *Works* (1528)

The words *shrew, shrewish,* and *shrewd* all come from Old English *scrēawa,* for a small, mouselike, insect-eating animal that is disproportionately fierce for its size. Shrews will fight one another to the death over a morsel of food and are so pugnacious that at one time they were thought to be poisonous to farm animals who happened to cross their path. Before long a person of unpleasant personality, particularly one who nagged or scolded, was called a *shrew* or *shrewish,* terms applied equally to a man or a woman. Similarly, *shrewd,* which now means "sharp-witted," used to mean "vicious." By the 14th century, however, only scolding women were called shrews, and although various later writers maintained that it was better to marry an ill-tempered shrew than a dull-witted, passive sheep, *shrew* and *shrewish* have largely lost the connotation of quick wits personified in Shakespeare's clever Kate (*The Taming of the Shrew*) and today are wholly pejorative.

▼*Skunk*

An important innovator of chemical warfare, the skunk, a native American animal, derives its name from Algonquian Indian words meaning "urinating fox." When attacked or threatened, the skunk discharges a yellowish, acrid, foul-smelling liquid by means of two musk glands located near the base of its tail. The muscles in that area are so powerful that the animal can spray its secretion as far as nine feet. Not only does the foul odor linger for a long time, but if it strikes the eyes it can cause a painful, burning injury.

Except for this disagreeable trait, skunks are docile creatures. They kill large numbers of mice and other rodent pests, as well as large numbers of insects. With their musk glands removed they can be gentle, lovable pets. Nevertheless, their unpleasant defense mechanism is what has undergone linguistic transference, and since about 1840 calling a person *a skunk* classifies him or her as "a stinker"—a mean, paltry, contemptible wretch. *To skunk* someone, on the other hand, means to win a game so overwhelmingly that one's opponent does not score at

all. Also of American origin, this expression dates from the late 19th century and possibly alludes to the overwhelming quality of the skunk's smell.

In World War II military jargon, a *skunk* was an unidentified surface craft, which might be either friend or enemy (a similarly unidentified aircraft was called a *bogey*).

That several foul-smelling plants should be called *skunkweed* is hardly surprising. Among them is the *skunk cabbage,* whose appearance is a sure sign of spring. The plant, *Symplocarpus foetidus,* grows in bogs, swamps, and moist open woods from Nova Scotia to Minnesota and south to North Carolina and Iowa. When crushed or torn, the huge cabbagelike leaves give off a rank, skunklike smell.

Far less obvious is the origin of *skunk works.* During the 1950s the Lockheed Aircraft Corporation had an experimental division for innovative defense projects. It operated in secret and was largely unencumbered by the elaborate bureaucratic procedures usually applied to such projects. Among its products were the U-2 aircraft in which Francis Gary Powers was shot down during a flight over the Soviet Union in 1960, and the F-117A stealth fighter, which was virtually invisible to antiaircraft radar. Someone at Lockheed named this division *skunk works,* both because of its proximity to a foul-smelling chemical plant and after the *Skonk Works* in Al Capp's comic strip, *Li'l Abner,* a manufacturing enterprise whose precise nature and product were a mystery (but probably were associated with producing Kickapoo Joy Juice, a moonshine whiskey). In subsequent years *skunk works* came to be used more generally for any innovative and secret laboratory or project.

▼ *Squirrel*

The name *squirrel* comes from Greek *skiouros:* from *skia,* meaning "shadow" and *oura,* meaning "tail." This bright-eyed, bushy-tailed little rodent gave rise to the expression *bright-eyed and bushy-tailed,* meaning wide awake and ready to go.

The squirrel's main diet consists of fruits, nuts, buds, leaves, bark, and seeds, which can make it the bane of farmers and gardeners. The squirrel also can damage newly planted trees and bulbs, and sometimes strips the bark off trees. Even more annoying is its habit of storing extra food for the winter months, either in a cache or in individual holes. This practice causes it to dig up lawns and gardens to find the acorns and other buried food. It also gave rise, in the first half of the 1900s, to the verb *to squirrel away,* meaning to store or hoard something.

Red squirrels are noisy, quarrelsome animals, and from this characteristic comes the adjective *squirrely* to describe a person who is jumpy or nervous, and who acts somewhat crazily. It is used more in Britain than in America.

Squirrels are sometimes put in a cage with a cylindrical framework that they rotate by running inside it. This gave rise to the expression *squirrel cage* to characterize a situation that seems to go on endlessly without any particular achievement or goal.

Tiger

Tiger, tiger burning bright
In the forests of the night,
What Immortal hand or eye
Could frame thy fearful symmetry?

—William Blake,
Songs of Experience (1794)

The tiger, whose name comes from Greek *tigris,* exists, other than in zoos, only in Asia. Known for its handsome striped coat, its strength, and its cunning, this fierce hunter moves effortlessly and quietly in pursuit of its prey. It has few natural enemies and occasionally becomes a man-eater that must then be eradicated by professional hunters. Calling someone *a tiger* or *tigress* (the female of the species) is synonymous with calling that person exceptionally fierce and courageous, and a formidable opponent. Similarly, *to have a tiger by the tail,* as though one could actually hold an untranquilized cat in this way, means to take on something unexpectedly difficult or formidable.

In poker, a *tiger* is a terrible hand. A *Big Tiger* is a hand with the king high and eight low, but with no pairs; a *Little Tiger* is one with the eight high, three low, and no pair. The names supposedly come from the fact that it takes great courage to hold and bluff when holding such poor cards.

More in keeping with the animal's image of ferocity, political cartoonist Thomas Nast chose the tiger to represent Tammany Hall, the powerful political machine that controlled the New York Democratic Party in the late 19th and early 20th centuries. His dramatic cartoons helped expose the corrupt Tweed Ring, named for Tammany head William March ("Boss") Tweed, which drained the New York City treasury of some $200 million through faked leases, padded bills, false vouchers, and kickbacks. Tweed finally was arrested and convicted in 1872, and he died in prison, but the symbol of the *Tammany Tiger* lived on.

Animal symbolism plays a large role in traditional Chinese customs and beliefs. The most important Chinese celebration is the New Year, which is always designated as the year of one of the 12 animals in the Chinese zodiac, including the Rat, Ox, and Tiger. Tigers still are found in China, although only in remote and sparsely settled areas. In ancient Chinese lore the tiger was the symbol of longevity, dignity, and military prowess. Its image, or just its head, was embroidered on robes, painted on shields, and hung by the door at the New Year to serve as a protection against evil.

Two terms with Chinese associations involve the great striped cat. In August 1941, five months before the Japanese attack on Pearl Harbor and the official entry of the United States into World War II, a volunteer group of U.S. airmen was formed under Major General Clare L. Chennault to support the Chinese against Japanese aggression. They fought fiercely and with great distinction, and soon were given the nickname *Flying Tigers*. In July 1942, they merged with the U.S. Air Force's 23rd Fighter Squadron.

Mao Zedong is thought to be responsible for the English term *paper tiger*, which presumably has existed in Chinese for a long time. In an interview with a Western journalist in 1946, Mao, then a leader of the Chinese communist army, said, according to the translator, that all reactionaries—that is, anticommunist forces and their supporters—are *paper tigers*, in that they appear to be strong but actually are weak. The term continues to be used for any seemingly powerful but actually ineffectual individual, group, organization, or nation.

Several older terms involving the tiger are virtually, but not entirely, obsolete. The bank in the card game of faro is called the *tiger*, and *to buck the tiger* means to play against the bank, that is, to gamble. A *blind tiger* is a place where liquor is sold illegally. The reason for the name is not known. One authority suggests it is connected to playing faro, which may have been done illegally in the same establishment; another speculates that stuffed animals, including toy tigers, were among the paraphernalia put on display in such an establishment to disguise the true nature of its business, but this idea seems a bit far-fetched.

▼Weasel

> All around the cobbler's bench
> The monkey chased the weasel,
> The monkey thought 'twas all in fun,
> Pop! goes the weasel.
>
> —Children's song

The weasel, from Old English *wesle,* is a small fur-bearing mammal found in many parts of Europe and from Canada to northern South America. In the northern areas of its range, where winters are long, the weasel changes its brown summer coat to a white one, which conceals it from both foes and prey in the snow. The color change is controlled by a pituitary hormone that is influenced by the amount of available daylight. The pelts of the white weasel, whose tail remains black in summer and winter, are called *ermine* and are considered a luxury fur.

The weasel is very small, less than a foot long, and has keen sight, smell, and hearing, and extremely long, sharp claws. It is a merciless hunter, pursuing mainly rodents, but it also eats birds and sucks the contents of birds' eggs. From this last behavior comes the term *weasel words.* In 1916, in a speech criticizing President Woodrow Wilson, Theodore Roosevelt said, "You can have universal training or you can have voluntary training, but when you use the word 'voluntary' to qualify the word 'universal' you are using a weasel word; it has sucked all the meaning out of 'universal.' The two words flatly contradict one another." Roosevelt himself did not invent this locution— it may have originated in a magazine article by Stewart Chaplin that appeared in 1900 in *Century Magazine*—but he did popularize it, and repeated it in another speech in the same year: "When a weasel sucks an egg, the meat is sucked out of the egg; and if you use a 'weasel word' after another word there is nothing left of the other."

Weasels are furtive creatures, sneaking up on their prey and, given their small size, able to get through quite small openings. These characteristics gave rise about 1920 to the verb *to weasel out,* meaning to evade something or someone, or to avoid committing oneself.

And then there is *Pop Goes the Weasel,* a children's song since about 1870 and remarkable largely because nobody is quite sure what the refrain means. One writer believes that the "pop" simply refers to vigorous movement, since weasels are extremely active and are good swimmers and climbers as well as fast runners. Perhaps the activity in question is erotic. The song originated in Britain and was published as "an old English dance" in 1853; it may have been meant to be sung to a dance. The British version has somewhat different words from the American one quoted above:

> Up and down the City Road
> In and out the Eagle,
> That's the way the money goes,
> Pop! goes the weasel.

The Eagle was a pub in the City Road, London, and *weasel* in 19th-century slang was a special narrow flat-iron, which resembled the animal's thin sharp face. (Another explanation has *weasel* meaning "overcoat.") "To pop" is slang for "to pawn," and according to one interpretation the song suggests that, after one has spent all one's cash in the pub, one can go and pawn one's flatiron (or overcoat), which can be temporarily spared for this purpose.

Still other theories concern two now extinct tools. According to one, which justifies the song's reference to a cobbler's bench, a *weasel* was a kind of awl with a threaded eye that was used by cobblers to mend shoes. But the weasel was difficult to push through a leather sole and had to be rammed through; as it came through, it made a "popping" noise. Another concerns a 19th-century device for winding yarn known as a "husband saver." As the arms holding the yarn rotated, a dowel-shaped piece, called the *weasel,* was forced aside until, after a given number of rotations, it "popped" back into place.

Whatever the original true meaning, the song continues to be popular with children in Britain and America, and the meaning to them no doubt is unimportant so long as "Pop!" is sung with sufficient emphasis and volume.

▼Wildcat

> *A simple man, perhaps, but good*
> *ez gold and true ez steel,*
> *He could whip his weight in wildcats,*
> *and you never heard him squeal.*
>
> —Eugene Field,
> *Modjesky as Cameel* (1882)

Wildcat, from Middle English *wilde cat,* is a general name for several kinds of cat found in the wild. In North America it is used for the Canadian lynx and the closely related bobcat (also called bay lynx), both of which belong to the genus *Lynx.* In Europe it is used for a similar feline, *Felis sylvestris* (Latin for "forest cat"). All of them superficially resemble the domestic cat but are far more ferocious and will, if necessary, attack animals considerably larger than themselves. Consequently, calling someone a *wildcat* credits him or her with exceptional ferocity.

As an adjective, *wildcat* has been used in the United States since about 1838 to describe a business undertaking as risky, precarious, and unsound. This sense was taken from the somewhat earlier (1812) noun use of *wildcat* for a rash prospector or speculator, later also called a *wildcatter.* It is an odd transference, since in the wild the animal does not seem at all impetuous but simply goes about its bloody business in order to survive.

The same element of risk is indicated in *wildcat well,* a term dating from about 1910 and meaning a deep well dug in hopes of discovering oil or gas but with the considerable risk that there will be none. A *wildcat strike* is one called by dissatisfied workers that has not been authorized by their union, or one that breaks out during the life of a labor contract in violation of a no-strike clause in that contract.

In the 19th-century United States a *wildcat bank* was one that issued far more bank notes than it could redeem. It usually was part of a branch banking system in which each branch could make or collect a loan, but only the main office would redeem the notes in specie (hard currency). That main office was in some backwoods location, a habitat more suited to wildcats than to civilized institutions like banks. In fact, it did not exist at all, and the notes were unredeemable. Common in such states as Wisconsin and Michigan, wildcat banking was eliminated with the passage of the National Banking Act of 1863, which established reserve requirements for all banks.

▼Wolf

> *I would have ye stur [work] honestly
> to kepe the wolf from the dur [door].*
> —John Heywood, *Proverbs* (1546)

The wolf, whose name comes from Old English *wulf,* is, like the fox, coyote, jackal, and domestic dog, a member of the dog family. It once roved the earth in great numbers. As humanity moved from hunting to herding to furnish itself with meat, the wolf became a serious enemy. No longer content with game, it attacked flocks and herds. Aesop's fables include at least three dozen concerning a wolf, and as often as not sheep figure in them as well.

The outstanding characteristic of wolves as transferred to describe human pursuits is their rapaciousness, their constantly ravenous appetite. *To wolf,* or *wolf down,* means "to consume greedily," scarcely bothering to chew, and to be *wolfish* is to be "fiercely greedy." Similarly, because wolves never seem to have enough to eat, they became symbolic of hunger and want. *To keep the wolf from the door* has meant to keep out hunger or to ward off starvation since at least the 15th century and was a well-known proverb by the time John Heywood included it in his collection. The Walt Disney film *Three Little Pigs* (1933) featured a song—"Who's Afraid of the Big Bad Wolf?"—in which, it has been suggested, the wolf had a double meaning of predator (attacking the pigs) and hunger.

The gray or timber wolf, the species most numerous in North America, tends to hunt alone or in pairs in summer, and in sizable packs in winter. Hence the term *lone wolf,* meaning a person who is by nature solitary or who likes to work alone, which H. L. Mencken claimed is the translation of an Indian chief's name. In World War II the Allies gave the name *wolf pack* to German submarines that pursued and attacked enemy shipping in a group.

One writer suggests that *to throw to the wolves,* meaning to sacrifice something in order to divert attention from something more important, originated in a situation such as that of imperiled travelers in a sleigh throwing food to a pursuing wolf pack in order to slow down the animals and permit the sleigh to escape. More likely it came from Aesop's fable about the nurse and the wolf, in which the nurse threatens to throw her naughty charge to the wolves unless the child behaves. (She does not do so, of course, and the wolf waits in vain for a tasty morsel.) Here, *to throw to the wolves* has more the sense of abandoning or dismissing someone to a terrible fate, the way the expression is most often used today.

Wolf in Sheep's Clothing

> *Yes, but they [wolves] gang in more
> secrete wise,
> And with sheepes clothing doen hem
> disguise.*
>
> —Edmund Spenser,
> *The Shepheardes Calender* (1579)

Among the most famous of wolf fables is that of the wolf
who disguises himself—in Aesop's version as a shepherd
and in the Biblical version as a sheep. Aesop's tale has the
wolf dressing up as a shepherd and sneaking up on the
flock, which are sound asleep beside the real shepherd and
his dog. The wolf tries to wake the sheep so as to draw
them away with him, but its efforts to imitate the shepherd's voice fail and wake both shepherd and dog. Worse
yet, the shepherd's cloak the wolf has donned prevents it
from running away or fighting, so it is killed. Aesop moral-
izes that deceit will never succeed, for truth will come out,
and whoever is a wolf had better not try to don a disguise.

In the Gospel of Matthew, Jesus warns of "false
prophets which come to you in sheep's clothing but

inwardly they are ravening wolves." There are comparable proverbs in both Greek and Latin, as well as in numerous modern languages. Presumably it is from this posing of an enemy as a friend that we derive the 20th-century *wolf,* the philanderer who makes sexual advances to women, along with *wolf call* and *wolf whistle,* the rude, oafish expressions of his admiration.

Cry Wolf

"The Boy would be crying a Wolf, a Wolf, when there was none, and then could not be believed when there was," according to Sir Roger L'Estrange's 1629 translation of Aesop's fable. A shepherd boy was watching the flock on a remote hillside and greatly feared an attack by a wolf. Moreover, he was lonely. So he summoned help by calling "Wolf!" even though there was none. After people had responded to his cries a number of times, they no longer believed him. When at last a wolf did approach, no one would come to help him. This fable appears in many forms in many countries, and *to cry wolf* still serves as a metaphor for sounding a false alarm.

Birds
of a
Feather

*Byrdes of one kynde and color flok
and flye alwayes to gether.*

—William Turner,
Rescuing of the Romish Fox (1545)

"Birds dwell with their own kind," wrote Ben Sirach, author of the Book of Wisdom (or Ecclesiasticus, one of the apocryphal books of the Bible) about 190 B.C., and the idea soon was applied to people as well. "Like attracts like," we often say.

The appearance, habits, and flight of birds are solidly entrenched in our language. Practically all the perceived attributes of birds are recorded: their clannishness (*birds*

of a feather flock together), nesting activity (*feather one's nest*), migratory habits (*bird of passage*), small size (*eat like a bird*), flight (*birdman; bird's-eye view*), capture (*bird cage; jailbird*), song (*twitter; warble*), superiority (golf's *birdie*), and intellectual inferiority (*birdbrain; featherbrained*). Quite a few of these terms are based on misconception. For example, birds actually eat a great deal relative to their size—some of the small ones eat the equivalent of their own weight every day—yet *eat like a bird* means to consume very little. Nor are all birds stupid; on the contrary, their brains are quite well developed.

In Old English, *brid* (and in Middle English, *byrde*) denoted the young of *foul* (or *foule* or *fowel*), a word that then meant all feathered animals and that today is used mostly for domestic birds (see under BARNYARD FOWL) or aquatic birds (*water fowl*). In the 13th century *bird* also meant "maiden" or "girl," which may have come from a blending with Middle English *burde,* for "young woman" or "young lady." In modern British parlance *bird* is slightly disrespectful slang for a young woman, much as *chick* is in the United States. On the other hand, *biddy* is reserved in America for an old hen and also is a distinctly unflattering epithet for a meddlesome woman, whereas in Britain it has no association with hens at all, but is a nickname for Bridget and by extension means any Irish maidservant.

To *get the bird* is also unpleasant. It means to be hissed at or otherwise given an unfavorable reception (and to *give the bird* means to do that to someone or something, or to show contempt by raising the middle finger, an obscene gesture). It most likely comes from the hissing noise made by geese and some other species of bird when they are provoked, but its specific origin is unknown.

Since the late 1940s and perhaps longer, in the United States, *That's for the birds,* or *strictly for the birds,* has meant that something is of no consequence or is unacceptable. One writer believes it comes from throwing crumbs to feed birds, crumbs being the equivalent of a trifling amount. Another source, quoted by Eric Partridge, suggests it comes from horse droppings left on the street in the days of horse-drawn carriages, from which sparrows and other small birds extracted seeds; this interpretation makes the expression a euphemism for "horse shit." This unpalatable etymology has not been verified, but the phrase persists. Another impolite reference, *bird shit,* comes from the Vietnam War, where it was military slang for paratroopers (who drop from the sky).

The diminutive *birdie,* for "little bird," dates from the late 18th century, and about a hundred years later it began to be used for the shuttlecock of badminton (also called *bird*), a cork sphere about an inch in diameter from which fourteen to sixteen feathers extend. The resemblance to a bird floating through the air is obvious. In the military, *bird* has quite logically been used as slang for a helicopter, a guided missile, and other pilotless vehicles, such as a satellite.

It is not birds' flight but their superiority that is referred to in the *birdie* of golf, which since about 1921 has meant making a hole with one stroke under par (making a hole with two strokes under par is termed an *eagle*). In the first half of the 19th century *bird* was a slang word for "excellent" or "first-rate," and although this usage is now largely obsolete its sense survives in the golf term.

The Bird Is Flown

> *The birds are flown.*
> —Charles Kingsley, *Westward Ho!* (1855)

Catching birds and caging them is an age-old pastime. The comparison of *bird cage* to prison is inevitable, and *the bird is (has) flown,* meaning the prisoner has escaped, was already a proverb by the mid-16th century, which also marks the advent of *jailbird,* for someone who has been or is currently incarcerated.

Even the most beautiful cage does not make captivity desirable, a fact pointed out by Chaucer in *The Mauncible's*

Tale: "Take any brid, and put it in a cage. . . . Although his cage of gold be never so gay, yet hath this brid, by twenty thousand fold, lever [would rather be] in a forest that is rude and cold." Indeed, we celebrate the natural condition of birds, unencumbered by land obstacles, in the simile *free as a bird,* used since about 1700 to signify being totally at liberty and, by implication, without obligations.

Even voluntarily trading one's freedom for wealth and comfort does not pay, as was related in the popular Victorian song: "Her beauty was sold for an old man's gold, she's a bird in a gilded cage." (This ballad, with words by Arthur J. Lamb and music by Harry von Tilzer, dates from 1900 and was launched in London by that grand lady of the music halls, Florrie Forde.)

Catching a bird is not particularly easy. In 16th-century England children were told they could do it if they *put salt on the bird's tail,* a piece of jocular advice that found its way into numerous literary works as an example of a vain enterprise ("Men catch knowledge by throwing their wit on the posteriors of a book, as boys do sparrows by flinging salt upon their tails."—Jonathan Swift, *A Tale of a Tub,* 1704).

Birds are not, as it happens, stupid, despite the fact that in America we have been accusing dumb or scatter-brained individuals of being *birdbrains* (or *birdbrained*) since the 1920s; the British have called such persons *featherbrains* (or *feather-brained*) since the 16th century. Perhaps the terms are connected with *flighty,* meaning, since the 16th century, capricious or given to flights of fancy. Even that connection does not make sense, however, since the migrations of birds follow extremely well-established patterns and are far from capricious. At least 100 species migrate each year from North America to winter in South America, each flock winging its way southward each time as though following an identical charted lane of traffic. Each species has its own pattern of speed (most fly quite rapidly) and timing (either day or night travel). Undoubtedly the paths are determined to some extent by available food supply, but how a bird so unerringly knows the food route of previous years, and even previous centuries, is a mystery. Since the late 18th century a migratory bird has been called a *bird of passage,* yet this term when transferred to human beings denotes a person who shifts restlessly from place to place rather than following the quite predictable pattern of the migrating bird.

Bird feathers also figure linguistically. *Fine feathers make fine birds,* holds a 16th-century saying that was first recorded in a Latin translation of Homer's *Odyssey* (1583). Transferred to humans, it is a comment on the benefits of fine apparel. Today we are more apt to say that someone is *in fine feather,* meaning they are "in excellent condition" in terms of appearance, emotionally, financially, or some other sense.

Bird's-Eye View

Long before human beings took to the air, they could well imagine how much birds could see from on high, and *bird's-eye view,* meaning a general overall view or large panorama, has been part of the language since about 1600. There are other terms involving birds' eyes, but they are based on their appearance—bright, small, beady—particularly in the names of various flowers, all small with bright centers, such as *bird's-eye primrose* and *bird's-eye violet,* and various fabrics with spots or markings resembling small eyes, such as *bird's-eye tweed* and the *bird's-eye cotton* fabric long used for babies' diapers.

When people finally did manage to fly, they were of course likened to birds. An aviator was called a *birdman.* In the 1950s a helicopter was sometimes called a *whirly-bird,* and an aircraft carrier a *bird farm.* In the era of containerized freight shipments, *birdieback* came to be used for a shipment combining the use of an airplane and truck (just as *fishyback* means ship and truck, and *piggyback* rail and truck).

A Little Bird Told Me

> *Curse not . . . for a bird of the air*
> *shall carry the voice, and that which*
> *hath wings shall tell the matter.*
>
> —Ecclesiastes 10:20

Speak no evil surreptitiously, because a bird will reveal your secrets, warned the author of Ecclesiastes about 250 B.C. Ever since, *a little bird* has stood for a secret source of private information, the source that investigative reporters often rely on and whose identity they conceal and defend, even on pain of imprisonment.

The ancients believed that birds in effect foretold the future. "Do not be a bird of ill-omen in my halls," wrote Homer in the *Iliad*. The raven in particular was thought to augur bad news and is so characterized by the Roman playwright Plautus. The owl, too, was thought to be "the prophete of wo and of myschaunce" (Chaucer); "the owl shriek'd at my birth, an evil sign," said Shakespeare's Henry VI. Worst of all, perhaps, *A bird in the house brings bad luck,* according to a saying that this occurrence indicates the impending death of one of the inhabitants. A swallow falling down a chimney was considered a sign of misfortune from the 17th century on. The superstition survived into the 20th century, although the bad luck so brought was less dire.

Not all birds were believed to augur ill. The cuckoo was the harbinger of spring, with its promise of renewed life. Nevertheless, the idea of bad news was more prevalent, so when this idea was transferred to human beings, it was a *bird of ill omen* that survived, as the bringer of bad news or impending misfortune.

Birdsong

> *Each bird is well pleased with his*
> *own voice.*
>
> —James Howell, *English Proverbs* (1659)

The calls and songs of birds generally are associated with their period of courtship and mating. This is probably the time when males sing most often, especially in the morning and again toward evening. Even though it is predominantly the males that sing, our transfer of *songbird* nearly always means a woman vocalist. (See also CANARY.)

Birdcalls are quite different in each species. Some calls consist of a succession of small, high-pitched, tremulous sounds called *twittering*, a word stemming ultimately from imitation of the sound itself. This term was transferred to humans, especially women, who chatter rapidly in a high, tremulous tone and then are said *to twitter*.

Many species of bird have a wide melodic repertory, especially those songbirds called *warblers*, a name of uncertain origin but probably derived from words meaning to whirl about (as the sound does). This term, too, has been transferred to human singers, and *to warble* meant at first to produce elaborate trills and other vocal ornaments but now more often means simply to sing softly and sweetly.

From about 1950 to the 1970s, one of the most famous jazz clubs was Broadway's *Birdland*, immortalized in George Shearing's song, *Lullaby of Birdland*. The club was named in honor of the renowned jazz saxophonist Charlie "Bird" (or "Yardbird") Parker, often called simply *Bird*. His name, however, came not from his music, influential and innovative as it was, but from his love of eating chicken, nicknamed "yardbirds."

A Bird in the Hand

> *I should be foolish to release the bird*
> *I have in my hand in order to pursue*
> *another.*
>
> —Aesop, *The Nightingale and the Hawk*
> (c. 570 B.C.)

Aesop told at least two fables that illustrate that it is foolish to give up something already gained in hopes of making some greater future gain, a lesson daily ignored by some stock market speculators. In one, the nightingale (or sparrow, depending on the translation) tries to convince its captor, the hawk, to let it go, since it is but a small morsel, and to search for bigger prey. But the hawk knows better. In another, a fisherman catches an anchovy that argues along the same lines as the nightingale. The proverb originated in Greek, was repeated in Latin—it appeared in Britain in *Latin Medieval Proverbs* (c. 1400) as a rhymed verse—and by 1450 or so had an English version. Today it is often put: *A bird in the hand is worth two in the bush.* Similar sayings appear in Italian (*better an egg today than a chicken tomorrow*), German (*one bird in the hand is better than ten flying over the land*), French (*better a sparrow than a goose in the air*), Spanish (*a bird in the hand is worth more than a hundred flying*), and presumably many other languages. Benjamin Franklin had his own version: "An egg today is better than a hen tomorrow" (*Poor Richard's Almanack*, 1734).

Kill Two Birds with One Stone

> *He thinks to kill two birds with one stone and satisfy two arguments with one answer.*
>
> —Thomas Hobbes, *The Questions Concerning Liberty, Necessity, and Chance* (1656)

Picking off birds with a slingshot presumably dates from Biblical times or even earlier, but trying to get two birds with one such shot seems just about impossible, unless a large catapult is used. Nevertheless, the idea of achieving two goals with the same effort dates from Roman times, although it was not always expressed in terms of birds (Plautus, for example, put it as catching two boars in one brake). John Heywood's collection of English proverbs (1546) has "stopping two gaps with one bushe" and Sir Thomas North (1557) quoted a proverb in which a man might take two pigeons with one bean. About that time the more conventional form—*kill two birds with one stone*—became current and it has since been quoted by numerous writers, including Henry David Thoreau, Mark Twain, and O. Henry. Today it is virtually a cliché.

The Early Bird

"The early bird catcheth the worme" is quoted in William Camden's book of proverbs (1605) and remains part of the work ethic of go-getters: those who get there first have the best chance of succeeding. Never mind that it may cause embarrassment in a social situation, such as a buffet supper, where greed is expected to be restrained in favor of good manners; such restraint can always be overcome with the excuse that someone has to be first.

Not only can human *early birds* gain such advantages as getting better seats at a performance, but in many places they can eat for a lower price. Numerous restaurants feature an *early-bird special*—meals reduced in price for those diners who arrive earlier than the most popular dinner hours—in order to attract a larger clientele.

Pecking Order

Among the unique characteristics of birds are their beaks. *To peck* means to strike with or take food with the beak, and the verb entered the language in the 14th century. Applied to humans, *to peck at one's food* means to eat rather little, in contrast to the British slang term *to feel peckish,* meaning to be rather hungry.

In 1922 T. J. Schjelderup-Ebbe published in a German journal the results of a study of the social life of chickens. In it he revealed that each flock has a social hierarchy based on, and reinforced by, pecking. (So much for the mannerly barnyard buffet.) Very soon afterward his German term for this hierarchy, *Hackliste,* was translated into *pecking order,* for who gets to go first, and was transferred to all kinds of human situation, ranging from the prerogatives of high society to those of the business corporation. The hierarchies, of course, are age-old, but the analogy to chickens and the term were new.

Feather One's Nest

> *Mr. Badman had well feathered*
> *his Nest with other men's goods*
> *and money.*
> —John Bunyan, *Pilgrim's Progress* (1680)

Birds' beaks are also their most important tool in building nests. Although nests are constructed for only a few weeks' use as a temporary shelter for eggs and young, they frequently are expert works of craftsmanship. In temperate climates it is the songbirds that build the most beautiful and elaborate nests, using straw, grasses, twigs, horsehair, cobwebs, and clay, with mud or saliva to stick it all together. A kind of tropical swift makes its nest almost entirely of dried saliva, the result being a thin white gelatin highly esteemed by the Chinese, who use it to make *bird's nest soup*. Many birds also use the softest of their own feathers to provide extra cushioning for their eggs and chicks, and it is this that is meant by *feathering one's nest*—that is, providing comfort for oneself, usually by laying by money and other forms of wealth. The expression appeared in a Tudor play in 1553 (*Respublica*, "Public Affairs"), and we still often use it to describe a public official who is making his or her life more comfortable through the perquisites—legitimate or not—of office.

In the days when practically every rural abode kept a few chickens, it was common practice to put an egg, either real or artificial, into a hen's nest to induce her to lay more eggs. It was called, logically enough, a *nest egg*, a term dating from the 17th century that soon came to be applied to a sum of money laid aside for retirement, an emergency, or an unexpected expense. The parallel is not too far-fetched: just as the presence of one egg inspires the production of more eggs, the initial savings can earn interest and thus multiply.

Albatross

> "God save thee, ancient Mariner!
> From the fiends that plague thee
> thus!—
> Why look'st thou so?"—"With my
> crossbow
> I shot the Albatross!"
>
> —Samuel Coleridge,
> *Rime of the Ancient Mariner* (1798)

The albatross is a large sea bird with a wingspan of up to thirteen feet and a body four feet long from beak to tail. Found in the Pacific and Antarctic oceans, it was so called by 17th-century sailors. The name is thought to come from combining Latin *alba,* for "white," with Spanish and Portuguese *alcatras,* for "pelican" or "frigate bird," in turn derived from Arabic *al-quadus,* meaning both "the water carrier" and "pelican-like bird." An albatross may weigh up to 25 pounds, so when it wants to rise from the water's surface it must run a long way before it can achieve flight. Once aloft, its enormous wings enable it to stay up for long periods, apparently hovering without moving its wings at all. While it seemingly hangs motionless in space, it really is balancing on a column of moving air.

Albatrosses are habitual followers of ships, and it must be extremely eerie to look up and see a huge bird floating motionless on outstretched wings and looking down at you. Not surprisingly they gave rise to superstitions, the most common of which was that it was unlucky to kill such a bird because it embodied the soul of a dead sailor.

Coleridge's famous *Rime of the Ancient Mariner,* quoted above, is a narrative poem about a sailor who does kill an albatross, and the terrible penalties he and his companions must suffer for this deed. Coleridge himself had never seen the actual bird, but the belief he recorded became the source of the figurative meaning of *albatross,* that is, a burden of guilt one must carry about, so heavy that it prevents progress or action. It often is put as *to have an albatross around one's neck.*

Not everyone believes the albatross is an ill omen. The French poet Baudelaire also wrote about the albatross, which he saw as a metaphor for the poet. The Maoris of New Zealand carve albatrosses into the bows of their boats to guarantee a safe and peaceful voyage. And in the 1930s in golf an *albatross* was a score of three strokes under par, but this term was later replaced by *double eagle.*

▼Buzzard

> *This have I heard ofte in saying*
> *That man (ne) maye, for no daunting,*
> *Make a sperhawke of a bosard.*
> —*Roman de la Rose* (c. 1240)

Most birds of prey are admired, but the buzzard, a member of the vulture family, is, like other vultures, hated and scorned. It is far from beautiful to look at, and it feeds on refuse and dead animals. Its name comes from Old French *busard,* and as far back as the 13th century it was said (as in the quotation above) that *one cannot make a hawk out of a buzzard.* This saying alludes to the fact that the buzzard was considered an inferior kind of hawk, useless for the very popular sport of falconry.

Actually, the original name meant "bold" and "hardy," but by the Middle Ages, in High German and Dutch, words similarly derived had a somewhat pejorative meaning—for example, "bastard." Indeed, *buzzard* long had the connotation of illegitimate birth. "I am a gentleman, though spoiled i' the breeding. The Buzzards are all gentlemen. We came in with the Conqueror." So speaks a character in Richard Brome's play, *The English Moor* (1650). Today this connotation is largely absent, and *a buzzard,* or an *old buzzard,* is merely a crochety, unlovable individual, and for some reason nearly always a man.

In the 1920s *buzzard* was the term used in golf for two strokes over par; the term was replaced by "double bogey."

One reader reported a 19th-century American folk expression, *hasn't enough sense to bell a buzzard,* but the precise analogy has been lost.

▼ *Canary*

> *But that which most doth take my*
> *Muse and me*
> *Is a pure cup of rich Canary Wine.*
>
> —Ben Johnson,
> *Inviting A Friend to Supper* (c. 1615)

The Canary Islands, a group of seven mountainous islands off the northwest coast of Africa, were occasionally visited by European travelers in the Middle Ages and came under Spanish rule late in the 15th century. For many years their main export was wine, notably a sweet white wine similar to sherry. This wine was well known in England by Ben Jonson's time and continued to please European palates until a grape blight destroyed the vineyards in 1853.

The islands' English name comes directly from the Spanish one, *Isla Canaria,* which in turn comes from Latin and means "Dog Island." Originally there were many large dogs on one of the islands. Also among the native wildlife was a finch that, it was found, could be taught to sing quite prettily by exposing it either to birds of similar ability or to instrumental music. Moreover, these birds bred well in captivity and had a relatively long life span, about fifteen years. The *canary bird* or *canary,* as it was called in English by the late 16th century, was introduced into Europe during the late 15th century and has been prized as a cage bird ever since. As such it can be the prey for other pets, especially cats, leading to the expression *look like the cat that swallowed the canary,* for looking extremely self-satisfied. (Also see page 3.)

Because the bird is valued for its singing, *canary* became, in the late 19th century, a slang word first for a woman singer and, in the 1930s and 1940s, for an informer who "sings"—that is, reveals secret information (see also under PIGEON).

In the wild the finches from which canaries are descended are usually gray or green, but breeding has produced yellow and buff-colored birds, as well as some with variegated plumage. Hence *canary* also came to mean a bright, clear yellow color.

▼ Cardinal

One of the very few red North American birds, the cardinal is a member of the finch family. Actually it is only the male that is all red, except for a black patch on its bill, whereas the female is yellowish brown with a touch of red. Both, however, have a heavy red bill and red crest, making them readily distinguishable from other red birds, such as the scarlet tanager and Baltimore oriole. The bird is so distinctive that it has been adopted as the state bird of Illinois, Ohio, Indiana, North Carolina, Virginia, West Virginia, and Kentucky.

One would think that such an attractive creature would have given its name to many things, but in fact it is the other way around. The bird's name comes from the red-robed official of the Roman Catholic Church, who in turn was named for being so important—that is, the adjective *cardinal,* from Latin *cardo,* meaning a "hinge" or "pivot." Anything cardinal was so important, in other words, that events depended (hinged or pivoted) on it. It was at first (6th century) applied to deacons and priests of the leading churches of Rome and bishops of neighboring dioceses who were close advisers to the pope. In the 12th century the College of Cardinals was organized along its present-day lines. At the first Council of Lyons, in 1245, Pope Innocent IV proposed that the cardinals all wear red cloaks and red hats, as a symbol of their willingness to shed blood for their faith. In 1567 the title of Cardinal was limited to members of the college, and in 1586 Pope Sixtus V set the maximum number of cardinals at 70, a tradition maintained until the time of Pope John XXIII, who greatly increased their number. By then, cardinals were chosen from all around the world, although a disproportionately large number of them still are Italian. When a pope dies, it is the College of Cardinals that chooses one of their number to be the next pope.

The name *cardinal* was used for the bird by early explorers and colonists from the 16th century on. Possibly even earlier the *cardinal flower,* a bright-red lobelia that is among the showiest of North American wildflowers, received its name from similar sources and for the same reason.

In 13th-century Britain the adjective *cardinal* was first applied to the four natural virtues—justice, prudence, temperance, and fortitude—and later also to the three theological virtues—faith, hope, and charity—so that *cardinal virtues* came to mean all seven virtues.

▼ Catbird

The catbird is, like most familiar North American birds, a perching bird. Its feet are well adapted for holding on to branches, since one of the four toes on each foot points backward. Most of these birds also have a well-developed vocal apparatus and are distinguished by their songs and calls. The catbirds are closely related to mockingbirds and sing almost as well; they are named for their mewing call.

And what has that to do with *catbird seat,* a term meaning a position of eminent superiority or advantage? It is thought to be originally a Southern phrase, coming from the bird's singing from an unreachable perch in bushes or trees. It was popularized in the 1940s by Mississippi-born baseball announcer Red Barber, who would say of a pitcher almost certain to allow no more hits, "Now he's in the cat-bird seat." Then it was immortalized by James Thurber's short story about a mild-mannered accountant contemplating the murder of a colleague who insists on using such terms as "in the catbird seat." In 1968, Red Barber and coauthor Robert Creamer came out with a book called *Rhubarb in the Catbird Seat.* Lexicographers William and Mary Morris report that in a letter sent in 1976, Barber says he originally got the term in a poker game where he bluffed all but one player into dropping out, and that player, who had an ace and an ace in the hole, had said from the start that he was "sitting in the catbird seat."

▽ *Coot*

> *He was ballid as a cote.*
> —John Lydgate, *Troy-Book* (c. 1422)

The common coot is a black water bird with a white bill that extends up to the forehead, giving the appearance of baldness because it contrasts so markedly with the bird's dark feathers. Its name, which dates from the 13th century, comes from Middle English *cote* or *coote,* and an early (before 1300) reference already calls it a *balled* [bald] *cote.* Though coots resemble ducks in appearance, they are not particularly fast and therefore are not considered respectable game birds (they are too easy to shoot). Consequently *coot* has come to mean a silly or foolish fellow, and, because of the association with baldness, a foolish old fellow; we also say *old coot,* which therefore may be a redundancy.

Occasionally one will hear the term *bald as a bandicoot,* which is alliterative but meaningless. A bandicoot is not a bird at all, but a name for two quite different animals, one an Indian rat and the other an Australian marsupial. Neither is bald nor gives the appearance of baldness. In the interests of alliteration, however, we do have *crazy as a coot,* a notion that dates at least from the 16th century, when John Skelton wrote about "the mad coote, with a balde face to toote" (*Phyllyp Sparowe,* 1529). It is not clear whether this allegation of lunacy arises from the bird's erratic winter behavior, when flocks of coots on a frozen lake or reservoir seem to fly at one another for no discernible purpose, or whether the craziness refers to the irrational behavior of a very old person. In 19th-century America a stupid person sometimes was called *a coot.*

▼ Crane

Years ago a coworker of mine, an amiable busybody with a blaring voice, was privately called the *whooping crane.* His rather narrow head seemed constantly to be swinging about on his disproportionately long neck, taking in every conversation and event in the office and filing it for future reports.

The crane, whose name comes from Old English *cran,* is a large, long-legged wader similar to the blue heron. It is five feet tall, with a seven-and-a-half foot wingspan. The whooping crane, named for its loud call, was in danger of becoming extinct and is still extremely rare; its relative, the sandhill crane, is more common and found throughout North America.

The crane's long neck caused its name to be transferred to the machine for raising heavy weights, which in turn gave rise to the verb *to crane,* meaning at first to hoist or lower with a crane (16th century), and then (18th century) to stretch one's neck in order to see better.

▼ Crow

> *We cut over the fields, straight as the crow flies.*
>
> —Charles Dickens, *Oliver Twist*
> (1837–38)

The second-largest of the common blackbirds (after the raven), the crow is easily recognizable for its loud caw. It lives on insects, carrion, and seeds, but also may eat bird's eggs, small birds, and small rodents. Farmers regard crows as pests because they feed on corn and other grains, and the stick figure they set in fields so as to frighten away all birds has been called a *scarecrow* since the mid-16th century. However, the crows' consumption of harmful animals may actually outweigh the damage they do to crops.

Crows normally head straight for their food supply, so *as the crow flies* means the shortest distance between two points. It was so used by poet Robert Southey in 1800 ("about fifteen miles, the crow's road") and presumably even earlier.

The nesting habits of crows were observed much earlier. Crows build a platform of sticks near the top of a large tree and lay three to nine eggs at a time; sometimes they produce a second brood in the same year. From the late 16th century on sailors called their top-of-the-mast lookout the *crow's nest,* a name also used today for similar platforms on fire towers, elevated traffic stations, and the like.

Like all the perching birds, the crow has well-articulated claws, enabling it to cling to branches. Because of the bird's large size, these leave well-defined footprints in soft ground. Since about 1350 the wrinkles that develop at the outer corners of human eyes as a result of aging and/or squinting have been called *crow's feet,* for their resemblance to the bird's footprints.

Another portion of the crow's anatomy gave rise to the name *crowbar,* a steel bar used as a lever for prying. It is so called because originally (c. 1740) this tool had a beaked end.

Since the 14th century, *to pluck a crow* has meant to quarrel or to find fault, or to have something difficult to settle. It is still in use in the southern United States and parts of Great Britain, with "to pick" sometimes being substituted for "to pluck."

Over the centuries something odd happened to the verb *to crow,* which means to utter the cry of a rooster, and, by extension, to celebrate, exult, or brag (*crow over* something or someone). The noun *crow* comes from Old English *crāwe* or *crāwa;* the verb *to crow* comes from *crāwan.* Originally it

almost certainly denoted the cry of a crow ("caw caw"), but early on it came to be used for that of a cock.

Eating Crow

> To cook crow for his own party.
> —*Scribner's Magazine*, February 1880

People presumably have been shooting at crows from the days of the earliest slingshots, but not usually to obtain their flesh, which doesn't taste very good. To *eat crow* means to eat humble pie—that is, to admit one is wrong and humbly make amends. It was part of American political slang by the time an unknown writer for *Scribner's* suggested "cooking crow" in an article on politics.

The term's true origin is not known, but there is a wonderful story, cited by Charles Earle Funk as having been published in 1888 in the *Atlanta Constitution,* that provides as colorful an etymology as anyone could wish. Toward the end of the War of 1812, the story goes, during a temporary truce a New Englander went hunting and mistakenly crossed over to the British lines. There he shot a crow. The shot was heard by a British officer, who came upon the American and decided to punish him. He was, however, unarmed, so he complimented the American on his fine shooting and asked to see his gun. When the ingenuous American handed it over, the officer pointed the gun at him, told him he was guilty of trespassing, and, as punishment, made him take a bite out of the crow. The reluctant soldier had to obey, but when the officer returned the weapon with a warning never to cross the lines again, the New Englander took his revenge, pointing the gun at the officer and forcing him to eat the rest of the bird. Since neither man had come off particularly well, the story would probably never have come out except that the officer decided to complain to the American authorities, claiming that the New Englander had violated the truce and therefore should be punished. The American commander called the soldier in and asked him if the officer's story was true and if in fact he had ever seen this officer before. The soldier, although much taken aback, managed to reply, "Yes, sir, I dined with him yesterday."

Jim Crow

A less than happy chapter of American history is the era of Jim Crow, associated with slavery and, after emancipation, another century of forcing black Americans to use separate accommodations, as well as other forms of racial segregation. The name *Jim Crow* was invented by Thomas Dartmouth Rice (1808-1860), a New York-born entertainer and showman who has been called the father of American minstrelsy. From a poor family, Rice took to the theater at an early age and eventually ended up in a stock company in Louisville, Kentucky. According to legend, it was there that he observed the shuffling dance of a crippled black stable hand as he worked and sang. Rice adapted both song and dance and introduced it about 1828 at the Louisville Theatre during his between-the-acts spot, calling it "Jim Crow":

> Wheel about, turn about,
> Do jis' so,
> And every time I wheel about
> I jump Jim Crow.

Rice imitated the stable hand right down to worn-out shoes and ragged clothes. He and the song were a big hit in the United States and eventually abroad. The song was even translated into French, and in England some years later an antislavery book entitled *The History of Jim Crow* was published. The character of Jim Crow became the precursor of the minstrel-show black man, and Rice was called "Jim Crow" Rice or "Daddy" Rice, the latter in acknowledgment of his fathering the minstrel show. Though he appeared in other shows later, Rice never again achieved the success he had won with Jim Crow.

The *crow* part of the name is obvious, since it simply means "black." In addition to becoming an insulting way of referring to black individuals, *Jim Crow* came to be an adjective applied to facilities, employment, or any other facet of life in which blacks were restricted. Thus a *Jim Crow car* was a railroad car in which blacks were forced to ride (while they were excluded from all other cars), *Jim Crow regulations* were laws concerning black–white segregation, and so on.

▼ Cuckoo

> *Sumer is icumen in, lhude sing cucu.*
> —Anonymous (c. 1240–1300)

The cuckoo, whose name comes from Old French *cucu,* a word imitative of the bird's repetitive call, has been considered the harbinger of spring since a monk in Reading Abbey, England, wrote the above-quoted early canon in Middle English (in modern English it reads: "Summer has come in, loudly sing cuckoo"). This migratory bird flies northward to the British Isles about April and deposits its eggs in the nests of smaller birds. Consequently it also came to be associated with *cuckoldry,* and in fact the word *cuckold* comes from *cuckoo.* The great lexicographer Samuel Johnson explained that one called out "Cuckoo!" to warn a husband that an adulterer was coming, but somehow the term was turned around and applied to the husband instead. This explanation itself seems to be turned around: surely it is the adulterer who needs to be warned of the husband's return. However, Dr. Ebenezer Brewer's remarkable compendium (*Dictionary of Phrase and Fable*) points out that the ancient Romans used to call an adulterer a *cuckoo* and quotes the playwright Plautus to prove his point. Whatever the ultimate origin, by Shakespeare's time the term was exceedingly familiar ("Cuckoo, cuckoo, o word of fear, unpleasing to a married ear!"—*Love's Labour's Lost, 1595*).

The cuckoo is an Old World (Eastern Hemisphere) bird, and the clockmakers of Switzerland, Austria, and other European lands became famous for their *cuckoo clocks*, which strike the hour with a cuckoo-like sound, generally accompanied by the appearance of a small bird figure through a little door.

First in early 20th-century American slang and later in British vocabulary, *cuckoo* came to mean "foolish," "crazy," or "somewhat demented." Possibly this usage comes from the cloud-cuckoo-land of Aristophanes' play, *The Birds*, an imaginary city built by birds that has come to symbolize a pipe-dream utopia. Or perhaps it came from the mindless repetition of "cuckoo" by clocks and other mechanisms. In any case, it has persisted in slang since its beginnings (c. 1915).

▼ Dodo

> *The Dodo never had a chance. He seems to have been invented for the sole purpose of becoming extinct and that was all he was good for.*
>
> —Will Cuppy,
> *How to Become Extinct* (1941)

The dodo, a flightless bird native to Mauritius and several smaller Indian Ocean islands, was so named in the early 1600s. Its name comes from Portuguese *doudo*, meaning a "fool" or "madman," and presumably it was so called for its clumsy appearance. The size of a turkey and unable to fly, it soon was killed off. Consequently we still have the alliterative simile, *dead as a dodo,* to describe something that is extinct, obsolete, or simply too old-fashioned to survive.

The noun *dodo* is also slang for a dull-witted person who is slow to react to circumstances. This usage, too, presumably comes from how the bird was regarded.

▼Dove

> But who does hawk at eagels with
> a dove?
> —George Herbert, *The Sacrifice* (1633)

Symbol of peace, innocence, and gentleness since ancient times, the dove was called *dūfe* in Old English and *columba* in Latin (*kolumbis* in Greek), all words meaning "diver." Since the dove is not a shore bird, it is thought to have been so named for its habit of ducking its head. In Genesis, the first book of the Bible, Noah sent a dove out of the ark to see if the flood had receded. At first it returned to the ark because it could not set down anywhere, the earth still being covered with water, but after seven days Noah sent her out again and she returned with an olive leaf, indicating that the waters were receding. The third time she was sent out, seven days later, she did not return at all.

In Christian art the dove is a symbol of the Holy Ghost and also of the soul. In modern times, Pablo Picasso designed a dove figure to be used as the symbol of peace. At first it was so used only by the Communist Party, but later it was adopted by many peace movements.

The juxtaposition of warlike *hawk* and gentle *dove* dates from ancient times as well. The Roman poet Ovid wrote in his *Metamorphoses* (c. A.D. 7), "as the hawk is wont to pursue the trembling dove." Centuries later, during the Cuban missile crisis in 1962, President John F. Kennedy's advisers were characterized as either doves (chief dove was United Nations Ambassador Adlai Stevenson) or hawks (Attorney General Robert Kennedy, Secretary of State Dean Rusk, National Security Adviser McGeorge Bundy), depending on whether they favored conciliation or taking a hard line against the Soviet Union, which had based missiles on Cuban soil, some ninety miles off the United States mainland. The dove–hawk polarization became even more prominent in the next few years, during the Vietnam War, with doves advocating that the United States withdraw from what they saw as a hopeless war and hawks insisting that the advance of communism (from North Vietnam to South Vietnam) must be halted at any cost. (See also HAWK.)

Apart from the symbolic characteristics of the dove, some of its physical traits have been transferred. Not all doves are gray—the mourning dove, for example, is brown—but *dove-color* is a warm gray with a pinkish or purplish tint and has been so called since the 16th century. In carpentry and cabinetmaking the *dovetail joint* is a feature of good workmanship. It consists of a tenon shaped like the dove's spread tail (similar to a reversed wedge), which fits into a corresponding mortise to form a joint. This term, too, dates from the 16th century.

The *dovecote* is not for doves at all but for their close relatives, pigeons, which have long been domesticated. Such structures have been used since pigeons were first raised, and so named since the 14th century. To *flutter the dovecote* means to alarm or cause confusion among quiet individuals, just as a cat or bird of prey might upset the inhabitants of such a structure.

Turtledove

> *As true as turtle to her mate.*
> —William Shakespeare,
> *Troilus and Cressida*

Doves have long been thought to be amorous birds, and the adjective *lovey-dovey* has been used for "amorous" since the early 19th century. Back in the time of Chaucer, one of the common European doves particularly known for its soft cooing noise was called not a dove but a *turtle,* and somewhat later a *turtledove.* It is this bird that is meant—and not the hard-shelled amphibian—in the Bible's Song of Solomon (2:12, King James Version, 1611): "The time of the singing of birds is come, and the voice of the turtle is heard in our land." Chaucer, Spenser, John Ray in his proverb collection, and Shakespeare all say that turtles (meaning doves) are faithful lovers, true to their mates. Much of this conjecture may come from the birds' *billing and cooing*—the touching of beaks and murmuring of soft noises—which also have been transferred to human behavior to mean kissing and whispering endearments.

▼Eagle

*America is fitly represented by an
Eagle, which Royal Bird is very
frequent there.*
—Samuel Sewall, *Phaenomena Quaedam
Apocalyptica* (1697)

The eagle, particularly the large golden eagle (*Aquila chrysaëtos*), is often called the king of birds. Powerfully built, it attacks fearlessly, feeding on such large game as fawns, hares, rabbits, squirrels, and grouse. However, the national bird of the United States is a different species, the bald eagle (*Haliætus leucocephalus*), so called because its head is covered with snowy white feathers which, from a distance, appear to be no feathers at all. Unlike the golden eagle, it feeds mainly on fish. Both species have a wingspread of six and one-half to seven and one-half feet, making them formidable fliers.

The emblem of the United States is a spread eagle, that is, an eagle with its wings outspread. The term *spread eagle* has been used since the 18th century for the position of a human body lying prone, face down, with arms and legs outstretched. In the days of sailing ships it was a common punishment to lash a sailor to the rigging, arms and legs outstretched, for flogging. More recently, the same term has been applied to acrobatic figures in skiing and ice-skating that involve a similar position. Because of the historic association of the spread eagle with national, royal, and imperial emblems—not just the American but those of imperial Rome, imperial France, Germany, Austria, Russia, and Prussia—the adjective *spread-eagle* came also to mean "noisily patriotic" or "bombastic"; the noun form, *spread-eagleism,* is a 19th-century American equivalent of the British term "jingoism."

Like all birds of prey, eagles have excellent eyesight. The golden eagle has been known to spot a rabbit on the ground from a distance of two miles. To be *eagle-eyed* has meant to have keen sight since the 16th century, and it sometimes is used figuratively for having keen intellectual vision. "Faith, being eagle-eyed, can . . . see the majestie of God," wrote William Barlow in 1601. Centuries earlier, Horace, in his *Satires* (35 B.C.), pointed out that those who are eagle-eyed in finding the faults of others are blind to their own. In modern times we have the slang term *legal eagle* for a sharp-sighted and sharp-witted lawyer. And the press nicknamed Charles Lindbergh *Lone Eagle* after his solo flight across the Atlantic in 1927.

The word *eagle* came in the 14th century from Anglo-Norman *egle,* in turn derived from Old French *aigle,* from Latin *aquila.* The eagle was the bird of the Roman god Jove (Jupiter) and was carried on Roman military standards. It was customary for an eagle to be set to fly up from a dead emperor's funeral pyre, representing the ascension of his spirit to the gods. In Christian times the eagle became the symbol of St. John the Evangelist and therefore was often represented on church pulpits (and still is).

The eagle is a mark of excellence in most, if not all, of its symbolic representations. *Eagle Scout* is the highest of Boy Scout ranks, and the eagle is the emblem of rank for

U.S. colonels in the Army, Air Force, and Marine Corps, and for captains in the U.S. Navy. In golf an *eagle* means a score of two below par for any hole (one better than a *birdie*), and three strokes under par is a *double eagle*.

At one time the eagle was a U.S. gold coin, with a face value of $10. U.S. servicemen during World War II sometimes referred to payday as *the day the eagle shits* (or, more politely, "screams" or "flies"), a term thought to date back as far as the Spanish-American War of 1898.

▼ Gull

> *If the world will be gulled, let it be gulled.*
>
> —Robert Burton, *The Anatomy of Melancholy* (1621)

The origin of the name *gull* for this large family of long-winged swimming birds is not entirely clear. In the 14th century *gull* meant an unfledged bird or gosling (baby goose), which may be why, by the 16th century, the word *gull* was used for a credulous person who is easily duped, and *to gull* meant to fool or to trick (whence the 19th-century *gullible*, for "easily tricked"). Certainly these characteristics are not related to the birds, which are quite cunning in hiding their eggs on sandy or pebbly shores, where nature provides camouflage. The herring gull, one of the most prolific species, also has proved resourceful in adapting its feeding and other habits to living close to human habitation. Some etymologists therefore believe that *to gull* comes from *gullet,* which has meant "esophagus" since the 14th century, and could be connected to swallowing untruths readily.

In Elizabethan times a *gull* was an easily duped person, especially a gentleman, and playwright Thomas Dekker's *Gull's Hornbook,* published in 1609, is a delightful satire about the wealthy but foolish young men who flocked to London to gain experience, secure patrons, and learn to strut and swagger. Dekker's hornbook is a primer for these obnoxious nuisances—sometimes called *coxcombs* or *woodcocks* as well as gulls—a mock-serious book of manners that pretends to guide them through a typical London day spent at St. Paul's, the inn, the theater, and so on.

▼ Hawk

> *We hate the hawk because he always lives in arms.*
> —Ovid, *Metamorphoses* (A.D. 7)

The hawk, whose name comes from Old English *hafoc,* is a magnificent bird of prey, strong, keen-sighted, beautiful in flight. It swoops down so fast that it appears to have been shot from a gun, and it strikes with great accuracy, rarely missing its victim. In the air, the hawk soars for hours without apparent effort, barely moving its wings to stay aloft.

The hawk's looks were early transferred to human beings. *Hawknosed* has, since the 16th century, described a person with a curved, beaky nose, and *hawk-eyed* since the early 19th century has meant keen-sighted (as has *eagle-eyed*). A person who preys on others is sometimes called a *hawk.* This may be why playwright Tom Taylor named the detective in his play *The Ticket-of-Leave Man* (1863), *Hawkshaw,* which subsequently became slang for "detective."

Ovid's remark about the warlike aspect of hawks was echoed in 1811 in John Randolph's epithet, *war hawks,* which is what he called the Republicans in the Twelfth Congress of the United States who vigorously supported policies of nationalism and expansionism. Among their leaders was Henry Clay of Kentucky, who was elected Speaker of the House, and John C. Calhoun of South Carolina, who with two others, Felix Grundy (Tennessee) and Peter Porter (New York), controlled the Foreign

Relations Committee. Most of the war hawks came from farming areas of the South and West, whose people would seem to be little affected by maritime issues but who chose to view Britain's seizures of American shipping and impressment of seamen as outrageous infringements on their country's rights. Also, the westerners wanted the United States to take over Canada, and the southerners wanted to take Florida away from Britain's ally, Spain. Their sentiments and Britain's continued acts of aggression led President James Madison to ask Congress to declare war on Great Britain, and on June 19, 1812, a state of war was declared.

The war hawks of the War of 1812 would probably have remained a self-contained chapter of American history had there not been a similar conflict between those who favored conciliation and negotiation and the rejectors of such "appeasement" in the 1960s. It began with the Soviet-American confrontation over the placement of Soviet missiles in Cuba in 1962 and, at almost the same time, American involvement in Vietnam. These *doves* and *hawks,* as they were called (see also under DOVE), remain fresh in our memory and speech, and the terms *hawk* and *hawkish* have been extended from those belligerent in foreign affairs to individuals behaving very aggressively in business, industry, and even day-to-day living. In commercial aviation, airlines personnel sometimes call a belligerent, unruly passenger a *hawk,* though others prefer the term *vulture.*

▼ Jay

Why a pedestrian who crosses the street at random instead of at a designated crossing point, or who crosses against traffic signals, should be named for a chatterbox of a bird is not known. In Britain *jay* was slang for a simpleton or a gullible person. In the mid-19th century United States a *jay* was a hick, a provincial. One writer suggests that when unsophisticated rural folks came to the big city they crossed the street wherever and whenever they liked, being unaccustomed to the presence of enough traffic to require some sort of system. Hence they were accused of *jaywalking,* or of being *jaywalkers,* a term that dates from about 1915. Another writer suggests that the jay is a noisy, boorish, impudent bird that shoulders smaller birds out of the way when it pecks for food, and may pay no attention even to a predatory cat. Therefore a *jaywalker* is so called for boldness and for ignoring potentially lethal traffic conditions.

Another lexicographer suggests that the term may have been reinforced by *jayhawker,* a name used for members of a guerrilla band in eastern Kansas who fought to keep their territory free of slavery during the 1850s and 1860s. This term, of uncertain origin, later meant any lawless marauder, and today it remains a nickname for any Kansan.

The word *jay* came into English in the 13th century from Old French *jai,* which in turn came from Latin *Gaius,* a proper name. And *Jay* still is a proper name in English.

Given the fact that the *blue jay* is one of the more colorful common birds, *naked as a jaybird* is a puzzling simile for "stark naked." However, like the young of other perching birds, the blue jay's young are born quite helpless and are scarcely covered with any down. Possibly that condition is the source of the expression.

▼ *Lark*

> Hark! hark! the lark at heaven's
> gate sings,
> And Phoebus 'gins arise.
> —William Shakespeare, *Cymbeline*

The name of the *lark,* known for its morning song, comes from Middle English *larke* and Old English *lāwerce.* Poets have extolled the beauty of its song since the times of the Greeks. "With the unmusical even, the lark is melodious," says an ancient Greek proverb, and Chaucer, Shakespeare, James Thomson, and Shelley are but a few of the poets who wrote paeans to this unremarkable-looking little brown bird. Hence we have *to sing like a lark,* meaning to sing beautifully. The bird's cheerful song also gave rise to *happy as a lark,* although we don't really know much about the bird's inner feelings.

To *rise with the lark* has meant to get up very early since the days of Theocritus ("Reapers rise with the lark, and with the lark to bed"—*Idyls,* c. 270 B.C.). Among the flippant sayings of the British military during World War II, especially in the Royal Navy, was, "Up with the lark and to bed with the Wrens," the *Wrens* being the Women's Royal Navy Service (WRNS), the female branch of the Royal Navy.

The *larkspur* beloved by gardeners was so named (16th century) because the spur-shaped calyx of its flower resembles the bird's long straight hind claw; its botanical name is *Delphinium.*

The noun *lark* also means "a spree" or "a frolic," but this usage has nothing to do with the bird. It appears to come from Middle English *laik,* for "play," and/or Old English *lac,* for "contest." One writer believes it comes from *larking*—that is, hunting meadowlarks, which were considered a small game bird in the 16th and 17th centuries. He claims that such hunts became a social pastime for young men and women, so a *lark* became "a pleasure jaunt." Unfortunately this pleasant etymology is no more than a flight of fancy. Meadowlarks are not even larks, zoologically speaking—they are a variety of blackbird—and the use of *lark* for "pleasure jaunt" dates only from the early 19th century.

▼Loon

The cry of the loon, a common Northern Hemisphere water bird that is a remarkable swimmer and probably the best diver of all birds, resembles crazy laughter, so *loony* came to mean crazy. So theorizes the same writer who thought meadowlark-hunting was the source of fun and games (see LARK). Not so, say more scholarly authorities. Long before it came to mean the bird, a *loon* was a rogue or scamp, and a worthless fellow, and where that came from is not known (possibly from Middle Dutch *loen*, for "stupid fellow"; or from Middle English *lowen*, for "worn out"). It was so used by Shakespeare ("The devil damn thee black, thou cream-faced loon! Where gottest thou that goose look"—*Macbeth*) and by Coleridge almost 200 years later ("Hold off! Unhand me, grey-beard loon!"—*Rime of the Ancient Mariner*).

The water bird was not called a loon until the early 17th century, and the source of that name is not known either, although it may have come from *loom*, which was the name for another species of sea bird also called the guillemot. It, too, is an excellent diver, and the etymology has nothing whatever to do with the bird's call.

So where do we get *loony bin* for "insane asylum" and *Looney Tunes*, the celebrated cartoons from Warner Brothers? It appears that they, along with *loony* for "crazy," are simply abbreviations for "lunatic," which came into the language in the 13th century and is derived from Latin *luna*, for "moon," because mental derangement was long thought to be related to the phases of the moon.

▽Magpie

The name of this noisy, mischievous relative of the crow dates from about 1600 and is a compound of *Mag*, an abbreviation of Margaret, and *pie*, for a kind of bird (probably a magpie). The ancients considered the magpie a bird of ill omen. By the 19th century this idea was somewhat mitigated, as Michael Denham's *Proverbs* (1846) put it:

> One [magpie] for sorrow, two for mirth,
> Three for a wedding, four for a birth,

Five for silver, six for gold,
Seven for a secret, not to be told,
Eight for heaven, nine for hell,
And ten for the devil's own sel [self].

While these superstitions are probably extinct, at least in America, the magpie is renowned for its noisy chatter, whence we call an incessantly talkative person a *magpie*. Magpies also are known for their habit of bringing back odds and ends to their nests, so the human *magpie* may be either a chatterbox, as above, or an indiscriminate hoarder of miscellaneous objects.

▼ Ostrich

To be an ostrich is to *bury one's head in the sand*—that is, to avoid unpleasantness or danger by simply turning away from it. The ostrich, the largest of modern birds, is flightless and thus cannot escape its enemies by taking to the air. However, it stands about seven or eight feet high and may weigh as much as 300 pounds, and it has long, powerfully muscled legs, so it can outrun many of its enemies, bounding along at 35 or 40 miles an hour in strides fourteen feet long.

There are two theories concerning the bird's habit of poking its head in the sand. One, proposed by a noted zoo director, holds that despite its rapid pace the ostrich often runs around in circles, making it easy to capture. Therefore it lies down and stretches out its long neck against the ground, hoping to be inconspicuous. Another theory holds that the ostrich is not hiding from danger at all—when cornered, it is a formidable adversary, able to kick quite dangerously with its powerful legs. Rather, when it burrows headfirst into the sand, the bird is probably eating, for it can feed on almost anything, including gravel and stones, which are used in its gizzard to help grind up tough food.

Whichever theory is true, it was long held that the bird hides its head in the mistaken belief that it then cannot be seen, and therefore the ostrich became a symbol for self-delusion. A 1623 document reads, "Like the Austridge, who hiding her little head, supposeth her great body obscured," and Thomas Carlyle wrote of King Louis XV that he "would not suffer death to be spoken of; avoided the sight of churchyards, funereal monuments, and whatsoever could bring it to mind. It's the resource of the Ostrich, who, hard-hunted, sticks its foolish head in the ground" (*The French Revolution*, 1837).

▼ Owl

> *The owl shriek'd at my birth, an*
> *evil sign.*
> —William Shakespeare, *Henry VI*, Part 3

The owl, whose name comes from Old English *ūle*, has been a symbol of wisdom since the times of the ancient Greeks. The owl was the companion of Athena, goddess of wisdom (and of her Roman equivalent, Minerva). An owl was stamped on all Athenian coins, and owls were protected in Athens, which therefore was infested with them. Thus *bringing owls to Athens* was the ancient equivalent of *carrying coals to Newcastle*—or so it was used by Aristophanes in *The Birds* (414 B.C.).

Owls are nocturnal birds of prey and are wonderfully equipped to hunt at night. Their eyes are set side by side at the front of their flattened head, and they are unusually large, making vision possible even in very dim light. To *fly with the owls* means to have nocturnal habits, or, more simply put, to be a *nightowl*, a term dating from the 16th century. Perhaps because they tend to perch in one spot in the daytime and their large eyes give them an exceptionally solemn appearance, the adjective *owlish* has, since the 17th century, been used for a person who looks wise but is actually rather silly. However, the similes *wise as an owl* and *solemn as an owl* are also based on the bird's appearance.

All owls have a syrinx, or voice apparatus, with which they produce a series of weird calls and screeches that can be terrifying in a lonely forest at night. Owls also tend to screech when a storm is coming, and so from Chaucer's time or even earlier the owl was thought to be a prophet of evil, pestilence, and death. "That prophet of woe and mischance," Chaucer called the owl (*The Legend of Good Women,* c. 1385), and 500 years later John Ruskin said he found "the owl's cry always prophetic of mischief to me" (*Praeterita,* 1887).

▼ P*arrot*

Parrots, known for their colorful plumage, the ease with which they are domesticated, and their remarkable ability to repeat words and sentences of human speech, are natives of tropical and subtropical climates. They were unknown in Europe until they were brought back by sailors, and they were not called *parrot*—a word thought to come from the French *Pierrot,* a diminutive of Pierre (Peter) used for any pet bird—until the early 16th century. Although parrots can mimic human speech quite well, there is little doubt that they do not understand it at all. Consequently a person called a *parrot* is one who repeats the words and/or actions of another without thought or understanding. Similarly, *to parrot* means to repeat or imitate another person with no thought as to the meaning of the words or actions.

▼ P*eacock*

> As any peacock he was proud and gay.
> —Geoffrey Chaucer, *The Reeve's Tale*

The peacock, with its gorgeous plumage and five-foot-long tail that can be expanded like a huge fan, has been a symbol of vanity and pride for centuries. Its name, from Middle English *pecok* and Old English *pēa* or *pawa,* dates from the 13th century and was already used figuratively at that time: a political song from about 1290 describes "a priest *proud as a Peacock.*" And a reader pointed out that in the Icelandic *Njáls saga,* also dating from the 13th century, a character named Óláfr Höskuldsson is so vain of his good looks that he is commonly referred to as *Óláfr pái,* or "Olaf Peacock."

Aesop tells of a jay who finds the plumes of a molting peacock strewn about and decks himself out in them. He parades up and down, strutting as a peacock would, but he gets a very cold reception and is scorned, hissed, and mocked until the true peacocks finally pluck off his assumed feathers. "The self-applauding bird, the peacock, see, Mark what a sumptuous Pharisee is he," wrote William Cowper in 1781 (*Truth*). This sentiment is echoed in Sean O'Casey's great drama about Ireland's Easter Rebellion, *Juno and the Paycock* (1924), about a supreme ne'er-do-well, Captain Boyle (the Paycock, or peacock), and his long-suffering wife (Juno), quietly courageous in the face of the utter ruin he brings on them.

▼Pigeon

> *Sure he's a pigeon, for he has no gall.*
> —Thomas Dekker, *The Honest Whore*
> (1604)

Pigeon, from French *pijon,* in turn from Latin words meaning "to chirp" or "peep," used to mean a young dove (14th century), and indeed pigeons and doves are very closely related. Like doves, pigeons are tractable, mild-mannered creatures. For a time *pigeon* also meant a young woman, but that usage became obsolete and was replaced by a different meaning—a simple-minded, easily duped person (16th century); fooling such a person then was termed *plucking a pigeon.* In the late 16th century

pigeon-livered meant meek and mild to the point of cowardly, a meaning that has persisted. In poker, on the other hand, *pigeon* is far from pejorative; on the contrary, it means a card drawn that greatly improves the hand.

The physical characteristics of pigeons were transferred to two descriptions of human orthopedic deformity: *pigeon-toed,* describing a person whose toes or feet are turned inward toward each other (so called since about 1800), and *pigeon-breasted,* a malformation of the breastbone so that it sticks out (used since about 1850 and also called *chicken breast.*)

Pigeons have been domesticated for centuries. Usually they are housed in multiple dwellings, called *dovecotes,* where a small hole is left so that the birds can fly in and out. Hence *pigeonhole* at first (16th century) meant a small compartment, in a desk or other piece of furniture, for filing papers. Eventually it also was used as a verb meaning to put something aside, or assign it to a certain place for the time being; that matter is then said to be *pigeonholed.*

Pigeons have a strong homing instinct, and since the 17th century they have been trained as *carrier* or *homing pigeons* to carry messages. They can fly as far as 2,500 miles in order to return home. How they accomplish this feat was long a mystery, but eventually it was found that, in the absence of visual clues such as sunlight, they are guided by the earth's magnetic field. However, an experiment in the 1970s, in which magnets were attached to the homing pigeons' heads, revealed that an overcast sky nevertheless confused and disoriented the birds.

Catching pigeons to train them for this purpose is not always easy. However, hunters earlier had discovered that one bird would attract others, so they would tie a pigeon to a stool or other perch to serve as a decoy and attract wild fowl. The same technique worked for attracting pigeons into captivity. By about 1810 *pigeon* was another word for "decoy," and about twenty years later *stool pigeon* began to be used for an informer or spy of any kind, but especially one working for the police in order to attract others to their trap. This meaning is still current, and the term is sometimes abbreviated to *stoolie.*

The term *clay pigeon* is used in skeet and trapshooting to mean the target, which traditionally is a clay saucer hurled up into the air from the trap.

▼ Raven

Quoth the raven, nevermore.
—Edgar Allan Poe, *The Raven* (1845)

The name of the raven, a close cousin of the crow, comes from Old English *hræfn.* The bird is known for its glossy black plumage and raucous cries. Both crow and raven belong to the genus *Corvus,* but the raven is almost twice the size of the crow, and while the crow caws, the raven's cry is a croak, like cr-r-ruck or pr-r-uk.

The ancient Romans regarded the raven as a bird of ill omen. Like crows, ravens feed on carrion, and one writer theorizes that perhaps because their acute sense of smell allows ravens to locate dead bodies from a great distance, they have become associated with death.

Raven-haired means "black-haired," but *ravenous* has nothing to do with the bird's feeding habits. Rather, it comes from the verb *to raven,* now obsolete, which meant to take by force (it comes from the same roots as *rape* and *rapine.*)

A reader pointed out that the Scots word for raven is *corbie,* also from Latin *corvus,* and a *corbie messenger* is a faithless or inept messenger, possibly from the raven Noah sent out from the ark, which did not return. And *corbie steps* are the steps on the gabled roof of a traditional Scots house, an obvious perch for ravens.

▼Robin

> *Who killed Cock Robin?*
> *I, said the Sparrow.*
> *With my bow and arrow,*
> *I killed Cock Robin.*
> *All the birds of the air fell a-sighing*
> *and a-sobbing*
> *When they heard of the death of poor*
> *Cock Robin.*
>
> —Nursery rhyme

The robin, a sure sign of spring in north temperate zones, is one of the most familiar of common birds. According to an old legend, when Jesus was on his way to be crucified a robin picked a thorn from his crown, and the blood that came from the wound fell on the bird and made its breast red. The bird's common name, *robin,* is in fact a shortening of *robin redbreast,* which is how the bird was first called. The *robin* part of it comes from the nickname for *Robert,* originally a French proper name, and reappears in two famous British folk heroes: *Robin Hood,* the legendary outlaw who helped the poor by robbing the rich, and *Robin Goodfellow,* another name for Puck, the sportive goblin celebrated by Shakespeare in *A Midsummer Night's Dream.*

The term *round robin,* on the other hand, appears to have nothing to do with the bird, other than that it, too, dates from the 16th century. Originally a round robin was a petition signed in circular form (that is, the signatures formed a circle) so that no one could tell who had signed first or last. Allegedly the practice was begun by seamen

presenting a grievance to their captain, who in the days of sailing ships had absolute authority. Though he might be inclined to punish any sailor questioning that authority, the captain could not mete out harsh punishment to the entire crew without suffering the consequences, and through the device of the round robin he could not determine who had originated the complaint. The "round" part of the term is obvious, but the "robin" is obscure. Some authorities believe it is a translation of the French *ruban rond,* for "round ribbon," referring to the string of signatures, but most etymologists say the origin is unknown.

Petitions of the round-robin variety are no longer common, but the term today is used more loosely for any letter or notice signed by a number of people in sequence. In sports such as tennis, a *round robin* is a tournament among a group of players who take turns playing one another, usually for a set period of time, and the losers of each round are not eliminated but continue to play until the end.

▼ *Snipe*

The snipe, so named since the 13th century (from Middle English *snype* and Old Norse *snipe* or *snīpa*), is a much prized long-billed game bird that lives on the boggy shores of small streams and in marshes. The verb *to snipe* means to shoot from behind cover, and a *sniper* is one who does just that, either literally, using a gun, or figuratively, with snide criticism and insults (usually hurled from a safe distance). Yet these meanings have little to do with actual snipe hunting, in which the hunter, walking into the bog, usually tries to walk straight up to the birds and flush them out, shooting them as they fly up.

A reader described another kind of snipe hunt, whereby a group of jokers trick one of their number. The victim is taken to a wooded area and is told to hold a sack while the others supposedly round up a snipe and drive the bird into the sack. While he or she stands there, the others go home or to a local watering hole, leaving the victim literally "holding the bag."

Probably because of the bird's association with mud and dirt, *snipe* was a term of abuse by Shakespeare's day; Iago used it to complain of Rodrigo (*Othello*). In the 19th century the Victorians coined the word *guttersnipe* for a street urchin who gathered scraps and rags from the street, as did many of the children who roamed the streets of Victorian London. It soon came to mean any lower-class person, and the term is still considered so insulting that it may not be used in debate in the House of Commons without risk of the speaker being ejected from the chamber. For a time in 19th-century America *guttersnipe* was Wall Street slang for a curbstone broker. (New York's American Stock Exchange was, until 1953, called the New York Curb Exchange because it began as a sidewalk, or curbstone, operation, moving indoors only in 1921.)

▼ *Swallow*

> *One swallow does not make a spring.*
> —Aristophanes, *The Knights* (c. 424 B.C.)

A friendly small bird, the swallow also was long regarded as the harbinger of spring and was so described by the ancient Greeks. Hence Aristophanes's warning (quoted above), which has been repeated many times since, sometimes with the substitution *summer* for *spring*. It has also been extended to mean that one small sign of an event does not ensure that it will actually occur.

Swallows are migratory birds, flying south to avoid the northern winter. Hence came the old proverb, *Don't take a swallow under your roof,* quoted by Erasmus (*Adagia,* 1523), meaning don't befriend someone who will abandon you during bad times.

▼ *Swan*

> The silver swan, who living had
> no note,
> When death approach'd, unlock'd her
> silent throat.
>> —Orlando Gibbons, *The Silver Swan*
>> (1612)

The largest of the waterfowl, swans are a traditional symbol of grace and beauty. One Eastern Hemisphere species, the mute swan, has been domesticated and is found in parks and ponds throughout the world. One variety of mute swan in Australia has black plumage, but all the other species are noted for their beautiful white feathers. In North America there are at least two kinds of wild swan, the whistling swan of the East, which makes loud, high-pitched cooing noises, and the trumpeter swan of the West, with a louder, shriller, honking call (although both species can sound lower-pitched tones as well).

The mute swan is not actually mute but is said to remain largely silent in captivity. It therefore gave rise to the legend that swans are silent until just before they die, when they suddenly burst into beautiful song. It was mentioned as long ago as 458 B.C. by the Greek dramatist Aeschylus (in *Agamemnon*) and was explained by Plato as the bird's expression of joy at going (in death) to join

Apollo, god of music. The myth has fascinated poets ever since. Shakespeare mentions it in at least three plays and in his long poem, *The Rape of Lucrece,* and Ben Jonson eulogized Shakespeare as the "Sweet *Swan of Avon.*" Franz Schubert's last songs were published after his death in a grouping entitled (by the publisher) *Schwanengesang* ("Swan Song"), and indeed any artist's last work is commonly called his *swan song.* All these terms are somewhat ironic, for the swan's actual call is far from beautiful, rather resembling the honking of geese.

Swans are, however, beautiful in the water, with their long necks and graceful swimming. From their dipping into the water to feed comes the term *swan dive,* for the human forward dive where the diver's head leans back and the arms are outstretched at shoulder height and then brought together above the head before the diver enters the water. See also *goose among the swans,* under GOOSE.

▼Vulture

> To *what vulture shall this corpse belong?*
>> —Martial, *Epigrams* (c. A.D. 85)

The much maligned scavenger of the animal world, whose name comes from Latin *vultur,* feeds on dead animals and refuse of all kinds. Awkward and ungainly, the vulture often gorges itself so completely that it has difficulty taking to the air. Vultures soar above the countryside searching with their keen eyes for some sign of food. Usually when one vulture spots food and descends to feed, it is followed by a flock of others, and among them they will leave little but bones and hide. The transfer of these characteristics to human beings took place long ago, and the name *vulture* has been attached to a predatory, rapacious person, especially one who profits from the dead, since about 1600.

Slithery Slimy

Creepy Crawlers:

Reptiles, Amphibians,

and Lesser Creatures

▼ Chameleon

> *'Twas brillig and the slithy toves*
> *Did gyre and gimble in the wabe.*
> —Lewis Carroll, *Through the Looking-*
> *Glass* (1872)

The chameleon, whose name comes from Greek words for "on the ground" (*khamai*) and "lion" (*leōn*), is a small lizard with the remarkable ability to change its color so that it blends in with its surroundings. The color changes depend on fluctuations in moisture, temperature, and sunlight, and are controlled by a tiny gland in its head; when the gland is removed, the chameleon loses its ability to change color. Chameleons can change to numerous colors—dark or light green, yellow, white, brown. While this may serve the purpose of disguising the animal from its enemies, one zoologist believes it is more likely a reflection of the chameleon's particular emotional state. Thus, many of these lizards change to brown when they are fighting, even in surroundings where green would be safer.

The chameleon's color changes were observed by the ancient Greeks; "more changeable than the chameleon," wrote Aristotle about 340 B.C. Thus *chameleon* was soon transferred to mean a fickle, inconstant person and has been so used ever since.

Because, like most lizards, it feeds so quickly, flicking out its long tongue—longer than its entire body—with unbelievable speed to capture insects (and, in the case of African chameleons, other small animals), it was at one time thought to live on air. Shakespeare likened the lizard to love ("The chameleon Love can feed on the air"—*Two Gentlemen of Verona*), but Jonathan Swift came closer to the mark when he wrote, "The chameleon, who is said to feed upon nothing but air, has of all animals the nimblest tongue" (*Thoughts on Various Subjects,* 1714).

▼ Crocodile

> She sailed away on a balmy summer's
> day
> On the back of a crocodile.
> You see, said she, I'm as safe as I can
> be,
> I'll ride him down the Nile.
> The croc winked an eye as she gaily
> paddled by, wearing a happy smile;
> At the end of the ride the lady was
> inside,
> And the smile on the crocodile.
>
> —Children's song

The crocodile, whose name comes from Middle English *cocodrille,* in turn from Greek words meaning "worm of the stones," is the largest modern reptile, sometimes as much as thirty-three feet long. One species used to inhabit the Nile River and was worshiped by the ancient Egyptians. Plutarch maintained that because the crocodile's eyes are covered with a thin membrane through which it can see but which makes its eyes hard to discern, the Egyptians likened it to an all-seeing god. Another species, however, the estuarine crocodile, found in southeast India, Asia, and the Pacific islands, is hated and feared. It is extremely aggressive and attacks human beings without provocation; in modern times its numbers have been periodically reduced by professional hunters.

Given the animal's fierceness and frightening aspects, with its huge teeth, large size, and great agility, it is unlikely that the ancients ever got close enough to a live crocodile to observe it with any accuracy and survive to report their findings. Indeed, the descriptions of these beasts by the Roman writers—Pliny in his *Natural History* and Seneca in his *Natural Questions*—are highly imaginative. It is from this time, apparently, that the myth arose that a crocodile weeps while consuming its prey. This myth was soon embellished, with the crocodile reputed first to lure travelers with its heartrending moans and sighs and then devour them, weeping all the while. It was quoted about 1400 by the English traveler Sir John Mandeville, who was not a particularly reliable reporter.

By A.D. 300 the Roman chronicler Aelius Spartianus was using the term *crocodile tears* figuratively to describe the hypocrisy of the Emperor Caracalla. Spartianus was quoted by Erasmus, who cited the Latin *Crocodili lachrymae* ("tears of the crocodile") in his proverbs about 1500. By the mid-16th century the expression *crocodile tears* as a metaphor for pretended grief was firmly entrenched in the language. There it remains, both as a metaphor and with a special medical meaning. Incomplete healing of the human facial nerve, when it is damaged by disease or injury, may result in partial paralysis and the profuse shedding of tears during facial movements causing salivation, such as chewing. Doctors refer to this phenomenon as *crocodile tears,* since no true grief is being expressed.

Like their cousins, the alligators and caimans, crocodiles rest on river banks during the day and do most of their feeding at night. A crocodile basking in the sun looks extremely content and its facial features resemble a smile—whence, perhaps, we can conclude that the song's "smile on the crocodile" was observed in the morning, following a nocturnal feast.

▼ Frog

Aesop had very little good to say about frogs, but the Grimm brothers did, and Mark Twain made his fortune with one. In at least three of Aesop's fables, frogs come off poorly: they ask Jupiter for a king, and he provides a heron that eats them; a frog helps a rat cross a river, stops midway so the rat will drown, and is attacked by a kite, which eats them both; and a frog boasts it is as grand as an ox in the field, swells up out of pride, and is trodden upon and killed by the ox. In Grimm's fairy tale, however, the frog turns out to be a prince in disguise; one writer believes this idea is derived from an old Roman proverb: *He who was a frog is now king.*

Mark Twain made his first great success with the story *Jim Smiley and His Jumping Frog,* published in 1865 and better known today as *The Celebrated Jumping Frog of Calaveras County.* In this tall tale, Jim Smiley, who loves to bet on anything, trains a frog to jump for flies and bets it can outjump any other frog in the county. A stranger takes him up on the wager, and while Jim goes in search of another frog for his to compete against, the stranger fills Jim's frog with quail-shot. It is now too heavy to jump, so, to Jim's chagrin, the stranger wins the wager.

The word *frog,* from Middle English *frogge* and Old English *frogga,* means not only the well-known tailless amphibian closely related to the toad (see TOAD), but also, since the 17th century, an elastic horny substance in the sole of a horse's foot, and from the mid-19th century, a grooved piece of iron at a place where railroad tracks cross that enables a train's wheels to cross from one track to another. And in the bows of violins and other stringed instruments, the *frog* is a device for tightening the bow's hair. The origin of these meanings is not known, though the horse's frog and the train track's frog may be related to the amphibian's jumping ability. A fourth meaning of *frog,* for an ornamental fastening for a military coat (earlier, an attachment to the waist belt for carrying a sword), appears to have come from Portuguese *froco* and Latin *floccus.*

Further, *frog* is a derogatory word for "Frenchman," and here the etymologists go to town. H. L. Mencken claims this meaning came to America from Britain during World War I. In Britain, says Eric Partridge, it dates only from about 1870, although in the 17th century it was used to mean a Dutchman ("Froglander") and also a Jesuit. However, prior to 1870 in England a Frenchman was called a *frog-eater,* which was then shortened to *frog.* (This in turn may have been borrowed from the German *Froschesser,* "frog-eater," dating from about 1812.)

The alleged reasons for the usage also conflict. One writer says it comes from the fact that an ancient heraldic device used in France consisted of three frogs or toads. Partridge suggests that in the 19th century the shield of the city of Paris depicted toads because there were actually a great many of them on the city's muddy streets. However, Mencken's idea that it comes from the French predilection for eating frogs' legs, a custom regarded with horror by the English, seems a more straightforward and logical conclusion.

Frogs are amphibians, meaning that most species are equally happy on land and in the water. The *frog kick* of the (human) swimmer's breaststroke resembles the animal's leg movements in water, that is, the legs are bent at the knee, extended outward, and sharply brought together, propelling the body forward.

Similarly imitative is the name *frogmen,* invented in World War II for swimmers who were equipped with rubber suits, flippers, and other gear, and who operated underwater to sabotage enemy shipping. The name is still used for divers in salvage operations.

The *frog's march* involves carrying a person (a drunk, a prisoner, etc.) face downward, with four men holding one limb each, to a police station or other such place. The person's body thus resembles that of a frog with limbs outstretched.

The children's game of *leapfrog,* so named since the 16th century although no doubt much older, consists of players taking turns vaulting, with legs spread, over another player who is bent over from the waist. During World War II the term acquired the more serious meaning of a military advance in successive waves, with troop 2 advancing beyond troop 1, troop 3 beyond troop 2, and so on. Both usages are related to the frog's jumping ability.

In the Middle Ages, throat infections such as thrush were sometimes treated by putting a live frog headfirst into the patient's mouth; by inhaling, the frog was believed to draw out the patient's infection into its own body. Happily the treatment is obsolete, but its memory survives in the 19th-century term *frog in one's throat*, still used for a hoarseness due to phlegm or mucus.

▼ Leech

> *Now to turn thyself into a leech and*
> *suck the blood out of these so-called*
> *pillars of the senate.*
>
> —Plautus, *Epidicus* (c. 200 B.C.)

Bloodletting was such an integral part of medical practice in ancient and medieval times that the word *leech,* which originally meant "physician," was transferred to the bloodsucking worm employed for this purpose—another case of man before beast. The leeches are a large class of segmented worms that feed on blood, attaching themselves to the bodies of fishes, turtles, and other aquatic animals in order to consume their blood. They digest and use this food so slowly that they do not need to feed again for months. Not only were leeches applied to treat specific human ailments, but many people believed periodic bleeding improved one's general health even if nothing was amiss.

The word *leech* comes from Old English *læce,* meaning one who relieves pain. Bloodletting used to be the job of barbers, who also were surgeons, and in fact the red-and-white striped pole still seen in front of barbershops originally represented blood and bandages.

Barbershops also often had a jar of leeches on display.

Although the remedy of placing a frog in the throat is no longer used (see FROG), leeches are still being applied to human patients, not only in "barbaric" places but in the most advanced countries. Microsurgeons have found that a small European leech, *Hirudo medicinalis,* helps in reattaching severed or damaged fingers. In such surgery, doctors reconnect nerves, arteries, and veins with sutures so fine they are barely visible to the naked eye. Often, however, the smaller veins are too delicate to suture. When fresh blood flows into the finger through the repaired arteries, there is no route for its return, and the blood accumulates, causing swelling and pain. Pressure builds, impeding circulation, and eventually cells are deprived of the oxygen and nourishment carried by blood. The stage is set for the death of the reattached finger. To save it until the damaged blood vessels can heal and restore circulation, doctors sometimes remove the fingernail or prick the fingertip so it bleeds. But repeated pricks damage tissue and do not always relieve the congestion. Enter the leech. This two-inch-long green and brown relative of the common earthworm can drain off about an ounce or two of stagnating blood—about six times its body weight—in twenty minutes. When the leech is full, it simply drops off. The puncture it made continues to bleed because the leech's saliva contains an anticlotting agent, as well as an antiseptic. When the finger turns blue again, the process is repeated with another leech. Leeches are used in other surgical procedures as well, mostly in delicate plastic surgery.

The word *leech* also has been used figuratively since at least the time of Plautus to mean a person who lives on the bounty of others and gives nothing in return—in other words, a parasite.

▼Lizard

The lizards are the modern reptiles that most closely resemble the great dinosaurs of bygone eras. Their name comes from Latin *lacertus* or *lacerta,* via Old French *lesarde.* Mainly carnivorous, they feed on small animals and insects, and they are, like all reptiles, cold-blooded, meaning they keep their bodies warm chiefly with heat from their surroundings. Therefore they often are seen on sunny walls, rocks, and fences, warming themselves and occasionally pouncing on prey. From these habits comes the term *lounge lizard,* a man who frequents cocktail

lounges, hotel lobbies, cafes, and the like in search of ladies who are richer, and usually older, than he, and on whom he sponges. The term originated about 1915 and was quite popular in the 1920s. It is heard less often today, though the practice certainly has not died out.

▼ *Snail*

> *You have beaten a snail in slowness.*
> —Plautus, *Poenulus* (c. 200 B.C.)

The snail, whose name comes from Middle English *snayle* and Old English *snægl,* is a gastropod, a single-shelled mollusk whose shell is usually a spiral structure. Most of these animals have an opening on the right side, and in growing larger the spiral grows to the right. As in all mollusks, the lower edge of the mantle produces the shell material and adds it to the margin of the shell opening. In this way, the shell can grow larger to accommodate the growing animal within. The fleshy part of a snail's body consists of a muscular foot, with definite front and back ends, and a soft body that is enclosed entirely within the shell. The foot, too, can be withdrawn into the shell. The flattened undersurface of the foot is used for locomotion and also to hold onto surfaces. A wavelike motion travels along the surface of the foot when the animal is in motion. A snail seems to move very slowly indeed as it glides along, but in fact, considering its size, it can cover a considerable distance in the course of a day. Further, it has no need for a fast escape, since it can protect itself by withdrawing all its parts into the shell.

Snails have fascinated people since ancient times. Their slowness gave rise to the term *snail's pace* as early as 1400, and the computer age spawned the expression *snail mail,* for ordinary postal service as opposed to E-mail and fax. The snail's ability to withdraw was also observed ("When [the snail] encounters a bad neighbor it takes up its house and moves away"—Philemon, c. 300 B.C.). The forward or head end of the foot contains sensory tentacles, a mouth opening, and sometimes part of a projecting proboscis (noselike structure). The tentacles have an eye near their tip and look like small horns. From this comes the expression *draw in one's horns,* which, of course, the snail draws in with the rest of its foot when it encounters danger. This term has been used to signify a retreat or backing down since at least the mid-14th century, when an unknown chronicler, writing about a campaign of Richard the Lionhearted, said, "They . . . gunne to drawen in her hornes as a snayle among the thornes."

Snails are considered a delicacy by French gourmets, who call them *escargots.* One kind of snail, however, is considered a menace to agriculture, and in 1992 Federal investigators launched a nationwide dragnet for the slimy, fist-sized banana rasp snail, or *Archacatina marginata,* which was illegally imported from Nigeria as a terrarium pet. It consumes one-fourth its weight in food every day, devouring bananas, melons, and vegetables, and can produce one thousand offspring during its lifetime.

▽ *Snake*

Perhaps no animals are feared as much as snakes. Numerous otherwise rational individuals are terrified of a quite harmless garden snake. Much of the fear is based on erroneous beliefs, such as that snakes use their tongues to bite, that they can charm animals (including humans) into paralysis, that they can jump at their victims or spring from the ground, that they can milk cows by sucking their udders, and that they swallow their young to protect them from danger and expel them, alive, when danger is past. All of these notions are myths.

Snakes use their long forked tongues as organs of touch and taste, and inject their venom by means of fangs, which are constructed like hypodermic needles. Any paralysis seen in human or beast encountering a snake is induced by fear. Snakes rarely spring from the ground—most must poise and partially coil their bodies in order to strike—and they certainly cannot reach as high as a cow's udders. As for swallowing their young, they do sometimes feed on the young of other snakes, but any live animal taken into a snake's digestive tract is completely digested and has no chance of remaining alive. Live snakes are sometimes found inside the bodies of larger snakes, but then only in the enlarged egg tube of a female snake, because they were about to be born when the mother died.

Nevertheless the snake, whose name comes from Old High German and Norse words meaning "crawler" or "creeper," has been hated and feared since ancient times. The Old Testament gives evil the form of a *serpent* in the garden of Eden. Aesop tells a fable about a peasant who kindly takes a freezing snake into his house, only to be bitten to death when the snake recovers from the cold. From this tale comes the saying *nourish a snake in one's bosom,* which is to the present day a metaphor for treason and ingratitude.

Virgil, in his *Eclogues,* wrote that one should beware of a snake lurking in the grass (*Latet anguis in herba*)—that is, a hidden enemy, especially one pretending friendship, whence our term *snake in the grass.* The idea was repeated by Dante (in the *Inferno*), Chaucer (*The Summoner's Tale*), Lyly, Shakespeare, Herrick, and Twain ("A guileful snake in the grass" in *Tom Sawyer*), among many others. Another term reminiscent of a snake's ability to deceive is *snake oil,* for a patent medicine of dubious value touted by a high-pressure salesman. Originating in the United States about 1925, the term later was extended to mean similar deception in other areas.

Not all the ancients' beliefs about snakes were negative. Although the Greeks pictured the evil creature Medusa as having hair of writhing snakes, they also admired the snake's ability to renew itself by shedding its skin. Further, the snake was associated with Hermes, the messenger of the gods, who is pictured holding a *caduceus,* a snake-entwined rod that enabled him to bring sleep to anyone. Hermes, called Mercury by the Romans, presented the caduceus to Aesculapius, the god of healing, and today this staff remains a symbol of the medical profession and also the insignia of the U.S. Army Medical Corps.

A Native American term dating from about 1770 is *snake dance,* a ceremony performed by various tribes, in which snakes—real or in representational form—are handled or mimicked by the dancers. (The Hopi, for example, use live rattlesnakes.) In the 20th century *snake dance* also came to mean a procession at a pep rally or similar occasion, in which the fans proceed in single file in a twisting, sinuous, snakelike formation in anticipation or celebration of an athletic victory.

The winding movement of snakes is referred to in the verb *to snake,* as well as in the names of various devices used to clean or clear obstructions from the inside of pipes. They include the plumber's *wind snake* and the flexible *snake* used to clean the bore of various wind instruments. These also gave us the verb *to snake out,* meaning to retrieve from an inaccessible place; it also is abbreviated to *to snake.*

In 1972 eight European nations established a *currency snake,* that is, a method of stabilizing their exchange rates by allowing them to fluctuate within narrow limits against each other (within the snake) but more widely against other currencies. This snake has been eliminated by the introduction of a single European currency, the euro, but conceivably could be revived in other parts of the world.

Most snakes live on land, and most American species hibernate during the winter. In some areas where the winters are especially severe, many snakes gather together for hibernation, and such a *snake den* may contain thousands of individual animals. Possibly it was this association that made M. J. Ward entitle her popular novel about the squalid and inhumane conditions of a mental hospital *The Snake Pit* (1947). On the other hand, she may have been referring to a barbaric form of execution—that is, throwing a person into a *snake pit*, a man-made pit filled with poisonous snakes. In any case, the term has since been used both for a squalid mental institution and, by extension, for any other horrible place or chaotic situation.

In gambling, *snake eyes* means a dice throw of a double one (two ones); the term originated in the United States about 1930. And during World War I *snake eyes* was military slang for tapioca, a dessert frequently served in the mess. The Pacific theater of World War II gave us *to snake-check*, meaning to look for snakes, scorpions, and similar wildlife before putting on one's clothes or getting into a sleeping bag. This term, too, is occasionally used figuratively, in the sense of checking out a statement or position to make sure it has no unwanted implications before exposing it in public.

Copperhead

> As a live Copperhead
> I'm a squirmulous vermiform wriggler.
> —F. Leypoldt (1863)

The copperhead snake is so named for its reddish brown color. At least two species have this common name, *Denisonia superba* of Australia and *Agkistrodon contortrix* of the eastern and southern United States, and both are extremely venomous. Unlike the rattlesnake, to which it is related, the copperhead gives no warning before it strikes. Therefore, it has come to be a metaphor for sneaky viciousness, or an unexpected enemy. For a time in the 19th century Copperhead was a pejorative name for a Native American, a usage that has long since died out. More commonly, the term was used for Northerners who sympathized with the Southern cause during the Civil War and therefore were considered traitors to their side. After the war the term was extended to any person disloyal to a group or cause.

Viper

No viper so little but hath its Venom.
—Thomas Fuller, *Gnomologia* (1732)

Technically vipers are a large group of venomous snakes that includes rattlesnakes and adders, among others. The name *viper* originated in the 16th century, probably from Old French and Latin words for "serpent," and was more or less a general name for any poisonous snake. Petronius, in his *Satyricon* (c. A.D. 60), rephrased the moral of Aesop's fable (see SNAKE above) as *nourishing a viper in your bosom* (*Tu viperam sub ala nutricas*), and it was so repeated in John Ray's *Proverbs* (1670) and Thomas Fuller's *Gnomologia* (1732).

In 1920s jazz slang in America a *viper* was a marijuana user, but this usage was not perpetuated by the drug users of later eras. However, *viper* is still used to mean an exceptionally spiteful or treacherous person.

▼Toad

*There is no man who eats Pitt's toads
with such zeal.*
—Lord Bulkeley, *Courts and Cabinets of
George III* (1788)

A fawning flatterer has been called a *toad-eater* since the 16th century and a *toady* since the 17th century. The toad, whose name comes from Middle English *tode* and Old English *tāde,* was regarded with considerable distaste, if not disgust and aversion. At one time it was thought to be poisonous; it is so referred to by Shakespeare and by John Ray in his proverb collection of 1678 ("full as a toad of poison"). Even today some people believe that handling toads will cause warts, a myth probably stemming from the fact that the toad's skin is covered with wartlike bumps that are actually glands.

Given these superstitions, the toad was a natural prop for the traveling medicine man. It became the custom of such mountebanks to have an assistant who ate—or rather, pretended to eat—one or more supposedly poisonous toads. The charlatan would then "save the life" of the assistant with some special medicine or treatment that counteracted the "poison." Thus there actually were toad-eaters, real or pretended, and the term was soon applied to any person who would stoop to perform a nauseating or distasteful act to please another. Subsequently the term was shortened to *toady*, which means the same in both noun and verb (*to toady*) forms—that is, to be an obsequious, cringing sycophant.

Considering the unpleasant associations of this little amphibian, it is curious that the British should prize a dish called *toad-in-the-hole*, which consists of a piece of sausage baked in batter. The name has been current since the late 18th century, and the dish, presumably, is still older.

▼Turtle

The turtle originated more than 200 million years ago and even then was so well equipped to survive that it has changed very little since. Its most distinctive feature is the bony box or shell in which it lives, providing an extremely effective armor. The shell consists of two portions which in most species can be tightly closed, covering all of the animal's soft parts. However, a turtle turned on its back is quite helpless and has great difficulty in righting itself, and when it is upside down enemies may be able to reach the fleshy parts of its legs. Hence *to turn turtle*, meaning to overturn or capsize, implies that one is helpless.

When the turtle does emerge from its shell, its head sticks straight out, and there is no differentiation in girth between head and neck. From this we have *turtleneck*, a word used since about 1905 to describe a high, close-fitting collar on a knit garment (shirt or sweater), which often is worn turned down.

Turtles are closely related to tortoises and terrapins, all three making up the order *Chelonia*. In present-day common speech the names are used interchangeably. Both *turtle* and *tortoise* may come from the Latin root *tort,* with reference to the animals' twisted feet. On land they are slow-moving creatures, but as the familiar fable of *the tortoise and the hare* points out, they plod along with great persistence (see under HARE). Nevertheless, we continue to call a slow person a *tortoise.*

Turtle is also an obsolete word for *turtledove* (the latter comes from the former), an Eastern Hemisphere bird noted for its cooing call. This word is thought to come from the Latin word *turtur,* which imitated the cooing sound. (See also TURTLEDOVE.)

▼Worm

> *The smallest worm will turn, being trodden on.*
> —William Shakespeare, *Henry VI*, Part 3

Even a miserable groveling creature like a worm will eventually turn on its tormentors, according to an English proverb published by John Heywood in 1546. Hence the saying *the worm turns,* meaning sooner or later the lowliest loser becomes a winner.

The word *worm,* from Old English *wyrm* and perhaps Latin *vermis,* originally meant a grander creature, a serpent or a dragon, in addition to the creeping, limbless, soft-bodied invertebrates that make up the numerous groups of animals we call worms.

There are many kinds of worm, but among the most familiar are earthworms, found in soil all over the world; various parasitic worms that attack the human body, such as the tapeworm and liver fluke; and the leech (described earlier in this section). It is the earthworm, most likely, that gave rise to the idea of being *food for worms* when one is dead and buried, which goes back as far as the Old Testament: "The worm shall feed sweetly on him" (Job 24:20). Earthworms do indeed take in decaying matter as they move through the upper layers of the soil. Tapeworms, on the other hand, live in the intestine of their host and feed on already digested food present there. In ancient times an aromatic but very bitter-tasting herb, *Artemisia absinthium,* was used as a remedy for intestinal worms and so was called *wormwood.* According to legend, this plant sprang up in the track of the serpent as it slid along the ground when driven out of the garden of Eden. Because of the herb's terrible taste, its name also came to mean anything bitter or extremely unpleasant. The Old Testament shows this figurative use as well: "For the lips of a strange woman [prostitute] drop as a honeycomb, and her mouth is smoother than oil: but her end is bitter as wormwood" (Proverbs 5:3–4).

The extreme lowliness of the worm also was transferred, so that an abject, miserable person was called a *worm,* a usage dating from the 9th century. The creeping, insidious, stealthy movement of worms gave rise to several verb forms: *to worm oneself into* the confidence of another, and *to worm out* a secret or information of some kind, both originating in the early 18th century.

The larvae of certain insects are soft-bodied creeping creatures that sometimes are loosely called worms. From this we have the *bookworm,* originally (16th century) the name for a maggot that lives on the pages of books, eating holes in them, but now simply meaning a person who is extremely fond of reading.

Worms are of incalculable usefulness, but perhaps none more so than to the fisherman who uses them as live bait. Generally one brings them along in a jar or other container, where they form an incredible tangle, wriggling about and entwining themselves with one another. From this came the expression *to open a can of worms,* meaning to introduce a complicated problem or insoluble difficulty.

Students of history are all too familiar with that unpalatable expression, the *Diet of Worms,* the famous imperial meeting held in 1521 in Worms, Germany, where Martin Luther was declared an outlaw. The "Worms" in question, however, is a perfectly legitimate German proper name and has nothing to do with the animals, which in German are called *Würme* (plural of *Wurm*). And *Diet,* although ultimately derived from the same Latin word (for "day") as *diet* meaning "edible fare," here signifies a public assembly.

Buzzing About:
The Bugs
and the
Bees

▼ Ant

*I'll get the ants out of those moonlit
pants.*
— George Kaufman and Moss Hart,
The Man Who Came to Dinner (1939)

The ants probably are the most advanced of all social insects, and every species of the ant superfamily, *Formicoidea,* has some form of social organization. Their behavior in some cases is so complex that they are suspected of having a level of intelligence like that of higher animals.

Ants are small, but they thrive under a variety of conditions. Their chewing mouth parts enable them to feed on many different foods, including nectar, plant and animal matter of all kinds, the secretion of aphids, bits of insects, and tiny fungi that they cultivate in "gardens" in their underground nests.

The name *ant* comes from Middle English *ante,* in turn from Old English *æmete,* made up of words meaning "cut off." Ants certainly can bite humans as well, and if they should get inside someone's clothing, they would cause that person to squirm with discomfort. From this we have *to have ants in one's pants,* a common expression for being extremely restless or jumpy.

▼ Bee

> *Lyk a bisy bee, with-outen gyle.*
> —Geoffrey Chaucer, *The Second Nun's Tale*

The bee, from Middle English *be* and Old English *bēo,* gives us examples of both industriousness and laziness. Honeybees have been cultivated for at least 4,000 years, and so there has been ample time to observe the complex activities of these remarkably advanced creatures. Three kinds of individual function in a honeybee hive: a single queen, who performs as an egg-laying machine, producing from 200 to several thousand eggs a day in her lifetime of three to five years; sterile females called workers, who perform most of the work of the hive, producing honey and beeswax, cleaning and guarding the hive, nursing the young, and gathering nectar and pollen in their brief lifetime of four to six weeks; and even shorter-lived males, called drones, who play very little part in the hive, as only one male out of thousands mates with the queen and the rest are driven off to die.

From this social organization alone come several common expressions: *queen bee,* used for any dominant or specially favored woman since the early 17th century; *drone,* for a parasitic loafer who lives on the work of others; and *beehive,* for an extremely busy place. The shape of the beehive, conical or domelike, also has been transferred: to a kind of hat, a woman's hairstyle, and an old-fashioned oven.

From the worker bees comes the term *beeline.* Originating in the United States about 1830 and signifying the shortest distance between two points, it is reminiscent of the route worker bees take in bringing nectar and pollen back to the hive. Edgar Allan Poe described it in his story, *The Gold-Bug* (1843): "A bee line, or, in other words, a straight line." It is also the workers that give us *busy as a bee,* a simile used since Chaucer's time, by

William Blake ("The busy bee has no time for sorrow"—*Proverbs of Hell*, 1808) and any number of other writers.

Bees in One's Bonnet

> *Their hartes full heavy, their heades be full of bees.*
> —John Heywood, *Proverbs* (1546)

A head full of bees—that is, full of cares and fancies—soon became a bonnet full of bees. The term *to have bees in one's bonnet* originally (16th century) meant simply to be eccentric or have odd ideas, but by the 17th century it meant both that and to have a fixed idea on some particular issue or point. Poet Robert Herrick wrote, "For pitty, Sir, find out that Bee which bore my love away, I'll seek him in your Bonnet brave" (*The Mad Maid's Song*, 1648). Ebenezer Brewer, self-styled chronicler of "literary bric-a-brac," theorized that the ancients saw a connection between bees and the human soul, and he cited both a 3rd-century Greek philosopher who mentioned "those souls which the ancients called bees" and the prophet Mohammed, who admitted bees to Paradise. Considering how long bees have been raised for their honey, it seems more probable that the expression arose among beekeepers who either were likening the humming of bees to the humming of ideas inside the head, or were referring to having been attacked by bees that got inside their protective headgear, which would certainly make one jump about crazily.

Spelling Bee

The origin of the word *bee* for a social gathering held to accomplish a task, play a game, or for pure entertainment is not known. The earliest recorded use of the term appears to be 1693, according to Stuart Berg Flexner, for a *corn-husking bee*. American both in origin and use, the term was first used in New England and New York, and may have derived from the idea of bees working together in a hive. Certainly these get-togethers were a welcome social occasion in rural and frontier areas, and they also served to accomplish tasks that might be terribly onerous or impossible for an individual or family. By the mid-18th century there were *spinning bees, logging bees, road-building bees, chopping bees, squirrel bees* (for hunting squirrels), *church-building bees*—bees for almost any chore. *Quilting bees* became especially popular in the early 19th century and reached a peak in midcentury. The *raising bee* of the 1830s involved erecting a log cabin or a barn in a single day. The only such bee still held on a regular basis is the *spelling bee,* a contest created in New England and quite popular after the Civil War. In 1925 the *Louisville Courier-Journal* founded a National Spelling Bee, which has continued to find sponsors and survives to the present day.

Another term with a puzzling origin is *to put the bee on,* meaning to try to get money or some other donation. One writer suggests that, cash being scarce in rural America, churches that could not pay their preacher in cash had the community organize a *bee,* in which people contributed work, clothes, food, and other essentials to the preacher. The organizers then would *put a bee on* anyone reluctant to contribute, that is, put pressure on them. Another lexicographer, however, suggests that the term refers to the bee's *sting,* in its slang meaning of "duping" or "cheating."

▼ Beetle

> The cliff that beetles o'er his base into the sea.
>
> —William Shakespeare, *Hamlet*

The beetles are the largest single group of insects, comprising more than 250,000 species, and they vary considerably in size. Some, such as the spectacular Goliath and rhinoceros beetles, grow to more than five inches in length, while others are so small they are scarcely noticeable. All beetles have antennae, or feelers, which are organs of smell as well as touch and may also include auditory structures. In the original Latin, *antenna* meant "sail yard." During the 15th century, Theodorus Gaza translated into Latin a work by the Greek writer Aristotle and used the Latin plural *antennae* as a translation of Greek *keraiai*, meaning "insect horns" or "feelers." It is this sense that then passed into English. Further, the word was extended to stand for an aerial, a conducting device for sending or receiving electromagnetic waves, and figuratively, for any strong sense of perception.

Beetles also have biting mouth parts, and they feed on an astounding variety of substances—plants, animals (alive or dead), bark, dung, wool, fur, hides, roots, and leaves, among other things. Indeed, the word *beetle* comes from Middle English *bityl* and Old English *bitela*, for "biting." The term *beetle-browed*, thought by some to refer to the tufted antennae of some beetles, came (in the 14th century) from the same roots and more probably relates to the aggressive aspect of some beetles, since it means heavy, prominently projecting eyebrows that tend to give a person a scowling look. Similarly, the verb *to beetle* means to overhang and therefore to threaten.

An inexpensive model of Volkswagen, a German make of automobile that was extremely popular in Europe and America from the late 1950s until about 1980 and was revived in the late 1990s, was popularly called a *beetle* or *bug* because the overall shape of its body superficially resembled the curved outer shell of many beetles.

Ladybird

> *Ladybird, ladybird, fly away home,*
> *Your house is on fire and your children all gone.*
>
> —Nursery rhyme (c. 1744)

The ladybird beetle or ladybug (*Coccinellidae*), especially the species whose body is red with black spots, is among the most familiar of all beetles. The nursery rhyme quoted above exists also in German, and Robert Schumann wrote charming music to these verses. Ladybirds are valuable insects because they prey on destructive aphids and scale insects and so can be effective in holding some serious pests in check.

The name *ladybug* originated in Britain in the late 17th century, and *ladybird* in America a few decades later. The lady in question is the Virgin Mary (in German the insect is called *Marienkäfer,* "Mary bug," or, in Schumann's song, *Marienwürmchen,* "little Mary worm"). One writer believes it is called the beetle of Our Lady because of its service in eating unwanted pests. Another holds that it tends to emerge around the time of the Feast of the Annunciation, also called Lady Day, March 25. It is considered a good-luck token in several countries, and in Germany and Austria small figures of the ladybird are used as Christmas-tree ornaments and for similar decorative purposes.

Snug as a Bug in a Rug

To most of us "bug" means the same thing as "insect," but entomologists differentiate between "true bugs," which comprise the order *Hemiptera* (meaning "half-wings"), and other insects. True bugs usually have a pair of thickened leathery forward wings that look like half-wings. They include bedbugs, chinch bugs, water bugs, and stink bugs, and are among the most destructive of all insects.

The origin of the word *bug,* used since the 16th century for various insects, is not clear. One group of etymologists points to its obsolete 14th-century meaning, an object of dread, which survives in *bugaboo, bogey,* and *hobgoblin*—all names for frightening creatures—and may have been derived from the Middle English *bugge* for "scarecrow" and "demon" (perhaps in turn from the Welsh *bwg,* for "ghost"). Another group believes it comes from Middle English *budde,* for "beetle," the *d* somehow having been changed to a *g.*

We speak not only of bugs that fly or crawl about, but of being afflicted with a *cold bug* or a *tummy bug*—that is, some infectious organism—or, by extension, of being "bitten" with the *computer bug*, that is, being extremely enthusiastic about or even obsessed with some particular object or activity. These usages, dating from the late 19th or early 20th century, led to such words as *jitterbug*, first (early 1930s) used for a nervous person and then (late 1930s) for the jerky, jumpy dance; *firebug*, a coinage of the 1870s for a person obsessed with arson (used figuratively by Oliver Wendell Holmes in 1872, who called someone "a political firebug"); and *litterbug*, from the mid-1940s, for a person seemingly determined to scatter about refuse.

A related use is that of *putting a bug in someone's ear*, that is, giving a hint about something important in hopes of arousing equal enthusiasm or action. Obsession can, of course, be carried too far, to the point of outright craziness. *To be buggy* has meant not only to be infested with bugs (18th century) but to be insane (it also was put as *crazy as a bedbug* from the early 1800s on), and *bughouse*, originating about 1890 as another word for "crazy," became an American slang term for "insane asylum" about 1900. It is not, however, populated by *bug-eyed monsters*, creatures that come to us from science-fiction aficionados who view outer-space visitors as having buglike (that is, bulging) eyes.

Since bugs are largely harmful creatures from the human viewpoint, it seems logical that since the late 19th century a *bug* has also meant a fault or delay in some enterprise or plan. "This new computer program has a bug in it," we say, or "Not all the bugs have been worked out of producing electric cars."

The best-laid plans of engineers, politicians, spies, and similar plotters and schemers can be disturbed by the use of another kind of *bug*, a concealed microphone or other electronic eavesdropper secretly installed in a room, telephone, car, or the like. To employ such devices is *to bug* something (a room, phone, car, etc.), a use dating from about 1945. This type of illegal activity was carried to nationally prominent extremes in the early 1970s by President Richard Nixon's administration and resulted in the Watergate scandal. Naturally enough the victim of such interference would feel annoyed and harassed at the very least, and in fact, *to bug* someone has also been a colloquial term for annoying someone since about the same time that electronic surveillance began to be used (the 1940s).

All these transfers reflect the negative aspect of bugs: their destructiveness, their ability to insinuate themselves in unwanted places (bedbugs) and to infest human lives in one way or another. Even *snug as a bug in a rug,* a rhyming locution first recorded in 1769 (*Stratford Jubilee,* author unknown), means exceedingly well entrenched and seemingly as comfortable as the destructive clothes-moth larva residing in a rolled-up carpet.

Unpleasant as they may be, bugs have nothing to do with *bugger,* a vulgar word for "sodomite" since the 16th century that was derived from various older words meaning "heretic" (among them "Bulgarian"); from it comes the equally rude *bugger off* or *bug off,* an exhortation to get out in no uncertain terms.

Humbug

> *Take the humbug out of this world, and you haven't much left to do business with.*
>
> —Josh Billings,
> *Josh Billings: His Sayings* (1865)

Nobody knows the origin of *humbug,* which has meant a hoax, imposture, or fraud, as well as to impose such a sham, since the mid-18th century—but it is easy to speculate. Most likely its source was a person who hems and haws—or hums—and in so doing is less than straightforward, if not downright deceptive. For example, there is A. A. Milne's beloved Pooh bear, who tries to hum and buzz like a bee so that the bees won't attack him when he goes after their honey. "Bah humbug!"—stuff and nonsense!—an etymologist might say, along with Dickens's Ebenezer Scrooge in his denunciation of Christmas.

▼ Butterfly

> *Float like a butterfly, sting like a bee.*
> —Muhammad Ali (boxing credo)

The butterflies, along with their close relatives, the moths, are among the handsomest members of the insect world. Collectors enjoy them, for they are fairly easy to capture and can be spread out, dried, and kept for years without losing their beauty. Their wings are covered with large numbers of tiny fine scales, marked with microscopic ridges. The ridges diffract the light passing through them, resulting in some of the characteristic colors and markings of these colorful insects.

The linguistic legacy of butterflies focuses on their bouncy, darting movement more than on their appearance. Thus we use *butterfly* for an individual who bounces from one notion or organization or group to another, particularly one who flits about socially—the *social butterfly*. Also, we refer to a nervous, anxious feeling as having *butterflies in the stomach*.

In cooking, to split a piece of meat such as leg of lamb and spread it apart so that it resembles the insect's spread wings is called *to butterfly*. Other objects resembling spread wings in this way are the *butterfly bandage*, used to close a minor cut; the *butterfly chair*, a sling chair in which the sling is suspended from the frame by the corners to form a back and seat resembling outstretched butterfly wings; and a *butterfly table*, with drop leaves that can be raised or lowered like the insect's wings.

In swimming, the *butterfly stroke* involves moving both arms out of the water in a circular motion while kicking both legs up and down simultaneously (called a *dolphin kick*).

And finally, we have the *butterfly kiss,* brushing one's eyelashes against another person's cheek, so called because it feels as light as the touch of butterfly wings.

▼ Caterpillar

> *The caterpillars of the common-*
> *wealth, which I have sworn to weed*
> *and pluck away.*
> —William Shakespeare, *Richard II*

The caterpillar, a hairy, wormlike larva of a butterfly or moth, never ceases to amaze us in that such an ugly creature can metamorphose into such a lovely one. Its name came into English during the 15th century, possibly from Old French *chatpelose,* for "hairy cat." A century later it became associated with *piller,* an obsolete word for "ravager" or "plunderer," as indeed caterpillars, who spend their entire life cycle feeding, are known to be. This is the sense Shakespeare intended above, that is, a person who feeds on others. Today we are more apt to think of the mechanical *caterpillar,* a steel track passed around and operated by two or more wheels of a tractor, tank, or other motor vehicle, enabling it to traverse very rough ground. *Caterpillar* is the trade name of vehicles with such treads, a product originally of the Caterpillar Tractor Company, and the name comes from the mechanism's resemblance to the caterpillar's method of locomotion.

▼ Cockroach

A household pest found throughout the world, the lowly cockroach was made famous by two 20th-century writers of very different aspect. The Czech writer Franz Kafka had Gregor Mendel, the protagonist of his novella *Metamorphosis,* change into a cockroach at the

222

outset of the story and view the world from this gloomy, anxiety-ridden perspective. In complete contrast, his American contemporary, Don Marquis, wrote a newspaper humor column featuring various gaily satirical characters, chief among them "archy the cockroach" and "mehitabel the cat," whose saga was eventually published in book form.

The name *cockroach* came from Spanish *cucaracha* in the early 17th century, and nobody knows where that came from. In the United States it is often shortened to *roach*. In 1920s jazz parlance a *roach* was a marijuana cigarette, and in the late 1930s the term was used mainly for the butt (unsmoked remnant). If such a roach were very small, one might use a *roach clip*, a 1960s name for a special device used to hold it.

▼ Cricket

> *Merry as a cricket.*
> —John Heywood, *Proverbs* (1546)

The name *cricket* comes from Old French *criquet* or *crequet* and possibly also from other words in Dutch and Low German, all of which are echoic, that is, they imitate the abrupt, dry sound made by this insect. Crickets are the main performers in the summer-evening insect orchestra. The males have rasping structures on their wing covers that produce a chirping sound as their rapid movement makes the wings vibrate.

In China crickets are both believed to bring good luck to a household and prized for their singing, so they often are caged like canaries. Many Europeans and some Americans share the Chinese belief and regard it as good luck if they see or hear a cricket in the house (and bad luck to kill it).

The cheerful chirping of crickets probably had nothing to do with *Jiminy cricket,* an exclamation of surprise dating from the mid-1800s. Rather, it was an elaboration of the earlier interjection *Jiminy*, which may have been a euphemism for Jesus (and the elaboration one for Jesus Christ) and which is heard less often today. Perhaps its best-known use was in Walt Disney's film *Pinocchio* (1940) as the name of the perky little character who functions as Pinocchio's conscience.

The sport of cricket, which gets its name from an Old French word for a stick used in a bowling game, is unrelated.

▼ **F***lea*

> *The horse he slipped and fell on the flea,*
> *And the flea said, Whoops! there's a horse on me.*
>
> —Children's song

Fleas are very small but sometimes very harmful insects that feed exclusively on the blood of warm-blooded animals, including human beings. (Hence the words of the song, of a type loved by children because it turns reality topsy-turvy.) Fleas have no wings, but they have long stout legs, and they are excellent jumpers. This ability was commented on by Aristophanes in 410 B.C. ("She jumps about like a flea on a blanket"—*The Clouds*).

Fleas have been considered a great annoyance for centuries, long before it was discovered that one species can spread bubonic plague from rat to rat, and from rat to human. It takes little imagination to see that having *a flea in one's ear* would be most unpleasant. The saying has been traced to about 1400, where it appeared in a Provençal play, and it originally meant to experience anything surprising or alarming; somewhat later it acquired the meaning of receiving a stinging reproof or rebuff (*to be sent off with a flea in one's ear*). It was so used in English from about 1580 on. Meanwhile, the expression also was used figuratively to mean being tormented by amorous desire; this usage is found in a 15th-century chanson by Charles d'Orléans and in Rabelais's *Gargantua and Pantagruel* (1546). Today the term is used more in the sense of giving someone a hint or suggestion, much like putting a bug in one's ear (see SNUG AS A BUG IN A RUG).

The word *flea* comes from the Middle English *fle* and Old English *flēah*. A single *fleabite* is not too bothersome and hence this word came to mean a trifling inconvenience or annoyance. But infestation with fleas can be most uncomfortable. The term *fleabag* originally (c. 1835) was slang for a bed or mattress of dubious cleanliness, and in Great Britain it still means a sleeping bag; in America in the 1920s it came to mean a cheap rooming house or flophouse.

The name *flea market* may have come from Fly Market, a market in New York City from pre-Revolutionary times until 1816, located at the foot, or valley, of Maiden Lane. Fly market in turn comes from Valley Market, which in Dutch was Vly or Vlie Markt, pronounced "fly" or "flea." Today a flea market is any open-air market of secondhand goods, with the implication that the used clothes and furniture sold there might be flea-infested. The name became common in the 1920s and may in fact have been simply a translation of a famous Paris secondhand market, Le Marché aux Puces (*puce* means "flea").

▽Fly

> *A fly in your ointment, a mote in your eye.*
>
> —Charles Lamb (1833)

The various kinds of fly, which along with mosquitoes, gnats, and midges are characterized by having a single pair of wings, have been pestering man and beast since prehistory. "Dead flies cause the ointment of the apothecary to send forth a stinking savor; so doth a little folly

him that is in reputation for wisdom and honor." So wrote the author of the Old Testament Book of Ecclesiastes more than two thousand years ago, and ever since, *fly in the ointment* has meant a trifling annoyance that spoils one's enjoyment.

The noun *fly*, originally meaning any flying insect, comes from the same root as the verb *to fly* (Old English *flēoge* and *flyge* for the noun, *flēogan* for the verb). The fact is, it is mainly the insect's ability to fly about that makes it such a ubiquitous nuisance. Clearly people have been swatting away at flies for centuries, and only the most dedicated pacifist *wouldn't hurt a fly*, a statement traced to approximately A.D. 50 and made in regard to the death of the Roman Emperor Claudius, possibly by Seneca. In the 19th century a person who was wide awake and extremely capable was said to *have no flies on him (her)*, presumably comparing that person to an animal that did not remain still long enough for flies to alight. Similarly, in Britain the adjective *fly* is slang for describing someone very knowing and alert.

Long ago people found that trapping flies might be more effective than swatting them. Sweet sticky substances worked best, as was pointed out about 1412 by Thomas Hoccleve ("A flye folowethe the hony"—*De Regimine*

Principum) and in 1728 by John Gay ("The fly that sips treacle is lost in the sweets"—*The Beggar's Opera*). But it was Thomas Fuller in 1732 who gave us "More flies are taken with a drop of honey than a Tun of Vinegar" (*Gnomologia*), and we still say *you catch more flies with honey than vinegar* to indicate that you can accomplish more by being pleasant than by being a sourpuss.

Nevertheless, driving off flies continued. "*Shoo fly, don't bother me, I belong to Company G*," went a Civil War song with words by Billy Reeves that was popularized by Bryant's Minstrels; *shoo* as an expression for "go away" dates from the 15th century. In the 1920s came *shoofly pie,* a sticky sweet Pennsylvania Dutch delicacy consisting of a single-crust tart filled with sugared crumbs and molasses, unaccountably named for its attractiveness to flies rather than any repellent qualities.

Flies tend to flock around anything they find attractive in large swarms, and indeed *like flies* has meant in large numbers since about 1600. It is this sense that appears in the phrase *to drop like flies,* meaning to collapse rapidly, or die, or drop out, and usually said of a group. For example, "Scots are not used to these temperatures, and the heat wave has them dropping like flies."

The persistent annoyance created by flies in the stable and barn (many species lay their eggs in manure and other excrement) also gave rise to the name *gadfly,* at first for species that plague animals (*gad* being an early term for "goad") and then (17th century) for a person who persistently annoys others or provokes argument through criticism. "What is the breeze in your breech?" asked a character in Beaumont and Fletcher's play, *Monsieur Thomas* (1619), *breeze* being another word for gadfly; thus the expression here is an early version of "Do you have ants in your pants?" (See also under ANT.)

The relation of flies to the *fly* or *fly ball* of baseball, a term dating from the 1860s, most likely just relates to the flight of the ball. It is, of course, a ball that is batted up into the air and, if the opposing team makes no errors, is caught before it bounces, resulting in an out for the batter.

Further elaborations are *infield fly* or *outfield fly* (depending on where it is hit), and *pop fly.*

A much newer word catching the eye of watchful lexicographers is *greenfly.* Originally (early 18th century) meaning a green aphid that attacks peach trees, it began to be used in the late 1970s for a devoted baseball fan who hangs around ball players' entrances, hotel lobbies, and the like in order to meet major league players, obtain their autographs, and perhaps also get some share of public attention (appear in television shots with them, for example). Presumably ball players regard them as pests, and hence the name. A similar term is *barfly,* originating about 1900, for a person who persistently hangs around barrooms and taverns, often for the purpose of cadging drinks from other patrons.

Annoying as they may be, flies are not very large, and the smaller ones could easily be overlooked. Hence we have the figurative *fly on the wall,* for an unseen witness to a private situation. It often appears in such locutions as "If only I were a fly on the wall when she finds out he's been cheating on her." Smaller yet is a *flyspeck,* a spot made by fly excrement. This word, too, has been transferred to mean anything trifling or insignificant. Still another allusion to the fly's small size is *flyweight,* the lowest weight class in professional boxing (109 to 112 pounds).

The use of *fly* for a horsedrawn coach and for a flap covering a fastening on pants or a tent would appear to have no relation to the insect, but the word is derived from the same root.

▼ Grasshopper

Even the peskiest of the grasshoppers, who have been so named since about 1275 for their grass-green color and jumping ability, are not very large. Hence *knee-high to a grasshopper* replaced, in America about 1850, the earlier *knee-high to a mosquito* (1824), *bumble-bee* (1833), and *splinter* (1841), all of them meaning quite small and, by implication, quite young. A murder mystery by Lee Thayer (*Accessory after the Fact,* 1943) mentions *knee-high to a woodchuck,* but that turn of phrase never caught on.

Grasshoppers are also commemorated in the *grasshopper,* a mixed drink consisting chiefly of the (green) liqueur, crème de menthe, and *grasshopper pie,* a one-crust pie containing crème de menthe and/or mint ice cream (also green).

▼ Hornet

In Britain *mad as a hornet* means "crazy," whereas in America it means "enraged." Anyone who has ever stumbled on or otherwise disturbed hornets, who live together socially much as bees do, will testify to the fact that they respond by flying at the intruder and stinging him or her repeatedly. The stinger is actually a modification of the hornet's egg-laying structure and thus is present only in females (queens and workers).

Hornets belong to a superfamily of wasps (*Vespoidea*) that also includes the yellowjackets and polistes wasps. In the course of a stinging attack, however, the victim often is too set upon to differentiate among the species of the attacker. It is not certain when *mad as a hornet* was first said, but *angry as a wasp* may have preceded it, dating back at least to a poem entitled *Alexander,* written about 1350 by an unknown author ("As wrath as a wasp"). By 1546 it was part of John Heywood's proverb collection ("Nowe mery as a cricket, and by and by Angry as a waspe"). To *stir up a hornets' nest,* meaning to set in motion a bustle of activity that is largely hostile in nature, dates from the early 18th century. (See also WASP.)

▼ Louse

The small wingless sucking insects known as lice are external parasites on many warm-blooded creatures, including human beings. Their presence usually indicates unsanitary conditions, and they were extremely common pests until fairly recent times. *Lousy* meant "full of lice" by 1377 or so, and by the mid-16th century it meant not only "filthy" but also "mean and contemptible." Since shortly before World War I a person displaying these characteristics has been called a *louse*. During the war, when conditions in the trenches were at best unsanitary, the prevalence of lice gave rise to *lousy with* in the sense of "full of," so one might describe the enemy as "lousy with ammunition," or a rich person as "lousy with money." In the mid-1930s the verb *to louse up* began to be used in America for "to ruin" or "to spoil."

▼ Mosquito

The name *mosquito* came from Spanish for "little fly" (little *mosca*) in the 16th century. Female mosquitoes feed on the blood of warm-blooded animals, and some species are responsible for transmitting malaria and yellow fever, as well as other diseases. These unpleasant characteristics were ignored, however, by whoever first called a small light vessel capable of rapid maneuvering a *mosquito boat,* presumably for its ability to skim over water just as the insects do. It originally (19th century) meant a small river craft carrying light guns, but in World War II the name was attached to PT (patrol torpedo) boats. Employed mainly to torpedo enemy ships, these boats were highly effective but they probably would not have become so well known were it not that John F. Kennedy, then (1943) a lieutenant junior grade in command of a PT boat in the South Pacific, had his ship rammed by a Japanese destroyer. Although injured, Kennedy managed a nine-day struggle for survival for himself and his men in enemy waters, for which he was awarded Navy and Marine Corps medals and the Purple Heart. Kennedy's heroic behavior stood him in good stead in his political future and attained a place for his boat, PT-109, in the annals of American political as well as naval history.

▼Moth

> There is no clothe so fine but
> moathes will eat it.
> —George Pettie, *Petite Pallace* (1576)

The nocturnal moth, whose name comes from Middle English *motthe* and Old English *moththe,* is readily drawn to the light, and in times when candles were the principal form of illumination it frequently singed its wings. This hazard was pointed out by Aeschylus, Shakespeare, and Byron, among other poets, who used it as a metaphor for fatal romantic attraction ("Maidens, like moths, are ever caught by glare"—Byron, *Childe Harold's Pilgrimage*).

Moths are extremely destructive during the larval stage of their development, when they occupy themselves entirely with eating. Among such larval destroyers are cutworms and armyworms (which feed on low-growing plants), corn earworms, gypsy moths, tent caterpillars, and the ubiquitous clothes moth. *To be moth-eaten* has meant to be damaged by moths since about 1350, and the expression acquired its figurative meaning of decayed and decrepit, and by extension time-worn and old-hat, about 1900.

Clothes moths tend to attack clothing and other materials that are not regularly worn. "The wasting moth ne'er spoil'd my best array; the cause was this, I wore it every day" (Alexander Pope, *Paraphrases from Chaucer*). Undoubtedly various preventatives and remedies were

tried until someone discovered that strong-smelling chemicals such as camphor and naphthalene repel moths. Early in the 20th century enterprising manufacturers began to produce *mothballs*, small balls made of such substances, which could be put away with clothes being stored. Before long the name attached itself to anything in storage or inactive, giving rise to the term *mothball fleet*, that is, naval ships put in storage for a period of time. This term, originating about 1946, may have come into use because ships stored after World War II had a plastic covering sprayed onto their gun mountings and other parts subject to corrosion, and thus resembled a moth's cocoon.

▽ *Spider*

> *"Will you walk into my parlour,"*
> *said a Spider to a Fly.*
>
> —Mary Howitt,
> *The Spider and the Fly* (1844)

The spider, whose name comes from Middle English *spither* and Old English *spīthra*, is notable chiefly for its ability to produce silken threads and weave them into a web. The production of silk, enabled by a spinning gland inside the insect's abdomen, may be the dominant activity of a spider's life. Each species builds its web in its own way, so that species can be identified by their webs. The main supporting strands are laid first, attached to some suitable support, and then the balance of the web is spun. A number of spiders build quite elaborate webs in which they capture insects, prompting the oft-quoted verse above. Since attracting prey to the web is considered a form of deception, it gave rise to such figures of speech as *web of deceit*, or, as Sir Walter Scott put it in *Marmion*, "Oh what a tangled web we weave, when first we practise to deceive!" Moreover, a person who entraps or lures others is sometimes called a *spider*.

A spider's network is also called a *cobweb*, a word derived from Middle English *coppeweb*, which combined Old English *(ātor)coppe*, for "(poison) spider," and *web*, for "woven." Since the spider's structure is relatively weak and flimsy, *cobweb* has been transferred to anything that is flimsy or insubstantial, as well as to a snare or network of intrigue (in reference to the spider's trapping of insects in its web). Further, since cobwebs make windows or other places where they are attached look blurry, their name has been used to describe mental confusion, as in "I'm exhausted and my head is *full of cobwebs*."

A fine, filmy cobweb on grass or shrubs or floating through the air is known as a *gossamer*. This word is a contraction of *goose-summer*, and the derivation is unclear. However, it is often presumed that when this word was first recorded in the 14th century, goose-summer referred to a warm period in early autumn when geese were plucked, and it is during just such a time that gossamer is most often seen. Within a century the word had been transferred to anything light and flimsy, and in the 19th century it was even applied to frivolous, capricious individuals.

Contrary to popular myth, few spiders are poisonous to humans. A notable exception is the American *black widow spider*. It probably is so named because the female of this species generally eats the male, a habit common in other spiders as well. This is also another instance where a human characteristic (in this case, widowhood) is transferred to the animal rather than vice versa.

The name *spider* has been transferred to various objects that more or less resemble its shape, consisting of an oval body from which extend four pairs of jointed legs. Among them are a frying pan that originally had legs or feet; a trivet or tripod used to support a cooking pot on a hearth; and a machine part having a number of radiating spokes or arms.

An exaggerated example of the spider shape is seen in the spider called *daddy-longlegs,* which has a compact round body and extremely long legs. It, like other spiders, is considered good luck, and an old American rural superstition has it that if one's cows stray, one should pick up a daddy-longlegs, dangle it, and recite, "Daddy, daddy longlegs, Tell me where my cows are, then I'll let you go."

▼Tick

This blood-sucking insect, whose name comes from Middle English *teke* or *tyke* and Old English *ticia,* feeds on warm-blooded animals, including humans, and can spread such diseases as Texas fever in cattle, biliary fever in dogs, and Rocky Mountain spotted fever, Lyme disease, tularemia, and relapsing fever in humans. The term *tight as a tick,* meaning extremely intoxicated, presumably comes from the comparison of a person full of drink to a tick engorged with blood. It originated in America in the mid or late 19th century.

▼Wasp

> *I'll use you for my mirth, yea, for my laughter, when you are waspish.*
> —William Shakespeare, *Julius Caesar*

The wasp, from Middle English *waspe* and Old English *wæps,* is differentiated from its cousins, the bee and hornet, by a longer, more slender body that is somewhat

234

indented in the middle. From this comes *wasp-waisted,* for a woman's slender waistline, a term originating in the mid-19th century when tight corsets helped achieve this fashionable silhouette. As with the bees and hornets, female wasps possess a stinger, and consequently it is as "perilous to anger a wasp" (Stefano Guazzo, 1574), as it is to stir up a hornet's nest (see HORNET). The wasp's venomous sting was noted by the Greek playwright Aristophanes, whose comedy, *The Wasps,* satirizes the Athenians' passion for litigation. The adjective *waspish,* for irritable, snappish, or petulant, has been applied to human behavior since the 16th century, by Shakespeare and numerous others since. Eric Partridge tells us that from about 1785 to 1850 in Britain *wasp* was a slang word for a prostitute with venereal disease "who like a wasp carries a sting in her tail."

In the 20th century wasp has twice become an acronym, in neither case at all related to the insect. During World War II the U.S. Women's Air Force Service Pilots were called the *WASP,* but that organization was eliminated in 1944 and its name all but forgotten. In 1962 an American sociologist, E. B. Palmore, published a journal article in which he abbreviated "White Anglo-Saxon Protestants" to *Wasps.* By this he meant the American privileged establishment or "ruling class"—that is, middle- or upper-class Americans descended from early English settlers who by definition are not subject to social, racial, religious, or ethnic bias. The term is often used with some disparagement and contempt, and continues to be popular.

Water Sprites:
Fish and Other
Denizens of the
Deep

▼ Fish

Fishes are the largest class of vertebrates and the dominant form of life in the waters covering the earth. The typical fish is spindle-shaped, its body tapering at both ends. Its sides are usually flattened and its tail is flat. The rod of vertebrae that transmits the force of the tail to the head is what gives fish their speed and maneuverability in the water. A similar movement by vehicles such as cars and airplanes therefore is called *fishtailing*, which in the case of a car causes it to swerve and in the case of an airplane causes it to slow down.

The word *fish* comes from Middle English *fisch* or *fyssh* and Old English *fisc*. In Christianity the fish became the symbol for Jesus because the letters of its name in Greek, *ichthus*, form an acronym for Jesus Christ, Son of God, Savior.

Probably the outstanding characteristic of fish is their watery habitat. Almost all fishes breathe by means of gills. Water enters the mouth and is swept back over the gills and out again. As it passes through the gills, the blood takes up oxygen and gives off carbon dioxide. A few kinds of fish can survive out of water for several hours if their gills are kept moist, but most fishes die when out of water because the gills cannot take oxygen from the air if they

are dry. Although this breathing apparatus may not have been completely understood in his day, St. Athanasius is credited with being the first, sometime before A.D. 373, to describe persons out of their usual environment as *fish out of water.* The simile reappears in Chaucer's *Troilus and Cressida* (1374), Langland's *Piers Ploughman* (1390), and numerous other works, and survives to the present.

No doubt it is the fish's breathing apparatus, which forces it to be open-mouthed most of the time and to look as though it were drinking, that gave rise to the expression *drink like a fish,* meaning to drink a great deal or to excess. "I can drink like a fish," wrote James Shirley (1646), and George Farquar's play, *Sir Harry Wildair* (1701), includes the line, "drink like a fish and swear like a devil."

Nearly all fish are cold-blooded creatures, whence we have the expression *cold fish,* for an unemotional, dispassionate individual. Shakespeare may have been the first to use it—"It was thought she was a woman and was turned into a cold fish" (*The Winter's Tale*)—although his meaning was slightly different.

As any careful consumer will tell you, freshly killed fish does not smell, and one's nose is an excellent arbiter of freshness. No self-respecting fish market will sell spoiled fish, no matter how vociferous a fishwife may be marketing the wares ("Did you ever hear a fishwife cry stinking mackerel?"—John Wilson, *The Cheats,* 1664). It was the loud coarse tongue of women fish-sellers in the Middle Ages that gave rise to the term *fishwife* for a scolding vulgar woman.

Although there is no biological evidence to support it, the proverb *A fish stinks from the head,* first recorded in George Pettie's *Civil Conversation* (1581), has survived. Today as then it is used as a metaphor for malfeasance by the head of a government, organization, or other hierarchy. Another proverb, of similarly old provenance and pinpointing the precise time of spoilage, is *Guests and fish stink after three days.* John Lyly put it: "Gestes and fish . . . are ever stale within three dayes" (*Euphues and His England,* 1580).

If a fish smells, its freshness is questionable. Therefore *fishy,* which for a long time meant simply "fishlike" in one way or another, came to mean, in the 19th century, "dubious" or "suspect." Benjamin Disraeli, novelist and orator as well as statesman, wrote in his novel, *Coningsby* (1844), "The most fishy thing I ever saw" in describing a suspicious circumstance.

Even earlier, across the Atlantic, the term *fish story* was invented by a journalist to describe a highly unlikely event. "A fish story! . . . In consequence of the shoals of whitefish which choked the channel the steamboat could not pass" (*St. Louis Enquirer,* December 8, 1819). The term clearly comes from the fact that fishermen, especially those who fish for sport rather than for their livelihood, are famous for exaggerating the size of their catch, and the term is still used to mean a tall tale. To bear this out, Eugene Field wrote, "Oh, you who've been a-fishing will indorse me when I say That it always is the biggest fish you catch that gets away!" (*Our Biggest Fish,* 1892).

Even if the biggest gets away, we may take solace in the fact that there are *lots of good fish in the sea,* a term used with dubious success to comfort a jilted lover or otherwise disappointed person since at least the 16th century.

Perhaps not for a fish trying to elude capture, but for some persons it is better to be *a big fish in a small pond (than a small fish in a big pond)*. In other words, it is easier to make one's mark when there is less competition.

Fish in Troubled Waters

> *A fisher in troubled water gains triple or double.*
>
> —Gabriel Meurier, *Trésor des Sentences*
> (c. 1550)

Allegedly fish bite more readily in rough seas, so *to fish in troubled waters* means to take advantage of turbulent times. There was even an old Latin proverb to that effect, *Piscatur in aqua turbida,* as well as similar sayings in French, Spanish, and other languages.

It is not clear what impatient fisherman first told a companion to stop procrastinating, lazing about, or daydreaming by saying *either fish or cut bait*. This phrase, still meaning to "get on with it" and make a decision—either continue angling or cut bait for another person—was used figuratively by Joseph G. Cannon in a congressional debate in 1876 and was repeated in the U.S. House of Representatives in 1882 by another congressman.

Of course one is never sure what a fishing line will bring up—trash or an old boot or a wonderful catch. The old saying, *He has fished well and caught a frog,* meaning he has brought little to pass despite all his hard work, was already a proverb in 1546 (John Heywood, *Proverbs*). That saying is largely obsolete, but *to fish for* something, which is almost as old ("I could not fish from him what was the matter" Samuel Pepys, *Diary*), survives, especially in the form of *fishing for a compliment*.

A related but newer term is *fishing expedition,* a hunt for information of a nonspecific nature. It originated, according to Eric Partridge, about 1930, from the practice of Japanese fishing boats entering foreign waters for purposes of spying. In succeeding years the term was taken up by the legal profession to describe the process of interrogating an adversary or examining an adversary's documents or property in order to discover evidence relevant to the case. As might be expected, lawyers have disagreed and argued as to how much "fishing" should be allowed and what kind of fishing is reasonable. There are even federal rules governing these procedures, and a person who is the object of a fishing expedition may seek a protective order to limit it. The term is also used by the police, private investigators, and the like for similar information-gathering activities.

Kettle of Fish

> Here's a pretty kettle of fish, cries
> Mrs. Tow-wouse.
> —Henry Fielding, *Joseph Andrews* (1742)

Whether it is described as *pretty* or *fine,* a *kettle of fish* always means a mess or a difficult predicament. The term is said to come from a Scottish custom of holding a riverside picnic, itself called *a kettle of fish,* where freshly caught live salmon are thrown into a kettle boiling over an open fire and then are eaten out of hand. Delicious as it may be, consuming fish in this way is bound to be messy, much like eating lobsters and clams at a beach clambake. A picnic of this kind was described by Sir Walter Scott in *St. Ronan's Well,* and the use of the term as a metaphor for a mess dates from the first half of the 18th century. It appears in writings by Samuel Richardson, Charles Dickens, Thomas Hardy, Bernard Shaw, and many others, although it is used less often today.

Also originating in fish cookery is the saying *to have other* (or *better) fish to fry,* meaning to have other, more important matters to attend to. The term dates from the 17th century and is still used.

Fish come in many shapes and sizes. Small tropical fish appeal to the hobbyist, and serious devotees now use elaborate, electrically lighted and heated tanks for their collections. In earlier times, a simple glass jar or bowl sufficed, as it still does for more casual fish fanciers, and one could observe the fish in it from all sides. In the early 1900s *fishbowl,* originally a simple container for this purpose, came to mean a place or situation where one's activities could be scrutinized by anyone and everyone—for example, a desk placed inside a glass-enclosed cubicle. H. H. Munro, remembered for his stories published under the pen name Saki, wrote, "I might have been a goldfish in a glass bowl for all the privacy I got" (*Reginald,* 1904). Some years later Raymond Chandler used *fishbowl* as a metaphor for "jail" in one of his detective stories.

Neither Fish nor Fowl

"Neither fish nor flesh nor good red herring," wrote John Heywood (*Proverbs,* 1546). The expression is believed to allude to the food for monks and priests (fish), ordinary folk (flesh, or meat), and the indigent (smoked herring, which was quite inexpensive). Consequently, if something was none of those, it fitted no known category. Later the phrase was shortened to the current *neither fish nor fowl,* which carries the same meaning—not one thing or another.

Quite another kind of food is *food for fishes.* Originally alluding to someone who has drowned and whose remains are consumed by meat-eating fish, this term, with its appealing alliteration, played on the much older *food for worms* (see under WORM). Rider Haggard was among the first to use it: "He was food for fishes now, poor fellow" (*Mr. Meeson's Will,* 1894).

▼ Barnacle

The barnacle has a strange history. It was long thought to be a mollusk, but in 1830 it was recognized as a crustacean. During the Middle Ages it was believed that the barnacle developed into a sea bird, a kind of goose called *barnacle goose*, and indeed its name comes from Old French *bernacle* and Medieval Latin *bernacula*, both meaning "a kind of wild goose." The name came into English in the 1400s and then was applied to the bird; only much later was it applied to the crustacean.

The characteristic feature of barnacles is that they attach themselves to stones, rocks, logs, wharf piles, ships, and even the bodies of other animals. Consequently *barnacle* has been transferred to a person or thing that clings tenaciously.

▼ *Clam*

Anyone who has ever tried to open a raw clam knows that the shells of these bivalve mollusks are very tightly shut. The very name *clam* comes from Old English *clamm*, meaning "fetter" or "constriction," and hence "clamp." It is hardly surprising, then, that *clam* eventually came to be slang for a closemouthed person, and *to clam up* came to mean to keep one's mouth tightly shut, both usages originating in America about 1915.

Clams are a staple seafood in New England, justly famous for the steamers (steamed clams) of its *clambakes* and the creamy soup called *clam chowder* (New Englanders disdain the Manhattan version, made with tomatoes instead of milk). Indians and colonists alike went clamming, using a kind of hoe to dig out clams from the sand at low tide. From clamming comes *happy as a clam*, which is short for *happy as a clam at high tide*, when the creature is safe from clam-diggers; it is only at low tide that clamming can be carried on.

Although the habitat of clams is certainly cold, damp, and sticky, the word *clammy*, which means all of that, is believed to come not from any association with the mollusk but from a related word meaning "clay," which also has these characteristics.

As for the slang use of *clam* to mean "one dollar," it began in the late 1930s in the United States and never became very widespread.

▼ Cockle

> Crying cockles and mussels, alive,
> alive oh!
>
> —*Molly Malone*, Folk song

The name of the cockle, another edible bivalve mollusk, can be traced to Greek *konkhulion*, meaning "little mussel." The word in English dates from the 14th century, and presumably the cockle has been cooked and eaten for far longer. However, *to warm the cockles of one's heart* has nothing to do with culinary matters, or even with seashells. Rather, it comes from the Latin term for the heart's ventricles, *cochleae cordis*, and it has meant to give great pleasure since about 1670. About that time one John Eachard wrote, "This contrivance of his did inwardly rejoice the cockles of his heart (*Observations upon the Answer to Contempt of Clergy*). The expression continued to be used so long and so often that Eric Partridge believed it was a cliché by the mid-19th century. It crops up less often today but is by no means obsolete.

▼ Crab

The name of the crab, a ten-footed crustacean, comes from Old English *crabba* and Old Norse *krabbi*, closely related to words meaning "to scratch and claw." From these roots also came the verb *to crab*, originally meaning to claw but later coming to mean to complain or criticize (from about 1810). From the same period comes the use of *crab* for a cranky, irritable individual and of *crabby* to describe such a person's behavior or disposition. A 13th-century word with the same meaning is *crabbed*

("Crabbed age and youth cannot live together"—*The Passionate Pilgrim*, c. 1559, author unknown), which today is used more for something intricate and hard to decipher, such as *crabbed* (that is, hard-to-read) *handwriting*.

The crab's ten legs give it a most peculiar gait. Depending on the species, it scrabbles about with jerky, darting motions, seemingly going in all directions, sideways and backward as much as forward. "You can never teach a crab to walk straight forward," wrote Aristophanes (*The Peace,* c. 421 B.C., cited by Erasmus). From this comes the adjective *crabwise,* originating in the early 1900s, for a sideways motion, like that of a person trying to move through a crowd. It also is the source of the name *crab canon,* a musical form in which the main theme reappears not in its original form but backwards (that is, with the notes in reverse order).

The exceedingly unpleasant pubic louse, *Phthirus pubis,* is also known as a *crab louse* because it looks like a tiny crab, and someone infected with it is said to *have crabs.*

▽ Eel

The eel's long slender body has only minute scales embedded in its skin, which therefore appears to be completely smooth. When it is wet, this snakelike body is very slippery, long ago giving rise to the simile, *slippery as an eel*. "You hold an eel by the tail," was an ancient Latin proverb, meaning you have to hang on tightly when you are dealing with a slippery elusive person. Chaucer used the simile, and about 1412 Thomas Hoccleve wrote, "Mi wit is also slippir as an eel."

▼Herring

An important food fish of the North Atlantic, where it swims in shoals that number billions of individual fishes, the herring has been a valuable catch for centuries. "Of all the fish in the sea, herring is the king," said an English proverb of the 17th century, and a Dutch proverb says, "A land with lots of herring can get along with few doctors." The enormous numbers of herring gave rise to such sayings as "Virtues thick as Herrings" (John Wolcot, 1795) and "People jammed inside like herrings in a barrel" (N. Gould, 1891). A number of writers, from Rabelais to Robert Browning, called the ocean, especially the Atlantic, a *herring pond*.

One reason herring are so valuable is that they lend themselves well to various kinds of preservation—drying, smoking, salting, canning, pickling—and so represent a long-lasting source of food. However, the fish is said to die extremely fast when it is out of water, whence the expression *dead as a herring,* meaning utterly dead; the simile was used by Shakespeare, Samuel Butler, and Tobias Smollett, among others.

The herring's skeleton gave rise to the term *herringbone* for a pattern used in various kinds of work, including masonry (an arrangement of stones or bricks), embroidery (a kind of stitch), and weaving (a twill with this pattern). The pattern basically consists of rows of slanted lines, each row slanting in the opposite direction, so that two contiguous rows form either a *V* or an inverted *V*.

Red Herring

> *Diverted from their own affairs by*
> *the red herring of foreign politics so*
> *adroitly drawn across the trail.*
> —W. F. Butler, *Life of Napier* (1890)

Smoking a herring changes its color from gray or silver to reddish brown and imparts a strong smell to it. In the 17th century, when hunting was an extremely popular recreation for gentlemen, it was found that hunting dogs could be trained to follow a scent by using a strong-smelling smoked herring as a lure. Such a powerful odor can also be used to divert a dog from its true objective, a fact found useful by criminals trying to escape bloodhounds, and so *red herring* soon came to mean any diversionary tactic.

In the securities industry a *red herring* is a preliminary prospectus for a new issue, which is given to brokers in order to attract buyers before the completed prospectus is available. Its name comes from the fact that on the front page, in red ink or red print, it announces that the information it contains is subject to change and thus does not constitute a firm offer. Such a red herring is quite respectable—that is, most such prospectuses do not deliberately attempt to mislead investors.

▼Mackerel

Another important food fish, the mackerel, with its attractive, wavy, cross-marked skin, gave its name to *mackerel sky,* a sky dappled with detached masses of cloud that resemble the fish's markings. The presence of such clouds usually means rain is coming, an observation made long ago. *A mackerel sky is never long dry* is an old Yorkshire saying quoted in a treatise on agriculture (1681).

▼ Minnow

The name *minnow,* from Old English *myne* and perhaps Old German *munewa,* refers to several species of quite small freshwater fish related to the carp. Minnows are often used as live bait to catch larger sporting fishes, and the saying, *Bait a minnow to catch a salmon,* meaning give up something small in order to gain something big, has been used since ancient Roman times. The word *minnow* is also still used to mean any small, insignificant object or person.

▼ Scallop

The most distinctive feature of the scallop, another edible bivalve mollusk, is its shell, which has approximately twenty radial ribs extending to the wavy outer edge. (The only part of scallops that is eaten is the big muscle that opens and closes the shell's two valves.) The name *scallop* comes from Middle English *scalop,* which in turn probably was derived from French *escalope,* for "shell." The scallop shell became the symbol for St. James of Compostela, supposedly because the shores near this Spanish town abound with the shellfish. It became the emblem first of pilgrims to St. James's shrine, and later of medieval pilgrims in general. The shells were worn on their hats, were blessed by priests, and were supposed to ward off evil. "Give me my scallop-shell of quiet . . . and thus I'll take my pilgrimage," wrote Sir Walter Raleigh (*The Passionate Man's Pilgrimage*). Much later the scallop shell became familiar as the logo of the Shell Oil Company.

Patterns resembling the wavy edges of scallop shells began to be called *scallops* or *scalloping* in the 17th century, and they continue to be used as a decorative edging on cloth, wood, and other materials.

▼ Sea Horse

The sea horses are small, attractive fishes, rarely more than six inches long. Their bodies are covered with rings of plates that form a kind of armor. Their heads are horse-like in shape, with a long snout, and they swim in an upright position. The male also has a long tail, whereby it can attach itself to small objects in the water. These characteristics account for the sea horse's zoological name, *Hippocampus,* a compound of Greek words for "horse" and "sea monster." In Greek myth, Hippocampus was a creature ridden by Poseidon and other sea gods, and it allegedly had a horse's body and a fish's tail.

A part of the human anatomy, one of two ridges along each of the brain's lateral ventricles, was named *hippocampus* because of its resemblance to the sea horse.

▼ Shark

In ancient times sharks were huge, fearsome creatures that probably dominated the waters of the earth. They still include many large, powerful, and even ferocious species, among them the great white, or man-eating, shark, which can grow to more than fifteen feet long and weigh 6,000 to 7,000 pounds. The name *shark* has been used to mean a large voracious fish since the 16th century, and to refer to a rapacious human extortionist since about 1700. Its original etymology is not known, but it may have come from Old German words meaning "rogue" and "to plague" or "vex." Presumably the application to human beings is that those who are so-called snap things up as the fish do—or perhaps it is the other way around: the fish are likened to humans who prey on others.

An obvious derivative is *loan shark,* a usurer who lends money at exorbitant interest rates. The term is American in origin and dates from the early 1900s. An only slightly more sympathetic figure is the *pool shark,* an avid, highly skilled billiards buff who preys on opponents of lesser skill, inducing them to bet at very favorable (to the shark) odds.

In the corporate world of the late 1980s the use of *shark repellent* became increasingly common. Originally a substance sprayed onto divers to ward off attacks by sharks, the name was transferred to measures that a company takes to protect itself against a hostile takeover by another corporation. Such measures may include requiring a large majority of shareholders to approve any proposed merger, or giving top executives extremely high severance pay that would make it very costly for a new management to eliminate the existing one.

▼ *Shrimp*

Shrimp has been the name for both a small crustacean and a puny person since the 14th century. It is related to Middle and Old High German words meaning to shrink or contract, presumably alluding to the animal's shriveled appearance. Although the kinds used as human food are anywhere from half an inch to three inches or so long, many of the smaller species are so tiny that they make up part of plankton, the mass of miniscule plants and animals that serve as food for larger sea creatures and that color the water.

▼ *Sponge*

> *An old sponger on other people's kindness.*
>
> —William Makepeace Thackeray,
> *Lovel the Widower* (1860)

The sponges, whose name derives from Greek *spongia* (via Latin and Old and Middle English), were the first successful group of many-celled animals, although they generally survived only in a marine environment. Except for one small freshwater variety, they live in shallow inshore waters and on the ocean floor at all depths. They are not related to any other animals. The typical sponge body consists of two layers of cells arranged in the form of a small vase, with a central cavity. The outer walls have hundreds of tiny openings that lead to a series of canals and finally to the central cavity. Water streams through the canals and into the central cavity, and then out through the large opening at the top of the vase. These currents of water are the source of the animals' food, for from it they extract tiny plants, animals, and particles of decaying matter, on which they live.

Its ability to soak up liquid has made the sponge useful for centuries, and diving for sponges dates from ancient times. The verb *to sponge on,* meaning to live like a parasite, soaking up the largesse of others but giving nothing in return, has been part of the English language since the 14th century. In the same sense, to be a *sponge* or *sponger* dates at least from the 16th century, and was so used by Shakespeare (in *Hamlet, The Merchant of Venice,* etc.), Dryden, and many other writers. The physical nature of the sponge is alluded to in *sponge cake,* a light cake with a porous texture so called since the late 1700s, and the actual use of sponges is referred to in *sponge bath,* dating from the mid-1800s and meaning a cleaning with sponges (or wet washcloths) rather than immersion in a tub of water.

Also of mid-19th century origin is *to throw up* (or *in*) *the sponge,* which dates from about 1850. It comes from prizefighting, where a damp sponge was used to refresh the contestants between rounds, and a fighter's second would throw his sponge in the air when his man conceded defeat. The expression has been used to signal surrender ever since, although occasionally "towel" is substituted for "sponge."

▼WALRUS

> *"A loaf of bread," the Walrus said,*
> *"Is what we chiefly need;*
> *Pepper and vinegar besides*
> *Are very good indeed—*
> *Now if you're ready, Oysters dear,*
> *We can begin to feed."*
>
> —Lewis Carroll, *The Walrus and the Carpenter* (1872)

Shellfish are the main food of the walrus, so Lewis Carroll's verses about the walrus and the carpenter devouring oysters are quite accurate. Its name comes from Dutch and means, literally, "sea horse" (its German name, on the other hand, translates to "horse whale"). The walrus is not at all horselike in appearance. Both male and female have two large ivory tusks projecting down from the upper jaw, often as long as two and a half feet. Their short broad muzzle is adorned with a mustache of stiff bristly whiskers that become shorter and thicker as the animal grows older. In the late 19th century it became fashionable for men to grow a thick shaggy mustache that hung down loosely at both ends, somewhat like the walrus's whiskers, and by the early 20th century it was called a *walrus mustache*.

▼WHALE

No doubt because of their great size, whales have long stirred the human imagination. They are the subject of many fables, myths, and stories of the ancient Egyptians and Greeks, and are frequently mentioned in the Old Testament of the Bible, where the story of *Jonah and the whale* is the most familiar example. By Aristotle's time people recognized the fact that whales differ from other fishes in that they bear their young live, which makes them, by definition, mammals. How they came to live in

the sea was unclear, however, until recent times, when the discovery of fossils showed that whales originally were four-legged land animals. Exactly when and why they became marine animals is still not totally documented, but it seems reasonable to surmise that it was a quest for food—fishes and plankton—that made them take the plunge.

The name *whale* comes from Old English *hwæl.* The largest surviving species of whale is 100 feet or more long, and it is their size that has found linguistic transference. Thus *a whale of a* something (a time, a job, etc.) means very much of something, or something very big or very fine, and has been so used in the United States since about 1890.

Despite their size, whales generally are not particularly belligerent, except for the species of dolphin called *killer whales,* which prey mostly on other cetaceans. However, the verb *to whale* has meant to attack or punch something or someone since about 1780 in America and since about 1850 in Britain. The origin of this phrase is not known.

Index